THE NEW RIGHT

Also by Norman P. Barry

Hayek's Social and Economic Philosophy
An Introduction to Modern Political Theory
On Classical Liberalism and Libertarianism

THE NEW RIGHT

NORMAN P. BARRY

CROOM HELM
London • New York • Sydney

© 1987 Norman P. Barry

Croom Helm Ltd, Provident House,
Burrell Row, Beckenham, Kent BR3 1AT

Croom Helm Australia, 44–50 Waterloo Road,
North Ryde, 2113, New South Wales

British Library Cataloguing in Publication Data

Barry, Norman P.
    The new right.
    1. Conservatism   2. Liberalism
    I. Title
    320.5′2   JC571
    ISBN 0-7099-1833-X

Published in the USA by
Croom Helm
in association with Methuen, Inc.
29 West 35th Street,
New York, NY 10001

Library of Congress Cataloging-in-Publication Data

Barry, Norman P.
    The new right.

    Includes index.
    1. Liberalism. 2. Libertarianism. 3. Laissez-faire.
4. Conservatism. I. Title.
JC571.B364 1987   320.5′1   87-9056
ISBN 0-7099-1833-X

Printed and bound in Great Britain
by Billing & Sons Limited, Worcester.

Contents

Preface

1.	Against the Consensus	1
2.	The Liberal Alternative — Economics	23
3.	The Liberal Alternative — Politics	56
4.	Conservatism	86
5.	Britain	103
6.	America	140
7.	West Germany	174
8.	Conclusion	190

Index 201

Preface

In recent years there has been much talk of the break-up of the 'consensus', both in current social and political thought and in political practice, and the emergence of something called 'new Right' social philosophy. The terms 'consensus', 'Right' and 'Left' have, perhaps, little exact descriptive meaning in political discourse, but they are nevertheless used repeatedly, if only for want of better terms. Some clarification is therefore essential.

The consensus, which is explained fully in chapter one, simply refers to the body of social and economic ideas that 'ruled' political thought and practice in most Western democracies from the end of the Second World War to about the mid-1970s. Of course, there was a great variety of policy positions covered by the term consensus, but there was sufficient common ground for it to function as a target for attack from heterodox political opinion. Consensus refers to a kind of agreement (genuine or otherwise) about ends and values: in this case the ends and values were economic growth, low inflation, a wide participation in politics, a more extensive social and economic equality, and the full range of civil liberties. These principles perhaps sound innocuous but what was distinctive about the architects of the consensus was the belief that the only *means* to bring about those ends were political and state actions. What was significant about the post-war years was not just the periods of high inflation, nationalisation and rapid extension of the welfare state but the common root from which all these phenomena stem — the pre-eminence of *politics* as a decision-making method for social problems. No doubt, this was democratic politics, or at least non-authoritarian politics, but it nonetheless evinced a firm rejection of market processes, or traditional rule-following, as solutions to economic and social problems. The public world of politics and administration gradually but perceptibly replaced the private world of individual choice and voluntary action as the focus of attention for political thought and practice.

The kind of new Right thinking that is described in this book is primarily the intellectual response to the consensus and the mode or style of politics associated with it. I attach little significance to the word 'Right'; I use it for no other reason than the fact that the political thought I discuss is commonly called 'right-wing'. However, I would stress at the outset that this book is not at all concerned with that old-style, neo-collectivist and anti-liberal 'Right' associated

with some types of European conservatism. Often this is monarch-
ical and religious and has little or no connection with the intellectual issues analysed in the following pages.

My concern is mainly with the classical liberal or individualist
response to the break-up of the consensus and, to a lesser extent,
with a certain type of conservatism. I maintain that in traditional
English political thought, at least, classical liberals and conservatives
have a lot more in common than the leading spokesmen of either
tendency are prepared to admit. This similarity is not explained
merely by the fact that it is Conservative political parties that have
adopted, to some extent, free-market policies in recent years; it is
more to do with a particular conservative tradition — a tradition
which, as I try to show, was all but obliterated by post-war consensus conservatism.

My main concern in this book is with political thought rather
than political philosophy. I have written elsewhere on some of the
more abstract and theoretical questions of classical liberalism and
individualism. Thus I am concerned with those aspects of classical
liberal political and economic ideas that have had a bearing on public
policy and institutional reform in the past decade, especially in
Britain and the USA. Although this is neither a work on public
policy nor contemporary history, I have found it useful in some areas
to look at those policy problems on which liberal ideas have had
a direct or, more likely, indirect, influence. This has meant that I
concentrate almost entirely on the utilitarian aspects of liberalism,
with only fleeting reference to the 'natural rights' or purely ethical
bases of individualist thought.

A word of clarification on my use of the term 'liberal' may be
appropriate. Most of the time I use it in its traditional sense in
reference to free-market and individualist ideas in economic matters.
In political matters liberalism describes key aspects of constitutionalism and the rule of law. The problem is that today, liberalism
is rarely used exclusively in those ways and has come to be associated
(erroneously) with many aspects of consensus-based social thought.
This is especially true of America, where liberalism is used in almost
the opposite sense to that intended by the founders of the doctrine.
I hope that it is clear to the reader which senses of this difficult term
is being used in the text.

The first four chapters are about the general problems of the consensus, liberalism and conservatism. I then look at the way the
doctrines of liberalism and conservatism have been understood in
Britain, the USA and West Germany. This has led to some unavoid-

able repetition, since liberalism, especially is characterised by certain more or less *universal* social economic and political propositions. A full explication of the doctrine necessarily involves some reiteration of its basic premises as we move from country to country.

The recent intellectual histories of Britain and America are in some ways remarkably similar. Writers in both countries have expressed considerable dissatisfaction with the prevailing semi-collectivist consensus and have gone back to some familiar but neglected political and social ideas of freedom. West Germany, as I shall show, is a somewhat aberrant case since for much of the post-war period, her economy and polity were conducted under more or less orthodox individualist principles. Political and economic policies that had become orthodox in Britain and the USA were not seriously entertained in the Federal Republic until the late 1960s and early 1970s. This is an interesting story in itself, which cannot be told here. It is sufficient to say that the principles of the German 'social market economy' are now prospering in countries which were formerly the bastions of consensus orthodoxy.

Many of the ideas outlined in the following pages have been clarified and developed over the years through conversations with many friends and colleagues too numerous to mention. However, I would like to express my thanks to John Burton, not for any direct connection with the contents of this book, of which he has read little, but for his knowledge of the subject matter, and his friendship, both of which have been invaluable. The manuscript was completed at Buckingham between 1985 and 1986 and, as on other occasions, I am indebted to my secretary, Sandra Gilbert, for her excellent typing.

Norman P. Barry
Buckingham

1

Against the Consensus

I

In almost all of what may be loosely called the Western democratic world (the notable exception was West Germany), the period from the late 1940s to about the mid-1970s experienced a remarkable era of intellectual stability. This is not to under-estimate the grave political and economic crises that regularly occurred, but only to suggest that they took place within the context of an ideological consensus comprising economic, social and political thought. The 'ends' of social and political life seemed not to be in dispute, though debate about the means to achieve those ends, and even about the precise meaning of the ends themselves, could be fierce as well as erudite. The ideological consensus might well be labelled as 'social democracy', except that this would imply that it was attached exclusively to the Labour Party of Great Britain and the Social Democratic parties of Europe. However, its most remarkable feature was the fact of its acceptance by the mainstream of conservative political opinion. There persisted an intellectual *ancien régime* of the 'reactionary Right', as well as of the Marxist Left and an *almost* senescent classical liberal stream, but the ideas of these groups, especially the last, were distinctly unfashionable.

The outlines of this consensus can be briefly summarised here (though the details will emerge later). The consensus begins with a rejection of the idea that spontaneous social forces, and the consequent traditional or customary modes of behaviour, are themselves sufficient to guarantee that level of economic development of which a community is capable. The experience of the Great Depression, with material and human resources lying idle for long periods of time, was sufficient to convince a whole generation of economists

1

that an unhampered market economy would periodically generate mass unemployment, which would not be eliminated spontaneously. The organisation of a market economy, at the macro-level at least, required a more active state than most European democracies had hitherto experienced (outside war-time).

It is no accident that the role of the state should be further extended into the interstices of economic and social life: for the existence of mass unemployment also highlighted problems of social welfare. Once again it was assumed that the state was superior to the private insurance market in fulfilling the role of protecting individuals against the vicissitudes of economic life. It was assumed that without the state people would be helpless victims of the 'blind' and unpredictable forces of the market. Furthermore, it seemed 'natural' that the state's welfare role should be extended into education and health. The rationale for this was not merely the relief of suffering (after all, state aid for the indigent had been accepted as an essential feature of public policy for centuries) but the creation of more equal opportunities. 'Social justice', where this term refers to the correction of a pure market determination of income so as to produce some desired social 'outcome', became perhaps the most predominant feature on the masthead of the new consensus. This contrasts markedly with the earlier idea of justice and equality — an idea much more limited, and confined to the guarantee of equality before the law and the application of fair and non-discriminatory rules to cases arising out of the relationship between essentially *private* agents.

It should be pointed out, however, that the extent to which social justice and equality should be pursued produced the most dissent amongst the adherents of the new orthodoxy. However, even here the critics of too extreme an egalitarianism were more concerned, in a utilitarian manner, to point out the effect this would have on incentives and economic performance, than to embark on any sustained defence of *individual* rights and claims to legitimately acquired property that were threatened by equality.

A further important element in the consensus was the acceptance of the power of organised labour and the attempt to incorporate trade unions more closely into the *political* decision-making process. Of course, the legal privileges accorded to unions, especially their exemption from the law of tort in relation to industrial disputes, preceded the period under discussion (in Britain the crucial legal land-mark is the 1906 Trades Disputes Act), but the post-war period witnessed the transformation of unions from economic agencies concerned with protecting the interests of their members in the workplace into bodies of great significance in legislation and politics. However, it was only in Britain that the *political* influence of trade unions was of great significance. In America the number of union-ised workers has always been low (at present little more than 20 per cent of the workforce — and this figure includes a significant number of public-sector employees); and in Europe the division between communist and non-communist unions prevented the organised labour movement from achieving that unity which is required for lasting political influence.

The greatest effect of the new union power was felt in the nationalised industries. The new consensus did not advocate the wholesale socialisation of the means of production but it did main-tain that certain 'key' industries, primarily in the areas of energy, communications and transport, were too important to be left to the 'vagaries' of the market. However, this had the unintended effect of taking wage determination in these industries out of the impers-onal market and increasing the power of the unions to secure 'economic rent' for their members — a process enhanced by the monopoly or quasi-monopoly status of publicly-owned industries. The emergence of the 'mixed economy' also brought unanticipated and unintended sources of conflict.

The major elements of the post-war period taken as a whole may be said to constitute an 'ideology'. It consists partly of a scientific (or perhaps pseudo-scientific) explanation of the way the social world works, and partly of a set of values, or more accurately, policy prescriptions, claimed to represent in concretised form the general agreement about the ends that exist in society. The particular strength of the post-war consensus was thought to lie in the fact that the policy prescriptions were validated by the conclusions of genuine scientific enquiry: a prosperous, harmonious social order became possible rather than merely ideal.

Another way of expressing this would be, to borrow a preten-tious term from the philosophy of science, to say that it resembled a 'paradigm'.[1] To avoid getting involved in the complexities of this concept it is sufficient to say that a paradigm consists of a com-prehensive and *internally* coherent explanation of the world which, although in large part supported by impressive scientific evidence, is, in its basic and fundamental tenets, impervious to rational refuta-tion or demonstration. Research consists of puzzle-solving and amending work conducted within the confines of the paradigm rather than challenging the basic postulates of the system of ideas itself. The overturning of one paradigm and its replacement with another is thought to be not a rational event, a revolution in a theory brought about by the conclusions of *objective* enquiry, but a change in attitudes of the intellectual class. Although this change is generated by continuing dissatisfaction with the growing failures (in predictions and so on) of the old paradigm and the belief that a new one is superior, the switch of the intelligentsia to a new way of thinking seems to be very subjective in nature.

In social thought there are some similarities to this process. The post-war ideological consensus that we are describing did broadly seem to come about in this way, though it is doubtful if there are any clear-cut and unambiguous paradigms in social enquiry. Certainly, however, the dissatisfaction with the hitherto prevailing 'model' of economic explananation, the neo-classical theory of the market determination of an equilibrium set of prices (of goods and factors of production) was generated largely by the apparent failure of this theory to account adequately for the experience of the 1930s. The Keynesian theory of the management of the economy by macro-economic methods looks suspiciously like an alternative paradigm: indeed a whole generation of economists seemed to be as much entranced as intellectually convinced by it.

Other aspects of the ideological paradigm, although they lacked the sophistication of the economic part, were nevertheless effective in attracting almost overwhelming intellectual support. Political scientists, sociologists and public administrators were almost entirely occupied in either the 'dispassionate' study of the new collectivist state or in seeking new and improved ways of administering its un-challenged goals. Thus, for example, in government and public administration, practitioners were far more interested in perfecting the administration of state services than in discussing the funda-mental issue of whether these should be delivered privately or pub-licly. In Britain especially, the seemingly endless rounds of reforms of central and local government and welfare organisations from 1945 to the mid-1970s, although of an administrative rather than a substantive kind, faithfully reflected the prevailing research interest of the social-science profession.

Not only did the more traditional academic social-science disciplines devote much of their attention to the exploration of the implications of the consensus, but new subjects were in effect 'invented' for this very purpose. Thus social administration and the other academic off-shoots of the burgeoning concern with social policy became the mechanical adjuncts of the normative ends

4

of the consensus.

At the same time as the acceptance of the social thinking of the new consensus became virtually complete, the influence of logical positivism, and its successor, the 'ordinary language' school of analytical philosophy, began to dominate academic political philosophy.[2] In fact, the rigour of conceptual analysis cut through the pretensions of traditional metaphysics (which underlay much received political philosophy) so successfully that the subject was proclaimed to be 'dead'.[3] In accepting the post-Humean view of reason as being impotent in the construction and justification of political and moral value systems, and incompetent to adjudicate between rival *Weltangschauungen*, the positivists virtually consigned political philosophy to the task of the dry analysis of concepts. An analysis of language that castigated all normative statements as 'emotive'[4] and designated empirical science and mathematics as the highest (if not quite the only) form of human knowledge was bound to have catastrophic effects on a discipline hitherto concerned with, for example, understanding the relationship between the individual and the state and demonstrating the nature of fundamental human rights.

In fact these philosophical movements had little effect on practical politics (despite the claims of many Marxists that philosophy's dismissal of political theory was a thinly disguised defence of the *status quo*). The argument that ultimate political principles could not be grounded in reason, that they rested on feelings and emotions rather than logic and metaphysics, did not tarnish the intellectual integrity of social democracy. Indeed, many of the analytical philosophers were overt advocates of the post-war semi-collectivist state and welfare society — though they were eager to point out that this advocacy had nothing to do with their professional philosophical interests. In effect, public opinion (as interpreted by the intellectuals — an important qualification, as we shall see) rather than reason became the source of political and moral value; and political *thought* replaced political philosophy as the formalised expression of that value.

However, analytical philosophy, and especially its positivist variant, left one important legacy for social science generally and for the rationale of the new consensus in particular: this was the emphasis on empirical investigation as the only genuine, incorrigible source of knowledge. The original, and extremely crude, positivist philosophy of social science had not only put a prohibition on value judgements acquiring any rational status, but had also limited scientific propositions to empirical generalisations: any statement of purported causality which was not, in principle at least, *verifiable* was dismissed as mere *a priori* speculation.[5] Whatever its epistemological shortcomings[6] (and there were many), this injunction was eagerly obeyed by the practising social scientists within the consensus. The literature of economics, political science and sociology soon began to abound with empirical studies; and while such 'information' that was acquired did not (as a matter of logic) convey any normative implications, it was undoubtedly used to buttress the prescriptions of the new moderate collectivism.

One classic example is always worth quoting: this is the case of homelessness, in which the cataloguing of vast amounts of empirical data about rising trends in the numbers of homeless people is always used to license demands for more public spending on housing. Yet scarcely any attention is given to the *theoretical* explanations of why this regularly occurs: in fact it is largely as a result of previous interventions in the housing market, normally by way of rent control and security of tenure legislation, which disrupts a potential equilibrium between the supply of and the demand for the housing stock.[7]

One lacuna in the theory of the consensus was to have very serious implications for its long-term viability: this was the lack of any real understanding of the nature of the state, coupled with a naïve belief in the efficacy of 'politics' as a problem-solving method. It was here that the withdrawal of political philosophy from substantive issues had perhaps its most damaging effect. In fact, the most important contributions to the theoretical understanding of state and politics were made by economists rather than political scientists or philosophers.

In this century the general view of the state in social democratic and moderate collectivist political thought has been benign. Its coercive features have been underplayed and it has been regarded as the purveyor of welfare and general beneficence rather than the embodiment of legalised force. Of course, the position was not quite as naïve as this simple statement might imply. No advocate of the mixed economy thought that all state action was necessarily good, but rather that the state was in some important sense *neutral* and therefore capable of being used for virtuous ends. As R.H. Tawney put it: 'Fools will use it, when they can, for foolish ends, criminals for criminal ends, sensible and decent men will use it for ends which are sensible and decent.'[8] There was little consideration of the possibility that the state might have its own mode of operation (which could be analysed by the social sciences) and that it might develop in such a way that it fails to reflect the prescriptions of 'sensible and decent men'.

This point, perhaps more than any other, serves to distinguish almost all varieties of social democracy or the new consensus, from their rivals on the Marxist Left and from the *laissez-faire* classical liberal school. The Marxists maintain an essentially 'exploitative' theory of the state: its institutions serve to preserve the (basically property) interests of the ruling class. The expression 'welfare state' should therefore be self-contradictory. However, the apparent successes of the post-war welfare state in meeting working-class demands is explained away as simply a 'concession' required to secure the loyalty of what would otherwise be a revolutionary proletariat.[9] However, it should be pointed out that some Marxist economists have produced quite sophisticated analyses of the 'fiscal crisis' of the welfare state[10] — analyses which show how the escalating costs of such concessions will eventually prove too great for mixed economies to bear.

The classical liberals have always been most critical of what they regard as a naïve conception of the state held by the social democrats. In their view the mistake was to interpret the motivations of public officials as being different from transactors in the private market. Thus, so far from displaying an altruism and devotion to public duty, public officials maximise their utility through the public sector — leading inevitably to its expansion (see below, chapter 3).

The assumption common to much social-democratic thinking was that 'public action' always meant action directed towards some discernible common good, while 'private action' denoted purely self-regarding behaviour which could have no socially beneficial consequences.[11] The original notion (from Adam Smith) that public benefit accrues almost accidentally from more or less self-interested behaviour was implicitly, and often explicitly, rejected. In its place there was a rationalist assumption that the public good was not only discernible but that it required deliberate prosecution, through statute law, regulation and economic guidance; in other words it could not be generated spontaneously. In this position, the social-democratic view is not that distinct, theoretically at least, from the authoritarian conservative Right, the theorists of which believe in the necessity of a strong state to preserve, and indeed create, a social equilibrium — though the extent of this state is more limited, and its mode of operation more coercive (for example, conservatism is less sympathetic towards civil liberties or the wide extension of individual freedom in private morality than social democracy).

This sanguine attitude towards the state was undoutedly encour-

aged by the experience of war. The success of the state in organis-
ing productive activity for the defeat of Germany not surprisingly
led many social thinkers to conclude that public administration and
centralised planning could similarly be used to combat the problems
of unemployment and social deprivation. Even the liberal economist,
Lionel (Lord) Robbins, who had been an intellectual opponent of
Keynes in the 1930s, admits to having his views modified by his
successful experience as an economic planner during the War.[12]
Furthermore, the high government spending during the War gave
an additional fillip to statist ideas, as well as partly anaesthetising
the population to heavy taxation. There was clearly a connection
between the post-war upward trend in public spending and the effect
of the War itself.[13]

Along with an expansionary state, the notion of 'politics' as a
decision-making process assumed new importance. The new consensus was not authoritarian; it did not believe that conceptions or
visions of the good society should be imposed (though, in the field
of welfare at least, there was a strong paternalistic streak), but neither
was there an acceptance of the workings of an impersonal market.
In the absence of general altruism on the part of individuals, the
only alternative method of decision-making was political, through
the democratic electoral process or through bargaining between
government and pressure groups.

The importance of the gradual 'politicisation' of social and
economic life cannot be over-stressed. It is measured not merely
in the increasing proportion of national income spent by the state
— though this clearly indicates an increasing predominance of
public over private ends — but also in the existence of a general
social and political environment which encouraged investment in
politics rather than in economic activity. The classical liberal critics
of the welfare state were quick to point out the enervating effects
which the constant pressure of group activities (consisting of organised minorities demanding privileges from the state) had on political
institutions. This point of view is shared by anti-liberal conservatives.
Despite their coolness towards the individualism of extreme market
philosophies, they have a similar scepticism about the possibility
of political action securing desirable ends. Politics should be limited
to preserving social order and not extended to the promotion of
substantive equality or social justice. This will only raise expectations that cannot be fulfilled and will result in a threat to the fabric
of the social order.

The most important effect of the more extensive role of politics was the rise in the *discretion* it granted to government officials, elected and non-elected. This led to a gradual desuetude of constitutional and legal constraints on political action. In fact, the prosecution of the social-democratic programme is almost inevitably accompanied by a decline in 'constitutionalism' or the 'constitutional attitude'. Legal rules that restrain political action and initiative are regarded, in almost Platonic manner, as unnecessary and reactionary obstacles that impede progress towards the achievement of the 'good'. The belief in the importance of such constraints, however, derives from scepticism about the value of purported social ends and a desire to ensure that formal procedures are followed. Furthermore, it is claimed that individual rights are more adequately protected by rules than politics.

It is worth pointing here to an analogy between economics and politics — between monetary constraints and constitutional constraints. The Gold Standard is an automatic rule that prevents governments destabilising the monetary system by inflating the currency. While there may be short-run advantages in terms of increased output and employment by increasing demand through inflation, the philosophy of the Gold Standard implies that such *discretionary* action must ultimately be very damaging to economic stability.[14] In the same way the relaxation of strict constitutional rules to secure some immediate utilitarian goal simple encourages an attitude of laxity on the part of political rules and renders them gullible to almost any political demands that might be made on them. It is not coincidence that the abandonment of strict monetary rules, a main plank in the social-democratic programme from Keynes onwards, should have been accompanied by a growing inclination to loosen more general constitutional ties.

Britain has always been in a peculiar position here since it has no written constitution. The doctrine of parliamentary sovereignty (leaving aside the minor dent in the principle caused by Britain's accession to the EEC) prevents any constitutional restraints being made permanent (they can always be overturned by temporary majorities of, in effect, the House of Commons). Furthermore, because there are no formal constraints on what Parliament can do, the lax and flexible 'British Constitution' turned out to be an admirable political instrument for the implementation of the various social-democratic programmes. Again, it is no surprise that the advocates of a new constitutional settlement for Britain [15] should also be critics of social democracy (though there is no logical necessity for this to be so).

Britain had, then, a 'constitutionalism' of a peculiarly permissive kind. What prevented this being used to override individual rights in the pursuit of collective ends in the past was the presence of a 'constitutional attitude'. This is no more than an intuitive under-standing of the limits on political action that ought to exist — a set of informal rules. Something like this must have operated in the past two centuries of British constitutional development, otherwise the principle of parliamentary sovereignty could have been used to very damaging effect.

Even countries with much more formal constraints, in the form of 'rigid' constitutions, proved to be incapable of resisting the trend. In the USA for example, despite the separation of powers, federalism and the absence of a sovereign legislature, social and economic policies markedly similar to those in Britain and Western Europe were implemented. Many of these, because they affected fundamental human and property rights, would have surely been ruled unconstitutional in the last century. However, the shifting opinions of the Supreme Court have proved to be the major determinants of social and economic changes, despite the presence of alleged strict rules.

The social democrats' lack of concern for the values of constitu-tional restraints, or more precisely the denial of their necessity, prob-ably sprang from their belief that the consensus was more widely based than it was in reality. The delicate problem of translating people's preferences into political reality, of constructing a constitu-tional order that enabled a genuine public opinion to be expressed at the level of government, was irrelevant to a school of thought that assumed that there were few differences in the preferences and fundamental outlooks of the people. However, it is plausible to argue that the consensus was of a political elite rather than of the majority and that lax constitutional rules permitted that social philosophy to predominate.

II

There is no one over-arching *theory* of the consensus we are describ-ing, no one book that encapsulates its major prescriptions and founds them on indubitable philosophical premises: as we have said, this was an age of political thought, not political philosophy. Furthermore, since a number of social-science disciplines con-verged on the the same theme, it would have been a difficult task for any one political theorist to master them all. The task was made all the more difficult by the increasingly specialised nature of the cognate subjects. More important, perhaps, was the fact that some of the inter-connections between the disciplines were missed: for example, many of the prescriptions of social welfare were made in ignorance of well-established findings of micro-economics. In fact there was a scarcely concealed contempt for micro-economic theory: a belief that this was a senescent doctrine that failed to describe accurately the features of modern capitalist economies. In fact, much of the social thought of the consensus consists of a reaction to the classical liberal system of ideas rather than a positive theoretical construction in its own right. In economics, the assaults on the received orthodoxy were directed at both the macro- and micro-levels. These assaults were of course designed to demonstrate the superiority of planning (albeit of a moderate kind) over spontaneity.

In a general sense, the Keynesian 'revolution' in economics sums up the whole attitude of the political consensus that was to emerge after the War. Keynes himself was certainly no socialist, least of all Marxist (he once described *Das Capital* as an 'obsolete economics textbook'), and he never really challenged the price mechanism, at the micro-level, as the best resource-allocation mechanism.[16] Rather, the Keynesian message derives from his belief that the tendency of the market to produce an 'equilibrium' (of full employment of all resources) was ill-founded: this he claimed was only a chance phenomenon that might occur, not an enduring property of the system. Although it is impossible to go into the details of Keynesian macro-economics here, some mention must be made of it since it constituted the economic corner-stone of the post-war consensus. There were a number of reasons why an unhampered market economy would not necessarily generate full employment for Keynes. The key issues were the roles of money, the rate of interest and the price of labour.

For Keynes, the demand for money did not comprise simply a transactions demand, i.e. a demand for money as a tool for facilitating exchange, but also included a 'speculative' demand — in other words, a demand for money to be held as an *asset* in preference to interest-bearing bonds on which a capital loss might be made if interest rates rose. The idea that money might be held and not spent or invested would be absurd to neo-classical theorists, but it was this speculative demand for money that accounted for the quite different function that money played in Keynesian macro-economics. The demand for money varied inversely with the interest rate and the latter's role was that of equating the demand for money with the available stock. This meant that the rate of interest could not be the instrument that equilibrated saving and investment so as to ensure the full employment of all resources.

More generally, Keynes did not believe that business activity was an efficient motor of the capitalist system. Business men were not the rational calculators that orthodox theory demanded. They responded in a 'herd-like' manner to irrational waves of optimism and pessimism rather than to fine changes in the rate of interest. Hence any attempt by the monetary authorities to get the rate of interest down may not succeed in inducing them to make the additional investment required for full employment.

While Keynes did not preclude the use of monetary policies to bring down the rate of interest, he thought that such policies would not be effective if liquidity preference is high (if people wish to hold money for speculative purposes). To the neo-classical argument that unemployment was caused by wages being above market-clearing levels, he said that to cut wages would further reduce demand, thereby creating unemployment. In a depression the only way to raise employment is to raise spending, and if private spending is inadequate, then only increased public spending, through budget deficits, can fill the gap. This, then, is the intellectual origin of 'pump-priming' and high government spending so characteristic of the post-war consensus.

The most important question was that of wages. Keynes accepted the wage rate set by unions as rigid — a kind of historical constant that could not be altered in nominal terms. Yet he knew that *real* wages would have to fall eventually if all willing labour were to be employed in a normally functioning economy and he thought that this would be achieved by mild inflation. In fact, the Keynesian system depends to a large extent on the existence of 'money illusion', i.e. the belief on the part of unions that their real wages are not falling under inflation. If they did realise this then they would simply demand higher wages — if this demand is successful, the real wage does not fall and therefore workers remain priced out of jobs. In fact, the critics of Keynes argue that this is exactly what has happened.

Behind the technical apparatus of macro-economics, however, lurked a general social philosophy. Although it was never articulated as such, and might be better described as an attitude of mind rather than a coherent doctrine, it was nonetheless essential to the economic theory and policy. Keynes was undoubtedly a utilitarian rationalist who believed that the human mind was capable of solving all social and economic problems without the aid of tradition, and without the need to rely on customary rules of behaviour.[17] His utilitarianism was 'act-utilitarianism', i.e an action (personal, political or economic) was justified if it produced an immediate discernible benefit. Such a utilitarianism, of course, licenses the over-turning of conventions and traditions if they can be given no rational justification. There can be no such thing as 'immanent wisdom' of 'tacit knowledge' that cannot be expressed in formal terms.[18] Despite being the author of *The General Theory of Employment, Interest and Money*, Keynes's political and economic policies were of a *particularist* kind, concerned with finding solutions to immediate problems. Furthermore, there was little analysis of the long-run effect of these policies. Had Keynes lived through the inflationary times of the 1970s (caused largely by the implementation of his economic policies), there is no doubt that he would have written another, different, *general* theory.

There was a strong paternalistic streak in Keynesianism, summed up by the expression 'The Harvey Road' mentality.[19] (Harvey Road was Keynes's home at Cambridge.) Successful government required that the right men with the latest 'knowledge' should be in power; unrestrained by archaic rules, such as the Gold Standard, a balanced-budget rule, or a written constitution. It was in many ways entirely inappropriate for the democratic age, in which politi-cians are compelled to respond to the demands of pressure groups and electoral politics. There was an implicit assumption that intellectuals could mould public opinion and even that the masses could be fooled (as the example of 'money illusion' indicates).

A further important legacy of the Keynesian revolution was the increased power which the implementation of demand-management policies gave to trade unions. The abandonment of the theory that unemployment was *always* caused by wages being too high relieved monopoly unions of that responsibilty. Yet wages had to be kept down if the 'stimulation' effects of inflation were not to be frittered away in higher prices. The Keynesian response, though it was *not* that of Keynes himself, was to institute prices-and-incomes policies. Apart from the economic effects of such policies there were also impor-tant political effects; for trade union 'agreement' to abide by them was almost always bought at the price of greater union involvement in other aspects of government policy

Nevertheless, with regard to employment policy, Keynes

had a much more realistic view of actual possibilities than did his acolytes who moulded the economic policy of the post-war consensus. He thought that an unemployment rate of about 7 per cent was feasible yet during the period under consideration as soon as unemployment went above 3 or 4 per cent, 'corrective' measures were taken.[20] It was this mistaken interpretation of the Keynesian message that did most to bring about the inflation that was ultimately to damage irreparably the economic policy of the consensus.

At the micro-level of the economy the analysis was less sophisticated, but the onslaughts against the effects of an untrammelled market were no less persistent. The major complaint was that the ideal picture of a market economy painted in orthodox textbooks of neo-classical orthodoxy no longer accorded with reality.[21] In theory the impersonal, perfectly competitive market is characterised by the absence of *power*. Each participant is an atomised individual who simply responds to price signals and is therefore unable to influence the course of events himself. Thus in an economic world inhabited by a large number of small firms, no one enterprise can determine price, so that inevitably competition drives down prices to marginal cost and 'entrepreneurial' profit is whittled away. The condition of freedom of entry means that oligopoly and monopoly are unable to survive: any potential firm that tries to raise price and reduce output so as to secure monopoly 'rents' will be quickly put out of business by competition. Above all, the consumer is *sovereign* — a rational and autonomous agent whose wants determine what is produced. The producer is powerless and simply acts at the behest of the consumer.

It was this vision that the social democrats, led principally by the American (but Canadian-born) political economist, John Kenneth Galbraith, attacked.[22] Their critique was intended to show that the market order, when uncorrected by social principles, failed to reproduce not merely the aims and purposes of social democracy, but also the ideals of its apologists, the classical liberals. The attack centred on two issues: the status and autonomy of the individual in a market system and the nature of competition itself under free enterprise. The first argument claims that there is an *interdependency* between supply and demand. This means that producers must not be seen as automatons who respond in a mechanistic manner to the demands of consumers; rather, they actively encourage, promote and create wants. The obvious target here was advertising, and it was claimed that quasi-psychological techniques of mass persuasion could induce people to purchase goods they did not 'really' need. The market was not a realm of individual autonomy and consumer sovereignty, but one of servitude. There seems here to be the assertion of a division between 'real' and 'apparent' wants. The latter consist of luxury goods and consumer durables characteristic of capitalistic affluent societies. In the writings of the neo-Marxist Herbert Marcuse,[23] a constant supply of consumer goods to the proletariat numbed the revolutionary impulses of that class and produced an acquiescent, supine population.

It is not clear what policy implications were to be drawn from these random speculations. They certainly cannot justify an increased democratic political control of economic life, for if individuals are incompetent to behave 'rationally' in the economic field, there is no reason to suppose that their behaviour will be any more prudent in the political arena. In fact, the assumption that individuals do not behave autonomously in supermarkets and are highly vulnerable to advertising is indicative of the elitism that pervades anti-market philosophy (even of a non-Marxist kind). Perhaps the real thrust of the argument is directed towards the point that a market system produces 'private affluence and public squalor', to quote Galbraith's notorious phrase. The obsession with luxury and personal consumption goods led to an economy characterised by a decaying infrastructure, poor public services and mounting 'negative externalities' (in the form of pollution and the despoliation of the natural environment). Thus, even on a more conventional utilitarian calculus, an unhampered market, it was claimed, failed to maximise the public welfare. Although the answers to these charges will be considered below, it is well worth pointing out at this stage that the social democrats' case seems to be a mixture of two not always consistent positions. One is a rather orthodox 'public-good' argument, i.e. certain goods such as defence and clean air cannot be priced in the market and therefore have to be delivered by the state. The other is simply the elitist argument alluded to earlier — that people do not choose autonomously and tend to prefer immediate satisfaction from consumer goods rather than to invest in, say, education or health. However, none of these positions was advanced very coherently — and indeed the claim that public squalor existed during a period when the proportion of GNP spent by the state increased inexorably sounds rather hollow.

The second part of the social democrats' argument about the nature of advanced capitalist economies was addressed to the rise of large corporations which, it was alleged, dictate terms in the market place. In other words, producers are not passive 'price-takers', compelled to price their output according to the conclusions of the impersonal processes of competition, but can themselves determine price without too much fear of economic retribution. The development of capitalism takes the form, it is argued, of the gradual elimination of smaller firms and the organisation of industry into larger units that are able to collude against the consumer. Of course, the demands of high technology and the soaring costs of research and development are said to be vital causal mechanisms in this process towards the atrophying of competition. Also, trade unions are not exempt from these strictures, since their large-scale organisation, itself a response to developments on the side of capital, both contribute to the erosion of the model of pure individualism, and also worsens the lot of the unorganised and relatively unskilled workers.

It was not denied that small firms do exist and provide much of the innovation, even in developed capitalist economies (to do so would have been to fly in the face of overwhelming empirical evidence). Galbraith himself seems to divide a typical capitalist economy equally between a sector largely independent of market pressures and one governed almost entirely by them.[24] What is not made clear is whether the alleged erosion of the market is a natural consequence of atomistic competition itself or whether it is also fostered by the growth of the state bureaucracy. On grounds of social democractic theory, the former must be preferred, yet Galbraith and his followers constantly stress that the ability of the large-scale corporation to insulate itself from competition is greatly helped by government contracts, especially in the field of defence. However, the two types of explanation of the decline of competition (itself an assertion rather than a reasoned or empirically based theory) were never properly separated out in the analyses of the consensus.

The consensus did believe in the mixed economy and rejected wholesale nationalisation as a solution to the problems allued to earlier. Indeed, outside the more metaphysical reaches of Marxism, competition was not condemned; it was looked upon more as a heady ideal which the spontaneous operation of the market would not necessarily generate. Therefore the role of the state was to act as a surrogate for a failed market. The theoretical aim was cashed out in policy terms by anti-monopoly law and extensive *regulation* of industry by the bureaucracy: if 'nature' prevented individuals from having the experience of real markets, then they could live a vicarious competive existence through a mixed economy ordered and tempered by the benign hand of political authority.

The major plank in the social democratic programme was social welfare: the role of the state in the provision of welfare was expected to increase (and, of course, it did so) even in conditions of rising prosperity. What theoretical arguments were used to justify this strange (at least superficially) proposition? One would have thought that the notion of individual autonomy would prescribe less direct *state* intervention in personal welfare in rich mixed-economies; and that this would be compatible with the pursuit of social justice if this were to take the form of income and wealth distribution.

Probably the only deep philosophical justification for the welfare and redistributive state was John Rawls's *A Theory of Justice*,[25] published, ironically, in 1971, just at the time that the ideology of the social-democratic consensus was beginning to experience its first sustained *public* intellectual assaults. Although many social democrats have used *A Theory of Justice* as an *ex post facto* rationalisation of the welfare state, it would be misleading to say that this work represents an explicit justification for that social organisation. It is true that Rawls specifies, by a contractarian method, the rational welfare function as one which maximises the well-being of the worst-off in society, and that he denies the right to pure individual ownership by claiming that property and natural talents constitute common assets to be distributed in accordance with the principles of justice; but his whole endeavour is an exercise in political *philosophy* rather than political thought.[26] The more mundane principles of the existing welfare state were constructed independently of *A Theory of Justice*.

In the British social reform tradition that runs from Tawney to Titmuss, equality is either asserted as an end to be pursued for its own sake, or as a means to the creation of a more fraternal society in which attitudes of voluntary co-operation replace the acquisitive, selfish instincts associated with individualistic market society. For the intellectual social democrat there seemed to be something intuitively 'irrational' about the persistence of economic inequality. When R.H. Tawney first published his famous book *Equality*[27] in 1931, he lamented what he called the 'religion of inequality' in British society. The problem for him was not merely that extreme inequalities of income and wealth existed, but that they were accepted as 'legitimate' by the working classes. The people accepted the *mana* and *karakia* of social, and especially economic, inequality in a similar manner that primitive peoples accept the ritual of tribal society. The rationale for this seems to be a form of the 'presumptivist' argument in social philosophy:[28] that is, there is a presumption in favour of equality, and departures from this are to be permitted only if some reason can be given (e.g. differential incomes might be sanctioned on grounds of incentives or desert); but otherwise, an egalitarian distribution ought to prevail. This prevented social democracy from slipping into the wilder extremes of socialist egalitarianism while at the same time putting the onus on the inegalitarian to justify his case. Although this argument is highly implausible,[29] and was never given a fully-fledged rationale, it is behind much egalitarian welfare thinking.

It is by no means obvious that the egalitarian aim should be implemented through collectivist welfare institutions: it might plausibly be argued that a cash redistribution to the poorest in society, leaving them to purchase education, health, social insurance and so on, privately, might be more efficient. However, the argument of Titmuss (in *The Gift Relationship*[30]) was that an egalitarian society required a different set of attitudes — those of giving and sharing rather than the maximising imperative of individualist society. Hence the case was made that the *common* consumption of welfare services would increase feelings of social solidarity and reduce differences between the classes.

There is one further argument used to support *compulsory* welfare, financed through taxation and national insurance. This is the argument from 'moral hazard', i.e., if people are left to spend their incomes on welfare without government interference many will not do so, thus leaving the state eventually with the task of baling them out. Of course, it doesn't have to, but the assumption is that the public will not tolerate a situation in which some people are in dire need even if it is their own fault. Such a situation could even be interpreted as a kind of 'negative externality', so that its correction by the state will increase everybody's welfare. But the knowledge that suffering will be alleviated anyway will increase the incentives for people not to provide privately for their own welfare. In which case, so the argument goes, compulsion is essential in the first place.

This point has important general implications; for it involves the whole question as to whether state action is more prudent, in the sense of taking care of the future, than individual action. The rationale for paternalistic action by the state is that individuals' time preferences, the rate at which they discount the future, is too high. That is to say, individuals prefer present consumption to future well-being and therefore will not invest enough of their income in, e.g., medical insurance and old age pensions. However, one of the most important features of the classical liberal's attack on social democracy, and the whole post-war consensus, is that it is governments that have too high time preferences. Governments are, because of the competitive nature of the democratic process, motivated to pursue policies that will ensure their re-election. This means that they are not likely to be too concerned about the effect of their policies on the distant future. In other words, their time-horizons, comprising at most four or five year election periods, are likely to be much shorter than individuals.

III

We have outlined the main elements of what may be loosely called the social-democratic consensus that ruled intellectual life from the late-1940s to the mid-1970s. In the last ten years the social sciences and political thought have been in their greatest ferment this century, with a number of competing explanations of the present political and economic 'crisis' and an equal number of prescriptions for its resolution. We shall concentrate on the classical liberal (and to a lesser extent, conservative) response. However, it would be quite wrong to suggest that there has been a 'paradigm switch', after the manner described earlier. Firstly, whatever *predictive* success classical liberal political economy has had (and it is quite considerable) it would be quite wrong to suggest that it has captured the economics profession. This is even less true of the other social sciences, where the liberal approach has never enjoyed more than minority support. In addition, it is certainly true that the liberal persuasion was never completely eliminated in social thought, but lay dormant in some places (and even dominant in others, notably the Economics Department of the University of Chicago), waiting for its confident prediction (namely, that the social-democratic consensus would break down) to be fulfilled. Furthermore, whatever success the liberal approach has had in influencing today's intelligentsia, this is not a consequence of its producing radically new explanations of social events, but rather, of its applying long-established but neglected theories to contemporary phenomena. There has been a recrudescence of an old intellectual tendency rather than the construction of a new paradigm. Nevertheless, it cannot be denied that the classical liberal world-view now has to be *countered* for the first time in decades.

Undoubtedly political and economic events were decisive in the shift of opinion. While it may be true that it is ideas, rather than vested interests, which ultimately determine events,[31] ideas take root in fertile intellectual soil. The growing fecundity of classical liberalism and neo-conservatism has largely been generated by the crises of inflation, high public spending and slow growth that social democracies have experienced in the last ten years. Whatever the theoretical vices or virtues of redistribution and extravagant welfare programmes, their practicability depended on continuing economic growth. The doubts about this have simply drawn attention to theoretical problems that were already there.

Although the major problems that afflict social democracy will be discussed in succeeding chapters, some of them may be profitably summarised at this stage. On the economic side, attempts to 'manage' the economy by controlling demand simply led to an escalating inflation. This was mainly because trade unions ceased to be victims of 'money illusion' so that attempts to get the real wage down by mild inflation failed. Unions were successful in anti-cipating future inflation through a learning process, and adjusted their wage claims accordingly. Furthermore, economists discovered (or re-discovered) the 'natural rate' of unemployment, i.e. the level of unemployment determined by structural factors (e.g. labour immobility), and any attempt to get below this level by monetary and fiscal stimulation would result in never-ending inflation.

In fact, Keynes himself cannot really be blamed for all this. Firstly, as we mentioned earlier, he had much more modest expec-tations of the rate of employment that could be secured through demand-management policies than did Keynesians. Furthermore, he also argued that while government deficits are essential to boosting output and employment during the recession, there must be government surpluses during the boom. In other words, the budget must be balanced through the course of the business cycle. This prescription was neglected by political economists and simply ignored by politicians. Deficits became a permanent feature of social-democratic governments, and they were largely caused by electoral pressure. It is no accident that the demand for a constitutional 'balanced-budget' rule has been a strong feature of the classical liberal and neo-conservative programme in the US.

The high public spending by all governments of Western democracies was itself a cause of inflation (though, of course, this does not have to be the case if it is financed by taxation). At a more general level, there was a definite revulsion in the mid-1970s against the inexorably increasing levels of public spending. Not only was government spending thought to be wasteful, and often dictated by special interest groups, but it was also thought to pose a threat to the political stability of liberal democracies, and the individual rights of their citizens. In 1976, Mr Roy Jenkins, a prominent member of Labour cabinets, caused a great controversy with his claim that liberal democracies could not survive for long if public spending exceeded 60 per cent of GNP. Classical liberals and neo-conservatives would claim that that figure is far too high.

Much of public spending goes on welfare and many critics of social democracy claimed that this had an enervating effect, not only on incentives but also on individual autonomy and personal responsibility. While conservatives might lament the decline in 'character' that too much state welfare was said to bring about, and indeed made moralistic comments about selfish and 'unsocial' attitudes of welfare recipients, classical liberals simply pointed out that those people were responding rationally to a situation which was not of their making. If high welfare payments made it not worthwhile for a person to seek employment, he would be foolish to do so.

It is clear, than, that practical circumstances and intellectual changes made the time propitious for the emergence of challenges to the hegemony of the social-democratic consensus. It is to these movements that we now turn.

Notes and References

1. T.S. Kuhn, *The structure of scientific revolutions*, 2nd edn (Chicago University Press, Chicago, 1970).

2. For a general introduction, see J. Urmson, *Philosophical analysis* (Clarendon Press, Oxford, 1956).

3. See T.D. Weldon, *The vocabulary of politics* (Penguin, Harmondsworth, 1953).

4. Described in J.O. Urmson, *The emotive theory of ethics* (Hutchinson, 1958).

5. See Weldon, *The vocabulary of politics*, chapter 5.

6. For Popper's critique of positivism, see his *Unended quest* (Fontana/ Collins, Glasgow, 1976), pp. 80-7.

7. See N.P. Barry, 'The political economy of housing', *C.B.I. Review*, Spring, 1977.

8. R.H. Tawney, 'Social democracy in Britain' in *The Radical Tradition* (Penguin, Harmondsworth, 1966), p. 172.

9. See I. Gough, *The political economy of the welfare state* (Macmillan, London, 1979).

10. J. O'Connor, *The fiscal crisis of the state* (St. Martin's Press, New York, 1973).

11. K.R. Popper argues forcefully that collectivism is not necessarily

opposed to selfishness, and that individualism is not hostile to altruism. See his *The open society and its enemies*, vol. i. (Routledge and Kegan Paul, London, 1945) pp. 100–1.

12. L.C. Robbins, *Autobiography of an economist* (Macmillan, London, 1971), chapter VIII.

13. See A.T. Peacock and J. Wiseman *The growth of public expenditure in the U.K.* (Allen and Unwin, London, 1967).

14. W. Rees-Mogg, *The reigning error* (Hamish Hamilton, London, 1974).

15. See N. Johnson, *In search of the constitution* (Methuen, London, 1980).

16. This is summarised in N.P. Barry, *Hayek's social and economic philosophy* (Macmillan, London, 1979), pp. 167–74.

17. See M. Polyani, *Personal knowledge* (Routledge and Kegan Paul, London, 1973), chapter 5.

18. Ibid.

19. Harvey Rd., Cambridge, was Keynes's home. The 'Harvey Road mentality' is described in D.E. Moggridge, *Keynes*, (Fontana/Collins, Glasgow, 1976), chapter 2.

20. See T.W. Hutchison, *Keynes versus the 'Keynesians'. . .?* (Institute of Economic Affairs, London, 1977).

21. An excellent description of a market system is to be found in A. Alchian and W. Allen, *Exchange and production: theory in use* (Wadsworth, California, 1969).

22. See J.K. Galbraith, *American capitalism* (Hamish Hamilton, London, 1957).

23. See H. Marcuse, *One dimensional man* (Sphere Books, London, 1969).

24. Galbraith's system of the 'dual economy' is described in his *Economics and the public purpose* (Deutsch, London, 1974).

25. J. Rawls, *A theory of justice* (Oxford University Press, London, 1972).

26. Most critics regard Rawls's social philosophy as moderately egalitarian or social democratic, but for a markedly different view, see B. Barry, *The liberal theory of justice*, (Clarendon Press, Oxford, 1973).

27. R.H. Tawney, *Equality* (George Allen and Unwin, London, 1964 edn.), p. 35.

28. The presumptivist argument in favour of equality is assumed in B. Williams, 'The idea of equality' in P. Laslett and W.G. Runciman, *Philosophy, politics and society*, 2nd series (Blackwell, Oxford, 1962).

29. A refutation of the presumptivist argument is to be found in R. Nozick, *Anarchy, state and utopia* (Blackwell, Oxford, 1974), chapter 8.

30. See R. Titmuss, *The gift relationship* (Allen and Unwin, London, 1970).

31. See N.P. Barry, 'Ideas versus interests: the classical liberal dilemma' in N.P. Barry *et al.*, *Hayek's 'serfdom' revisited* (Institute of Economic Affairs, London, 1984), pp. 45–64.

2

The Liberal Alternative — Economics

I

It is undoubtedly the case that the main intellectual challenge to the consensus has come from the ranks of classical liberals. Many of these thinkers remained 'underground' during the dominance of the Keynesian and welfarist orthodoxy and simply waited patiently for its disintegration. As is the case with conservatism, liberalism did not so much represent a new theoretical response to social democracy (although, as we shall see, there have been some significant innovations in liberal social and economic thought in the past twenty years), as constituting a reassertion of some traditional social values.

Before analysing the nature of these values, a simple terminological point must be cleared up immediately. This concerns the use of the term 'liberal'; for it would be true to say that this word has been hi-jacked by intellectual spokesmen for political and social ideas alien to the original nineteenth-century conception of liberalism.[1] The change in meaning has primarily affected economic ideology. Whereas classical liberals have always favoured a market allocation of resources and income, the state being precluded from a redistributive role through taxation, the contemporary 'liberal' has an almost obsessive concern with the alleged injustice of this form of income determination. Furthermore, the contemporary 'liberal' does not have the classical liberal's faith in the equilibrating properties of the market, and thus recommends a wide role for the state in macro-economic management. The differences between the two forms of liberalism can be vividly illustrated by their rival conceptions of the government budget. To a classical liberal, the budget is simply the means of financing necessary

23

government services (those that cannot be provided by the market); and it should always *balance*. To the modern liberal, public finance also has a redistributive role, together with the task of creating employment in a recession (hence the frequency in the modern world of unbalanced budgets) by adjusting the level of demand.

The only real connection with traditional liberalism lies in the belief that the new commitment to economic activism can be combined with the older concern for the protection of civil liberties. It is indeed true that the emergence of permissive attitudes concerning personal morality (and the repeal of repressive laws regulating sexual conduct and artistic expression) was largely engineered by an intellectual elite also committed to a more *dirigiste* economic philosophy. However, even here civil liberties were extended beyond traditional individualism to include 'positive discrimination' with regard to race and sex, and other controls over private choices. The transformation of liberalism from an individualistic to a collectivistic ideology has been virtually completed in the US where a 'liberal' would be 'social democrat' in the conventional European nomenclature. As we shall see later, the development of the US Constitution in the twentieth century has produced a remarkable expansion of civil liberties *pari passu* with a contraction of economic freedom.

Despite these conceptual and terminological mutations we shall use liberal in the older sense, without always adding the adjective 'classical'. Although Americans now tend to use the word 'libertarian' to describe social and economic individualism, this word is much less familiar to European ears and, furthermore, in American usage it tends to connote a more extreme social philosophy.[2] What is equally important is the fact that liberalism will be used here exclusively in the description of certain philosophical, economic and political attitudes, and not in connection with particular political parties. Liberal attitudes can be found in almost all of the major political parties in Western democracies, and in recent years the most receptive parties to *economic* liberalism have been conservative ones. Although in the US and Britain, for example, the Republican and Conservative Parties have been reluctant to incorporate into their programmes the social and *personal* liberties associated with the purest form of the doctrine.

II

Although the popular image of liberalism, even amongst informed intellectual circles, is that of a unified, coherent and even monolithic body of social and economic doctrine, this is something of a caricature: for while there might be broad agreement on basic policies, a cursory analysis of the doctrine reveals a myriad of differing schools of thought and political tendencies which, if not pointing in radically differing directions, occupy parallel lines on an hypothetical ideological diagram rather than exactly the same space. It would be even more misleading to place contemporary liberals in some kind of Left-Right political spectrum, even though classical liberalism has been stuck with the label 'radical Right' for some time.[3]

The reason is simple: as we saw in the previous chapter the Right is traditionally associated with conservatism of an anti-rationalist kind. Here obedience to the state, an authoritarian structure of law and a reluctance to embrace radical reforms emanating from any source produce anti-individualism. Although private property, the market and personal liberty all feature strongly in most formal expressions of conservatism, they do not often rest on individualistic philosophical foundations and are almost always subordinate to the demands of stability and continuity. On some issues at least liberals might find themselves on the left side of this hypothetical spectrum. Furthermore, there is in liberal thought the absence of that mystical reverence for the state that dominates much conservative philosophy.

The major figures and movements in contemporary liberalism are easily identifiable. It is to be noticed that most of these writers were originally economists who either applied traditional economic analysis to familiar social problems or developed political theories on economic foundations. In either enterprise liberals challenged the *autonomy* of politics and constructed social theory on the basic individualistic postulate of micro-economics. In this they have departed strongly from orthodox conservatism; this does subordinate economic factors to the wider consideration of social order, stability and continuity. As we shall see, liberals have recognised that there is some truth in the frequent accusation of 'economism', i.e. that they have no social theory apart from the application of economic principles to all social phenomena (on the assumption that human behaviour is always of a self-interested kind). Almost all liberals would now concede that economics alone is not a sufficient foundation on which to base a viable social theory — a concession reflected in the recent re-emphasis on ethical, legal and constitutional factors. Although economism is readily apparent at the policy level, most contemporary classical liberals embody their positive economic prescriptions in a more comprehensive and general social theory.

The dramatis personae of the new liberal movement is easy to identify. The original dissentient voices against the consensus did undoubtedly come from the field of economics. Indeed the very existence of micro-economics, a subject that is entirely concerned with valid deductions that can be made from postulates of *individuals* in market situations, is itself a recognition of at least one aspect of the liberal credo. The most articulate, lucid and persuasive proponent of the new economic liberalism is undoubtedly Milton Friedman (although his brand of liberalism has many other representatives from Friedman's university, Chicago). Although his major technical work is in macro-economics,[4] his individualist political philosophy is vigorously expressed in *Capitalism and Freedom, Free to Choose* and *The Tyranny of the Status Quo* (the last two written in collaboration with his wife, Rose Director Friedman). Perhaps the other most important members of what is known as the Chicago tradition are George Stigler and Gary Becker. Again, these two writers are economists whose work has an indirect application to politics.

What unites all the writers in this tradition is an enthusiastic commitment to *positivism* — the methodological doctrine that holds that the only true propositions in social science are those that can be established by empirical observation. Chicago economists also maintain another postulate of positivism — the doctrine of ethical non-cognitivism. This is the view that propositions about good and bad, right and wrong, just and unjust and so on, do not convey any objective information about the world, but merely express the subjective opinions of the utterer. Thus for Friedman, the only way that normative disputes can be settled is by converting them into empirical arguments: values are things about which men can only 'ultimately fight'. Chicago economics, then, is very much in the orthodox social-science tradition: it merely claims that empiricism vindicates liberalism. On the assumption that most men (including socialists) agree on the ends of prosperity and liberty, it is argued that the liberal institutions of free markets and limited government will maximise these better than any known alternative.

The other alternative to the Chicago tradition in free-market economics is the 'Austrian' School. Although this dates back to the work of Carl Menger in the last century, it all but vanished into obscurity for much of this century. The tradition was kept alive by Ludwig von Mises (1881–1973),[6] although he became better known as an ideological, and sometimes over-belligerent, defender of liberalism than for his technical work in monetary and trade-cycle theory. However, its most important representative is F. A. von Hayek[7] (born 1899), whose ideas have been influential in contemporary policy-making. However, his construction of a liberal order is as much a product of certain political, philosophical and legal ideas, derived generally from the Scottish Enlightenment, and particularly from David Hume and Adam Smith, as it is by pure Austrian economics.

The contrasts between Friedman and Hayek are not often appreciated. Although both adhere to the free market, the justification of it for Hayek (and others in the Austrian tradition) depends less on empirical demonstrations of the efficacy or otherwise of policies than on the delineation of certain universally true features of human action from which can be derived the necessity (if men are to advance their ends) of certain economic and political institutions. Furthermore, as we shall see later in this chapter, there is a specific disagreement between Austrians and Chicago political economists over the appropriate monetary policy for a free order.

A crucially important feature of the new liberalism is the analysis of the behaviour of public officials. An unexamined assumption of the apologists for the consensus was that officials, elected and non-elected, could be relied upon to behave in a virtuous and publicly oriented manner. However, the inexorable growth of government activity, much of which was not directed towards public ends, cast doubt on this blithe assumption of the essential benevolence of political actors. It was the Virginia school of public choice economists, led principally by James Buchanan and Gordon Tullock,[8] which provided a theoretical support for the intuitive distrust of the proposition that government action is benign felt by the traditional liberal. By applying the individualistic calculus of micro-economics to public action, they were able to show that utility-maximising politicians do not necessarily maximise the public interest. Their search for appropriate rules to constrain public figures brought the problem of constitutionalism to a prominent place on the liberal's agenda.

Closely allied to this theoretical approach is Mancur Olson's analysis of pressure groups and special interests in two important books on political economy and social theory.[9] The general conclusion of Olson's work is that the traditional political scientists' view that the activity of special interest groups is a benign, and indeed necessary, adjunct to the formal political process is false. Classical liberals have always accepted that the concept of the public interest has cognitive significance — i.e. it is not merely an emotive slogan designed to dissemble the privately oriented nature of all policies. The public interest refers to those policies (and institutions) which promote the interests each individual has as an *anonymous* member of the public. For the liberal these will be limited, perhaps, to zero inflation, the rule of law, and government activity restricted to the production of genuine public goods. Olson explains how modern democratic systems provide incentives for groups, or combinations of groups, to secure privileges which ultimately defeat the public interest. Ironically, the more stable a political system is, the more it will encourage the proliferation of such groups.

The above writers may broadly be termed utilitarian liberals in that their analyses are conducted in consequentialist terms; at the very least they are concerned with explaining (and, indeed, predicting) the adverse consequences that accrue from systematic attenuation of the market. The ends of human action are taken to be prosperity and liberty, but no specific *moral* arguments are used to establish those principles, and furthermore, objections to intervention are not primarily focused on the 'rights-violating' nature of such intervention. Some of the above writers are explicitly opposed to philosophical theories of natural rights. It is true that in popular discussion, the legitimacy of the liberal order is made to turn on 'rights' and 'freedoms', but it is undoubtedly the case that its major contemporary intellectual exponents place little direct reliance on morality. The significant exception is Robert Nozick. His *Anarchy, State and Utopia* caused a tremendous stir when it was first published in 1974[10] — partly because of the extremely limited role of the state (restricted to a police function with no welfare role or authority to prohibit any act between consenting adults), and partly because his political theory of individualism was rights-based and specifically anti-utilitarian. Against any form of collectivism that sacrifices individuals to social ends, Nozick writes: 'there is no social entity with a good that undergoes some sacrifice for its own good. There are only individual people, with their own individual lives. Using one of these people for the benefit of others, uses him and benefits the others.'[11] His theory of liberalism is based entirely on the argument that there are moral side-constraints on action which limit what men may do (as individuals or through the state) to one another.

However, in the following reconstruction of the basic principles of liberalism, I shall be mainly concerned with broadly utilitarian arguments. These are the terms within which the public-policy debate has been discussed, and which have been most influential on contemporary non-socialist governments in the West. Nevertheless, we should not lose sight of the fact that at the heart of liberalism lies a doctrine about the autonomy and sovereignty of the individual, even if the philosophical development of that doctrine is at the fairly rudimentary stage.

III

The most difficult feature to explain in a reconstruction of the liberal order is the role of reason in it. At first glance a clear contrast between liberalism and conservatism would seem to be that policy decisions for a conservative seem to depend far more on intuitive judgement, or on a special kind of 'political' faculty, than on a carefully worked out scheme of reasoning in which policy judgements emerge in a determinate manner from a fully-articulated set of premisses. Yet this latter method seems to be a strong feature of classical liberalism. Policy recommendations, such as the inadvisability of prices-and-incomes policies, seem to derive entirely from the assumed self-correcting properties of the market: any coercive intervention in wage- or price-fixing by the state will disrupt the automatic signalling process by which factors (labour, capital, and so on) are allocated to their most productive uses. This conclusion follows ineluctably whether or not liberalism is of the empiricist kind, in which meticulous observation and sophisticated econometric testing establishes policy recommendations, or of the *a priori* kind in which conclusions are demonstrated by pure deductive reasoning. In neither case are non-economic factors, such as considerations to do with the 'socially just wage', allowed to modify or correct the process.

Yet it does not follow from this that liberalism is entirely rationalistic: indeed, classical liberals, such as Hayek, are explicitly anti-rationalistic in their intellectual foundations. This anti-rationalism rests upon the utilitarian belief in the superiority of spontaneous forces over conscious decision-making and control in the production of desirable social ends. Although this argument became prominent during the debates in the 1930s and 1940s over the logical possibility of a rationally planned socialist economy,[12] its origins lie deep in the history of political thought.

The first systematic expression of spontaneity was probably in the eighteenth-century Scottish Enlightenment, particularly in the philosophies of David Hume[13] and Adam Smith.[14] Hume's assault on the pretence of reason was designed to show that appropriate rules and institutions emerge by a process of trial, error and evolution rather than by deliberate design. Indeed, since reason can only be the 'slave of passion'; all of our values and ends must ultimately be dictated by emotion. However, far from this sanctioning any kind of *irrationalism*, or a belief that we cannot discriminate at all between rival social doctrines, Hume showed that people tend to approve of those rules and institutions which promote utility. Smith gave the argument a specifically economic twist by describing how the co-ordinating mechanism of the market, operating through a benign self-interest, *accidentally* promoted a desirable end which was no part of any one person's deliberate intentions. As Smith put it, the individual, 'by pursuing his own interest . . . frequently promotes that of society more effectively than when he really intends to promote it. I have never known much good done by those who affected to trade for the public good.'[15]

It is these insights that have been taken up by contemporary classical liberals. Writers such as Hayek and Polanyi have continued Hume's enterprise of using reason to 'whittle down the claims of reason'. Hayek writes frequently of the need to supplement the thesis of the division of labour in economy and society with a thesis about the division of *knowledge*.[16] By this he means that in a complex society, knowledge (or information) is dispersed amongst millions of actors, each one of whom can be acquainted only with that knowledge that affects him personally. The idea that social and economic knowledge (of production costs, consumer tastes, prices and so on) can be centralised in the mind of one person, or even in one institution, is an epistemological absurdity for Hayek.

Michael Polanyi (1891-1976) makes a similar distinction between *articulated* and *tacit* knowledge. The former refers to that knowledge which can be expressed precisely in the form of words, maps or symbols. It is perhaps exemplified best by knowledge in the physical sciences. However, the important point is that the sum of human knowledge is not exhausted by the articulated form. Tacit knowledge or 'unformulated knowledge, *such as we have of something we are in fact doing*, is another form of knowledge'[17] (italics added). The fact that spontaneous social processes generate tacit knowledge is a crucial element in liberal political theory, for its existence casts a serious doubt on the ability of planners, who have only a fragile reason to guide them, to bring about desirable ends. One important point is that much of social and economic knowledge is of a fleeting and ephemeral kind (this is itself largely a product of the unpredictability of human action). The only way a rationally designed plan could work effectively would be if human action, in terms of, say, choices, were regular and predictable: then, social 'states' could be reproduced mechanically. This, of course, does not preclude some regularity in human action: the *tendency* for individuals to maximise their pecuniary self-interest makes a science of economics possible, but this is quite insufficient to make exact quantitative predictions in social affairs.

It follows from this that the market analysis of human affairs is not necessarily rationalistic — for the objection to arbitrary interventions by government in the exchange process is that they disrupt and attenuate the flow of knowledge. Thus prices-and-incomes policies, by disturbing the signalling mechanism of the market, prevent an efficient allocation of resources and reduce the productivity of an exchange economy. The same applies to the familiar example of rent control, which by placing a ceiling on prices reduces the supply of rented accommodation. These cases illustrate the point that spontaneous, decentralised processes exhibit a greater 'rationality' than that of centralised control mechanisms. In advance of there being a market there would be no way in which a planner could *know* what the demands of individuals are.

It is true that classical liberalism takes a rationalistic form when it is asserted that all or almost all social problems can be settled by the application of the principles of market economics. There has always been a problem as to what areas of social life the market should reign over and what activities should be directed by the state. Liberals become rationalistic when, as in the cases of extreme *laissez-faire* or anarcho-capitalistic doctrines, they argue that market mechanisms are always superior to the state. However, most liberals do depend very largely on tradition and experience in areas of life where the application of market principles is not compelling. In Hayek's words, freedom means submitting to general rules 'so long as one has no definite reason to the contrary'.[18] Apparently, there is no alternative between accepting the blind forces of tradition and the orders of a superior.

It is not just in the market that liberal anti-rationalists detect the pervasive forces of spontaneous adjustment. Arising out of the belief in the hidden wisdom of tradition is the argument that a more efficient legal system is *common* law rather than statute law.[19] The basis of this is that judges proceeding in a case-by-case manner are more likely to produce a more complex (but predictable) set of legal rules than that contained in *codes*. The designer of an efficient statute system would have to be omniscient if he were to produce a system capable of dealing with all possible circumstances. However, the anti-rationalist liberal maintains that the dispersed nature of knowledge and the unpredictability of human action preclude this. A major liberal objection to the consensus is precisely the fact that *public* law has gradually replaced *private* law in large areas of social and economic life.

However, it cannot be denied that the question of the appropriate legal rules for a free society has been a difficult one for liberals. Most, including Hayek, would agree that even a common-law system is not always self-correcting in the way that a market is, and legislative intervention may be required to provide a coherent framework for the co-ordination of individual ends. This clearly relates to the role of the state, but before this can be considered, a clearer understanding of what the contemporary liberal means by the market is required.

IV

Although it is the most talked about feature of classical liberalism, the 'market' is probably the least understood. Furthermore, misunderstandings about the nature of the market tend to parallel misunderstandings about 'competition' and the competitive process. The curious thing about the critics of the market is that much of their fire is directed not so much at the market as such, but at the degenerate forms in which it is alleged to exist in Western democracies. Indeed, few people would deny that if markets worked 'perfectly', they would have considerable virtues in comparison with bureaucratically directed and politically organised production systems. There is in fact a long tradition in socialist thought that specifically argues that markets are only possible under collectivism and that it is the existence of private-property capitalism that prevents them working efficiently.[20] A further point often made is that the state's coercive power is used to support monopolists and other beneficiaries of market imperfections so that the liberal ideal of open competition is a sham. The upshot of considerations such as these is that there is a difference between a genuine market system and a capitalist system: that capitalist economies are no more than ersatz versions of some competitive ideal.

It is clear, then, that the notions of competition, property and capitalism require some conceptual clarification before the liberal system can be properly described, let alone evaluated. A crucial question is whether a competitive market is conceivable without a capitalist system of property ownership. In principle a market is no more than an exchange process through which each participant hopes to maximise his well-being. What makes the idea of a market prima facie favourable to the liberal ideology is that its mechanisms are entirely individualistic. The market has no ends and purposes (indeed, it is misleading to speak of *the* market as such); market phenomena are merely what emerge from the actions of individuals pursuing their ends and purposes. The basic point about exchange processes is that from them every participant benefits — or else why would he make trades? Leaving aside for the moment the important questions about the *origins* of the things that are exchanged and the conditions under which exchange occurs, the liberal claims that the *values* of all things are revealed only in the exchange process. In markets, then, the value of any good (or service) is entirely *subjective*. The market simply allocates subjectively valued goods and services according to supply and demand.

Exactly the same process that occurs in product markets takes place in factor markets (i.e. labour, capital and land). Thus the wage represents the price of labour on the labour market, interest on capital lent and rent is the return to land ownership. Competition in a perfect market will drive returns down to that minimum level required to keep these factors in operation.

To the liberal, property is essential to the operation of the market because without it there would be nothing to exchange. Indeed, it is openly admitted that (as Marxists say) a person's labour is a *commodity* which is sold on the market. However, so far from this negating individual freedom, as collectivists imply, the liberal argument is that in the absence of a free market in labour which allows individuals to choose their occupations in accordance with their subjective valuations, people would have to be allocated to tasks by centralised command. The additional point made by classical liberalism is that the market combines the ethical value of freedom with the value of efficiency in the allocation of resources. The efficiency claim follows from the point made above about social knowledge, i.e. that no central planner could have the information about the marginal productivity of labour in order to allocate that factor efficiently.

However, the claim made by social democrats and all varieties of collectivism is that real-world markets are quite unlike those described either in the texts of micro-economics or in the classics of liberal theory.[21] In existing markets competition appears to operate less than perfectly: for example, if a producer secures a monopoly, then he is able to raise his price and lower output so as to secure a 'profit' over and above that *return* on capital required to keep him in operation. Producers may collude (often with labour unions) against the consumer and technological advances by large corporations may make it difficult or impossible for smaller firms to enter the market (in the jargon of economics, 'increasing returns to scale' might exist in some enterprises). Furthermore, the existence of 'negative externalities' or 'neighbourhood effects' are said to undermine whatever intuitive plausibility the idea of an unregulated market may have. These occur when profit-maximising firms employing the least-cost methods of production impose 'social' costs (in the form of pollution and damage to the environment) on others.

In sum, these features of markets are said to impose 'welfare' losses on the community — losses which can be eliminated by appropriate state action. Such corrective action should take the form of measures such as nationalisation, regulation or anti-monopoly legislation. In addition there is the argument that an uncontrolled market produces quite unacceptable outcomes in terms of income and wealth distributions. The concept of 'social justice' (which morally sanctions redistributive measures by the state) will be considered in more detail below, but it is worth stressing at this stage that this operates as an 'external' corrective principle to the internal (and 'blind') process of the market.

The contemporary liberal response to these objections is to question the notion that the ideal of 'perfect competition' of pure theory has any real evaluative applicability to economic policy.[22] To put the point more precisely, in the appraisal of policy, the comparison should not be between flawless perfect competition and flawless government intervention but between necessarily imperfect markets and necessarily imperfect government intervention. There are two reasons, the liberal claims, why government action is likely to produce worse outcomes than those in less than perfect markets. The first is that there are sound economic reasons why even well-motivated governments may not improve on the automatically self-correcting processes of the market. The second is that we cannot assume that governments are 'benevolent': this is especially so in modern democracies where governments are always likely to be deflected away from the pursuit of some economic 'optimum' by the *sectional* demands of pressure groups and by the electoral timetable.

It has been a considerable achievement of contemporary liberal economic thought to exorcise the ghost of 'perfect competition'. This ideal presupposes a large number of buyers and sellers, perfect knowledge on the part of transactors and costless entry. In such an ideal world everybody will be a 'price taker' (i.e. a producer will be unable to influence price but will be compelled to accept that decreed by an impersonal market) and prices will exactly reflect marginal cost. The difficulty with this theory, however, is that it describes a situation which has been brought about by a *competitive process* rather than depicting the essential properties of that process itself. In fact, it is a static 'end-state' vision of the world rather than a dynamic one in which 'rivalrous' competition between transactors gradully pushes the economic system towards an hypothetical 'equilibrium'. In Frank Knight's phrase, 'in perfect competition there is no competition'. Furthermore, there is no 'profit' in the equilibrium end-state of perfect competition since it is assumed that this has *already* been whittled away by competition.

The theoretical differences between 'general-equilibrium/perfect-competition' theories and 'market-process'[23] theories need not detain us here. What is relevant is the implications which the competing theories have for the role of the state in economic policy. Thus for example, the justification for anti-monopoly policy rests on the assumption that the central economic planning could 'know' what an equilibrium price for a particular product would be. Yet this is precisely what is assumed when economists try to calculate the 'welfare loss' to society caused by the existence of monopoly.[24] In fact, the whole of the 'trust-busting' and anti-monopoly legislation of the US, Britain and West Germany, while claiming to be consistent with the preservation of a market philosophy, rests upon the contentious assumption that the efficacy of a market depends upon it resembling perfect competition.

From Adam Smith onwards, however, the liberal idea of market competition has never been that of 'perfect competition' (as described in general equilibrium theory). This latter interpretation is in fact closely connected with 'rational' socialist economic planning.[25] Here it is assumed that 'efficiency' (in the sense of an optimal use of the factors of production to satisfy consumer demand) can be achieved without the familar imperfections (including entrepreneurial 'profit') associated with *capitalist* market economies.

The liberal argument is that the process of exchange between individuals is constantly correcting the imperfections that exist in the real-world markets: for example, a monopoly, if it emerges independently of the granting of government privilege, is still subject to *potential* competition as long as there is unrestricted entry into the activity in question.

The liberal idea of a market process envisages public benefit accruing *unintentionally* from individual maximisers pursuing their self-interest. Therefore, the possibility of a market process working effectively without private property is inconceivable. The classical liberal justification for private property is both utilitarian and moral. The utilitarian argument focuses upon the role of private property as that motor of change and adjustment which makes co-ordination and efficiency in a free market possible. The moral case for property rests upon the claims of entitlement that individuals have as a consequence of its creation through their own efforts (from labour and exchange) or through gifts or bequests from other legitimate property-holders. It is the former argument that is germane to the present discussion.

The obvious advantage of an economic system that permits exchange of property rights is that it provides incentives for transactors: without the prospect of profit, the tendency towards an efficient use of resources would not occur. Since real world markets are always imperfect (i.e. there are price differences, and therefore opportunities for profit to be exploited), the real question is whether private individuals risking their own resources and subject to the discipline of profit and loss are better than political actors in this activity. There is a number of reasons why liberals suggest that this should be so: but the liberal is not content merely to enumerate the incidence of government failure in enterprise, with Britain providing the most spectacular examples; he also seeks to ground an explanation of this phenomenon in a general social theory.

The first reason has already been considered but is worth reiterating in this specific context. This is that governments, because they are centralised institutions, cannot have the knowledge of economic opportunities that is possessed in a dispersed form by decentralised economic agents. The American 'Austrian' economist, Israel Kirzner, in a series of important works,[27] has emphasised the role of the *entrepreneur* in a market system. Put simply, entrepreneurship is the capacity to spot or be alert to profitable opportunities that will always exist in necessarily imperfect markets. It is the capacity to detect some differences in price (a difference that would not exist in perfect competition where all prices are correct) that can be exploited for profit which constitute entrepreneurial action. All economic action in a liberal market economy, then is a type of arbitrage and the process of competition will select out people who are especially proficient at this. The utilitarian virtue of this process is that the system is gradually 'nudged' towards an efficient allocation of resources (a state of affairs desired, presumably, by collectivists and non-collectivists alike). Of course, there is little likelihood of such an economic nirvana being reached since the incessant change that characterises human action will always generate new opportunities for entrepreneurial alertness.

It is to be noted that although property is required for a liberal market to work, it is not true that entrepreneurship is to be identified with the possession of property. This is far from being the case, although the easy identification of the two by liberalism's critics is a constant source of misunderstanding. The ability to be alert to a profitable opportunity is a mental attitude, or a category of human action which does not depend on ownership. Of course, a structure of property relationships is required for this alertness to be translated into practical action, but the entrepreneur *in principle* needs few resources. What he has to do is to discover opportunities. Those who lend capital will earn a return while he will secure 'profit'. It is this profit that is absent in the equilibrium models of a market economy, yet it is essential to the operation of a competitive system.

According to liberals, the alternative method of production, the planned system, lacks the requisite knowledge and an appropriate incentive structure. Some recognition of these factors was made by governments during the consensus period when successful entrepreneurs were appointed to manage publicly owned enterprises — presumably in the hope of simulating private-market conditions in the state sector. However, this shows a serious misunderstanding of the nature of the entrepreneurship. For the entrepreneurial qualities, if exercised in the public sector where there is no calculus of profit and loss to guide action, will not necessarily be directed towards the public interest. As the liberal political economist, von Mises wryly observed, it is better to have civil servants following rigid rules in charge of public enterprises, rather than entrepreneurs, since these will prove equally adept at manipulating public money.[28] However, since public-sector enterprises are not (normally) allowed to go bankrupt, entrepreneurial activity here is not subject to necessary constraints.

In liberal political economy, as Armen Alchian has pointed

out,[29] the idea of market processes may be likened to the evolutionary processes explained in theoretical biology, for competition does weed out the unsuccessful firms through time. Firms rise and fall in an *unpredictable* fashion in such a way that a mechanism equivalent to natural selection may be said to be at work. Of course, this 'natural selection' process goes on between social and economic *institutions*: it is the 'survival of the fittest' among firms, not people, that is under review. As long as the market is kept 'open' — i.e. with no restrictions on entry — the liberal argument is that experimentation and innovation will flourish in the absence of intervention.

The most crucial demand that the liberal makes for the effective functioning of the market is that politics be separated, as far as is possible, from economics. Since it is assumed that the market is self-correcting, and that the price mechanism automatically directs factors to their most productive uses, there is little need for conscious direction and control by political authorities. The utilitarian value of the system is said to lie in its very *anonymity* — that it is the public in general that benefits from its operation, and not named individuals or groups. The market system is 'optimal' in the sense that it increases 'the changes of any member of society taken at random of having a high income'.[30] Thus the role of politics should be limited to the enforcement of those general *rules* of just conduct which guarantee some predictability and certainty for transactors in an otherwise unpredictable and uncertain world.

The effect of government action in the economy is to disrupt the flow of information which is spontaneously transmitted to transactors and thereby prevent the efficient allocation of resources. The most obvious example of this, at the micro-level, is government support for industries which would otherwise be eliminated, and the factors of production associated with them re-allocated, by the evolutionary process described above. If efficiency is the sole criterion for the conduct of policy (and, of course, critics of liberalism would deny this), then government action cannot improve on the market but only direct factors *away* from the production of goods which consumers demand.

Worse from the liberal point of view is the fact that the replacement of decentralised economic decision-making by government action increases the influence of politically significant pressure groups in society. The anonymity of the market is replaced by the personal power of known groups. This may come about through the electoral process, in which coalitions of groups may combine to defeat the public interest, or by direct action of politically powerful groups on executive government. The liberal criticism of what may be called (albeit inelegantly) the 'politicisation' of economic life is that there are fewer constraints in the public world than the private. There is no real equivalent to loss and bankruptcy in political action.

The most serious example of disruptive group action on the spontaneously adjusting market process is the trade-union movement — precisely because trade unions advance *sectional* demands which are incompatible with the promotion of the general interest. In most Western democracies, certain legal privileges, such as immunity from the laws of tort and a tolerant interpretation of the right to picket, have reduced competition in the labour market. Trade-union pressure means that wages are kept above the level that would clear the market, thus causing involuntary unemployment. The influence of trade unions, however, varies from country to country; in comparison with the British case, union influence in America is weak. Nevertheless, the years of the consensus undoubtedly saw a greater involvement of trade unions in political matters in Western democracies — an influence which was in turn reflected back on to the economy.

It is not only trade-union action which has the effect of attenuating the market: employers, especially the managements of large corporations, are equally assiduous, if ultimately less successful in attempting to secure privileges from government. Such privileges take the form of protection from potential competition by the granting of monopoly rights in the production of goods and services. Thus, liberalism is *not* to be identified with the virtues and attitudes of the business community, but in the impersonal processes of exchange and competition.

In Britain especially, the age of the consensus witnessed the emergence of what came to be known as 'tripartism' (a variant of the better-known 'corporatism'). This involves the direction of economic events not by the impersonal forces of the market, but by (unenforceable) agreements between government, trade unions, and the leaders of big business. This seemed to have two aims: first, the control of inflation by prices-and-incomes policies rather than by strict monetary methods; and second, the 'regeneration' of British industry through government aid and subsidies rather than by the spontaneous corrective mechanisms of the market. The liberal objections to this were not merely economic but also involved political considerations, for it was argued that the direction of events by pressure groups threatened both individual liberty and the survival of *parliamentary* government.

For liberal political economy, it is clear that dislocations and break-downs in the market system can only occur through impediments to the exchange process. Such impediments come from exogenous factors, i.e. actions emanating from *outside* the market, normally government. If there are break-downs — and the recurring bouts of *involuntary* unemployment constitute the most spectacular examples — then we must look for distortions of the signalling process of the market, which would otherwise direct factors of production (including labour) to their most efficient use. It is argued that it is always government intervention that atrophies the market so that the flexibility and quick response to changing circumstances that the evolutionary process requires is stunted. Of course, this is not to deny that liberal political economy requires governmental action in some areas.

From this it follows that liberalism is primarily about micro-economics, not macro-economics. Without delving too much into the vexed question of the differences between these two branches of the discipline, it may be said that micro-economics deals with the functioning of the price system at the level of exchange between individuals and firms and so on, while macro-economics is concerned with the relationship between 'aggregates' describing features of the whole economy, such as the money supply, the level of employment and the rate of interest. Although liberal political economy does not always reject the notion of macro-economics (nevertheless some do),[31] it does claim that, to be meaningful, its propositions must ultimately be reducible to individualistic (micro) foundations. In practical terms, liberals claim that economic transactors are not moved to action by changes in the relationships between large-scale variables but by changes in individual prices. Thus, even the avowed macro-economist, Milton Friedman, would vigorously deny that changes in the money supply can, in the long run, influence the level of employment. Employment can only be guaranteed when wages are allowed (naturally) to find that level which will clear the labour market, and when all impediments to the mobility of labour are removed. These, of course, are micro-economic propositions.

Although individual liberal economists disagree about particular aspects of monetary theory and policy and about the effects of inflation, they agree ultimately that reform of the micro-economic structure (especially the labour market) is the only way that the present mixed economies can move into an era of higher employment and resumed economic growth. Thus they would eliminate the state from any economic management role. Paradoxically, liberal economic policy is, strictly speaking, no policy. Even the imposition on governments of a legal obligation to adhere to strict monetary rules and balance their budget (two requirements demanded by Milton Friedman) does not really constitute 'policy' because they are designed precisely to remove any element of political *discretion* in the handling of economic affairs.

As to the question of unemployment, the general liberal argument is that it is soluble only by letting the price mechanism operate fully in the labour market. Labour is indeed a 'commodity', and therefore has a price like any other. If there is excess supply of the labour commodity, then its price must fall if it is to be purchased. Of course, macro-economic phenomena, mainly the persistence of inflation, introduce all sorts of complexities into the argument, but ultimately supply-and-demand analysis must be paramount in any causal explanation of idle labour.

The factors which make the labour market especially rigid in Western democracies are trade-union power, which keeps wages above market-clearing level; and that plethora of welfare and housing legislations which reduces the mobility of labour. The fact that in most Western countries unions are immune from tort actions means that employers cannot sue for damages in connection with industrial actions (strikes) which have a far-reaching effect on economic progress. As we shall see, immunities have been more extensive in Britain than elsewhere. Furthermore, closed-shop agreements and tolerant picketing-laws enable unions to keep out competitors who would otherwise bring the price of labour down to market-clearing levels. An even more serious effect of union power is felt in nationalised industries; for in the absence of a real possibility of bankruptcy the deleterious consequences of this power can be postponed almost indefinitely.

The effect of generous welfare and unemployment benefits is obviously to make low-paid work unattractive: at the *margin* the income from wages will be very small. The liberal is making no *moral* criticism (as conservatives often do) against those who do not choose to work in such circumstances: those individuals are simply maximising their utilities in the manner prescribed by neo-classical economics textbooks. In addition, the existence of subsidised rented public housing tends to make labour much less mobile. Again the question hinges on the real value of working compared with not working — for if, in order to gain employment, a person has to give up a subsidised house with no guarantee that he will get a similar property in the new area, the real value of the wage is reduced accordingly. This may to some extent explain the persistence of pockets of unemployment in certain parts of Britain.

The factors sum to form what is sometimes called the 'natural rate of unemployment' by liberal economists.[32] Although this may be difficult to calculate, its meaning is clear enough: it is the rate of unemployment determined by structural and institutional factors which cannot be lowered by monetary or fiscal measures. Any attempt to reduce unemployment below the natural rate by stimulating demand, according to liberal political economy, will simply raise prices (though there are significant time-lags).

This, then, is the fundamental objection to Keynesian demand-management policies; and although liberal political economists differ in analysis and prescription at the level of detail, they are united in their conviction that a market economy cannot be controlled or regulated by monetary or fiscal measures to produce some desired outcome. The result of repeated attempts to do this has been persistent inflation.

It is appropriate at this stage to consider briefly 'monetarism' and its connection with liberal economic values. Adherents of the doctrine of monetarism prefer this to be called the 'quantity theory of money' and like to distinguish it, as a scientific theory, from the political economy of liberalism. Strictly speaking, this is correct, for it would be possible for someone to believe that the quantity theory of money is *true* yet reject other typical liberal values, such as a belief in the virtues of private enterprise, individualism, limited government and a limited welfare state. Yet the strong connection between faith in the quantity theory and liberal political economic values is no coincidence. A correct description would be to say that belief in the quantity theory constitutes a necessary but not a sufficient condition for the structure of liberal ideology.

Briefly, monetarists [33] claim that there is an empirically predictable relationship between increases in the supply of money and increases in the general price-level. Thus if production remains the same and the supply of money and credit is increased, there will be an increase in prices. Although in the short run, in a situation of less than full employment of all resources, an injection of money will lead to an increase in economic activity, *ultimately* the permanent effect will be a general increase in prices (inflation) with no effect on production. Inflation is everywhere a monetary phenomenon normally determined exogenously by government as the monopoly supplier of the medium of exchange, and not by, say, the actions of trade unions in pushing up wages ('cost-push' inflation).

One feature of the economic policy of the consensus was a belief in the existence of a 'trade-off' between inflation and employment — that is to say, a government could choose a desirable level of employment and inflate the money supply accordingly to achieve this. In the jargon, a 'negatively sloped' Phillips curve[34] was postulated. In policy terms, the argument was that governments could *choose* between inflation and unemployment; and that although inflation might have some undesirable features, it was at least preferable to unemployment. This view was predominant in Britain, mainly because in the twentieth century, economic dislocation in this country had appeared most dramatically in the form of mass unemployment. Here, the initial *uncritical* acceptance of the Phillips-curve hypothesis was possibly as much psychological as intellectual.

It is a major claim of liberal political economy that governments are not presented with such a choice; that in the long run, inflation is harmful and is itself a cause of unemployment. It is one of the many achievements of Milton Friedman's macro-economics that it shows this to be the case. The argument is that the persuasiveness of the Phillips-curve hypothesis depends on a confusion between *real* and *nominal* wages.[35] Increasing doses of inflation will lower the real wage and therefore increase employment: in the short run, therefore, the Phillips curve is negatively sloped. However, trade unions learn that their real wages are being cut and they anticipate, more or less correctly, the future course of inflation, and therefore take account of this in their wage demands. This means that in the long run, the real wage will not fall and all we will see is accelerating inflation. In the late 1960s and throughout the 1970s, empirical evidence seemed to confirm this with the phenomena of rising inflation *and* rising unemployment. Ultimately, then, monetary policy, for a liberal political economist, cannot be used to stabilise the economy or to get unemployment below the 'equilibrium' or natural rate (the rate determined by social factors noted above).

All this illustrates how liberal political economists have decisively rejected 'money illusion', i.e. the idea that people will not notice a cut in their real wages if their nominal incomes rise because of inflation. Of course, in conceding that real wages must ultimately fall if employment is to rise, Keynes was accepting a fundamental axiom of liberal political economy. It is just that Keynes and Keynesians had a rather complex method of reducing the real wage, a method that liberal economists always claimed would lead to inflation. When monetarists say that 'money matters',[36] they mean precisely that mismanagement of the money supply has a profoundly destabilising effect on a free economy. Against the Keynesian view that monetary policy can have little effect, Friedman argued that the massive cut in the money supply, engineered (mistakenly) by the Federal Reserve Board between 1929 and 1933, produced a deflation which was the immediate cause of the Great Depression.[37] In the post-war years, money has still mattered but has produced a reverse effect (inflation).

The 'Hayekian' anti-inflation theory is subtly different from orthodox Chicago monetarism.[38] Hayek's argument has less to do with changes in 'aggregates' that result from profligate monetary policy, and much more to do with the change in *relative* prices that this brings about. 'Cheap' money sends a misleading price signal to economic transactors and encourages malinvestments — i.e. investments in enterprises which can only be sustained if the inflation continues. Thus, inflation does not merely change the general price-level, it also produces massive distortions in the structure of the economy. This can only be solved by ending inflation immediately, which in turn must be followed by a painful period of re-adjustment (in terms of a fall in employment) as labour factors are re-allocated. Thus, although the simple quantity theory of money is true, it goes nowhere near far enough in explaining the connection between money and real factors in a private enterprise, free-market economy.

Of fundamental importance is Hayek's argument that even if the basic propositions of Keynesian theory were correct, governments would lack the knowledge to 'fine-tune' the economy in the manner prescribed. He argued in his Nobel Lecture, 'The Pretence of Knowledge', that

> when we are asked for quantitative evidence for the particular structure of prices and wages that would be required in order to assure a smooth continuous sale of the products and services offered, we must admit that we have no such information.[39]

In other words, governments can never have the knowledge of prices that would (hypothetically) clear all markets, including that of labour, so that the attempt to create employment by monetary or fiscal measures is to pursue an illusion.

The particular solutions recommended by liberal political economists will be discussed in later chapters, but a few general observations would be appropriate at this stage. It is clear that the principal liberal argument is that the root of the problem is the *discretionary* control over money that governments have acquired during this century. Clearly, in a genuine free economy, spontaneous action by individuals would generate a stable medium of exchange. Whatever paper money was used would retain its value because it could be converted into a commodity: historically, of course, gold has been the ultimate guarantor of monetary stability. All 'monetarist' 'policy' recommendations can, in fact, be seen as variations on the theme of the need to eliminate the need for monetary policy on the ground that a market system itself provides stability and continuity. In this important matter there is common ground between 'radical' liberal political economists and 'old' conservatives, who regard the existence of 'sound' money as an essential condition for a stable and free economy and society.

The liberal objections to inflation itself are quite straightforward. It is true that if everybody could anticipate correctly the future course of price increases then inflation would have no effect on the real economy, since people would make contracts and other arrangements that took these increases into account. Although people do this to some extent, especially in wage negotiations, it would be absurd even to imagine that this could be done for all transactions. Societies are inhabited by *human* actors prone to error. Inflation increases uncertainty and therefore the likelihood of error: this has been demonstrated by the Hayekian explanation of the change in *relative* prices that monetary laxity brings about.

In addition, there are familiar liberal objections to inflation. It redistributes income in a more or less arbitrary manner between individuals: in particular, those on fixed incomes suffer severely from the process. Moreover, in a bid to mitigate the effects of expected price increases, individuals will invest in goods likely to retain their value — for example, property, jewelry, works of art and so on. These investments, although of benefit to individuals, may not necessarily be of benefit to *anonymous* society. Lastly, and of perhaps the greatest importance, inflation produces divisiveness, bitterness and envy in society — a point emphasised by 'old' conservatives. A consequence of these effects, according to the liberal, is an inevitable increase in the power of the state.

VI

There is a number of varying liberal responses to the problem of money. They involve technical economic recommendations for monetary stability and also more general observations on the social and political effects of the various attempts to deal with inflation. Despite their differences, all are consistent with two overriding liberal economic principles: firstly, that the market is a self-correcting mechanism, at the macro- as well as the micro-level, and therefore requires very little in the way of conscious direction and control; and secondly, that attempts to improve on its working by monetary and fiscal measures produce results which are *unanticipated* by the authors of the measures. These effects are normally inflation and the consequent disruption of the signalling processes of the exchange system. The root cause of the problem is the intrusion of politics into the (for the liberal) autonomous area of economic activity. The fundamental reason why the liberal requests this self-denying ordinance from politics, or, better still, enforces it by a constitution, is that governments respond essentially to short-term pressures (from electorally significant groups or sectional interests), while economic processes are long-term, the benefits of which are diffused widely across an anonymous public and promise no *immediate* benefit to named segments of society.

The liberal argument is that the removal of government from its dominant position in the creation of money is the only permanent way of avoiding inflation. As to the question of how this is to be done, however, opinions differ. In the background to the discussion is the Gold Standard — the traditional method of restraining governments in the monetary field. There is no doubt that historically, the obligation of government to redeem paper money in gold was eminently successful in ensuring reasonable monetary stability: throughout the nineteenth century, and for part of this century, its existence coincided with very minor changes in the price level. Furthermore, this stability did not prevent remarkable economic growth and reasonably full employment. Economic history suggests that the liberal is correct in assuming that exogenously determined stimulants are not required for economic prosperity. Indeed, inflation has accelerated as countries have, one by one, abandoned gold during this century. The last remaining link with the Gold Standard was broken in 1971 when the US suspended the obligation to pay gold to foreign holders of dollars on request.

In fact, the existence and historical efficiency of the Gold Standard pays a curious tribute to the anti-rationalism of liberal political economy. To the modern technological (or 'scientistic') mind, it seems absurd that men should depend on the expenditure of resources in digging metal out of the ground for the organisation of a monetary system. Yet the apparent irrationality of this masks a hidden inner wisdom, for gold only developed spontaneously as the basis for monetary transactions because it had some ultimate *use value*. Thus it is not so much the psychological hold over people's minds that made gold effective but the fact that it is ultimately a *commodity*. Indeed, the modern paper-money systems could very well be called irrational because their designers did not take into account the *unintended consequences* of entrusting the management of the currency to politicians.

Nevertheless, the idea of a commodity-based currency does not have the hold it once did on liberal political economists. Although the Gold Standard is often *theoretically* praised as the ideal monetary system, very few liberal theorists have systematically analysed the possibility of a return to it. The exception is William Rees-Mogg's book, *The Reigning Error*[40] — though this is written from a general conservative standpoint rather than that of an explicitly *laissez-faire* perspective. The assumption has normally been that present circumstances make it impracticable for a return to gold. One important point is that such has been the experience of political discretion over the currency that governments of any ideological persuasion cannot be relied upon to accept the restraints that the rules of the Gold Standard imply. Nevertheless, to the extent that all the known liberal alternative monetary arrangements are surrogates for these, then presumably, the same problem would arise if any of them were to be adopted.

The most well-known contemporary liberal alternative is Milton Friedman's idea that increases in the money supply should be limited by a fixed rule — a rule that tied these to increases in production.[41] By this method the dangers of both inflation and deflation would be avoided. This is normally held in conjunction with the doctrine that the international value of a currency should be determined by the market — a policy in fact adopted by most Western democracies with the abandonment in the 1970s of fixed exchange rates between currencies — a mechanism established by the Bretton Woods agreement of 1944 (which also created the International Monetary Fund). These were replaced by the *superficially* more liberal policy of allowing currencies to 'float' freely on the international money markets. These policies have always been opposed by liberal political economists of the Hayekian or Austrian persuasion. The monetary rule has been objected to because of the difficulty of determining what things shall count as money for the measurement of the money stock. 'Money' does not take just one exclusive form, and in a complex economy forms of credit will function as near-moneys and the authorities will find it impossible to control these. Hayek's more radical suggestion is that legal tender laws should be lifted so that citizens can use any currency they wish.[42] This would mean a 'free market' in money so that competition would eliminate unsound currencies. In such circumstances a government would be deterred from inflating its own currency through fear of it being driven out of the market.

In the unlikely event of such a radical scheme being implemented, the general non-Chicagoan liberal position is that governments should deflate as quickly as possible. In fact, Austrian economists do not fear deflation, a genuine reduction in the amount of money and credit in the economy, in the way that even Chicago economists do. The claim is that a short period of severe pain, in terms of increased unemployment, is preferable to a long drawn-out process of monetary correction. They would claim that if all prices were flexible, as they would be if there were no exogenous impediments to free exchange, then there would be no need to increase the money stock at all. Increased production would simply bring about a gently falling price level.

Again we find Hayek in opposition to Friedman over the question of 'floating' currencies in the international markets.[43] Obviously, the declining value of its currency will signal to the government that it should take corrective action, but Hayek argues that this still gives governments too much monetary discretion. By the time that they act to stem the fall in the international value of the currency very serious harm to the economy may have been committed. For this reason Hayek always favoured fixed exchange rates between currencies since that imposed an *immediate* constraint on governments (though of course currencies were devalued during the period that this system operated). It is to be noted that nevertheless, the introduction of freely floating currencies in the 1970s was regarded as something of a triumph for economic liberalism. Perhaps this indicates how little the doctrine was understood at the time.

VII

One particular point of criticism aimed at the consensus concerned the use of prices-and-incomes policies to correct inflation brought about by governmental monetary policy. It is not merely that such policies never succeed (apart from in the very short-run) in the aim of controlling prices (and liberal political economists display a malicious delight in going back to ancient Greece and Rome in their historical demonstrations of such failures), it is that *general* reasons can be produced why this must always be so. Furthermore, liberals are equally keen to expose the unintended, malign consequences of such policies.

Prices-and-incomes policies fail because the natural economic pressures become too great when there is too much money and credit circulating in the system. Repressed inflation is, in fact, thought to be much worse than open inflation. If prices and wages are kept below their 'natural' levels then individuals will simply evade them. To prevent such evasion, which inevitably creates bitterness between such groups, some of whom are more successful at evasion than others, governments are driven to more and more Draconian measures to enforce the policy. Furthermore, because an economic society is a human society and therefore subject to constant change, the successful enforcement of a prices-and-incomes policy would have deleterious effects on efficiency. This is because if *relative* prices are not allowed to change, then that array of prices enforced by government will not accurately reflect values in the economic system. It is to be noted that Keynes himself did not favour prices-and-incomes policies; he was more favourable to the allocative mechanism of the market at the micro-level than is often supposed. Later Keynesians, however, have been driven to them because they have tried to get unemployment down, by monetary and fiscal measures, to a level that would have been thought impossible by the author of the *General Theory* (see below, chapter 5).

In truth a prices-and-incomes policy can only be operative effectively (leaving aside the question of economic efficiency) in a completely planned economy where there are few limits on the coercive power of the state. In post-war social democracies, governments in the consensus era were not prepared to make those assaults on personal and economic liberty which the logic of some of their macro-economic policies implied. In Britain, especially, attempts were made to secure voluntary incomes policies, but to the liberal this entailed a further politicisation of economic life since such voluntary agreements required 'deals' with trade unions: and labour leaders would only participate if they were granted further political and legal privileges. These usually included additional exemptions from the rule of law in industrial actions. Since union leaders could rarely deliver their side of the bargain, pay restraint, the net result was the break-down of the anti-inflation policy and the persistence of the privileges — i.e. further erosion of the self-correcting properties of the market.

VIII

The theory of the market in liberalism represents two complementary but distinct social values: efficiency and liberty. So far we have considered in detail only the efficiency argument, but no matter how effective this might be, it is of little ideological value if it is not ultimately grounded in some plausible account of human liberty. Contemporary critics of liberalism, from both conservative and collectivist sources, have tended to concentrate on what they see as inadequacies in individualistic accounts of the person and freedom.

Although this topic extends beyond the realms of public policy, and ultimately into metaphysics, it does have some relevance to the contemporary economic debate — for the liberal is accused of presenting a puny, morally emaciated individual, a mere utility maximiser who is arbitrarily wrenched from any genuine social or communitarian context. Yet, it is contended, this abstract individual cannot be understood as a properly *autonomous* agent since his tastes and preferences are vulnerable to advertisers and the persuasive techniques of large corporations. Liberal society is not then a free association of independent agents, held together by contracts freely made, but an unstable collection of *passive* individuals subjected to a constant bombardment of consumer goods.[44] In the jargon of contemporary collectivist economics, there is an 'interdependency between production and consumption'. The consumer is not *sovereign*; he does not dictate to the producer but is himself a 'willing victim' of a covertly oppressive system. It might be said that because socialist planning has failed to deliver the goods, the collectivists are now claiming that the goods ought not to be delivered anyway.

It is true in a sense that liberal economists have encouraged this line of criticism — albeit accidentally. This is because they resolutely maintain that the science of liberal political economy assumes 'wants' to be 'given'. From Bentham onwards, liberals have made it an act of faith that the individual is the best judge of his own interests. They have asserted that however foolish a person's choices might be, to deny him the right to make them cannot possibly 'liberate' him from self-destructive desires, but will serve only to subordinate his personal ends to those of some paternal authority. However, it is not perhaps the limitations of the liberal view of personal autonomy that have encouraged collectivist criticism but the failure of socialist economics to fulfil the hopes of the planners. It is the case that original socialist economic planners (such as Lange and Lerner) and Keynesians worked with a concept of man not fundamentally dissimilar to that of orthodox liberal political economy. It is only in recent years that socialists, under the influence of neo-Marxist thinkers, have questioned the appropriateness of the depiction of man as a mere calculator. Although liberals have not devoted much attention to such criticisms — indeed, most would claim that to enquire into the origins of wants is to go outside the legitimate realm of a predictive social science — their case has not gone entirely unanswered.

The criticism seems to depend on a distinction between genuine or 'innate' wants (the demand for which it would be easy to satisfy) and created wants, or wants for objects that only exist *because* they are already being produced. It is assumed that the latter need not be produced and therefore that resources invested in their production should be redirected towards other things (no doubt, public goods). The liberal counter to this is to say that while there may be an analytical distinction here, in the sense that one could identify innate wants for food, shelter and clothing in primitive conditions, this can have no relevance to civilised societies, even those much less advanced than our own — for here it is the case that the desire for most valued things must emanate from circumstances in which the goods already exist. That we value consumer goods, automobiles, exotic foods and so on (items that we do not technically or biologically need) does not prove that we are coerced into buying them. As Hayek has argued: 'To say that a desire is not important because it is not innate is to say that the whole cultural achievement of man is not important'.[45] Although it is true that producers will try to influence individuals, this effort will only be one of a whole congeries of factors which go to make up the act of consumption. Also, it could be argued that what characterises a liberal society is not some idealised, and most probably unrealiseable, conception of individual autonomy, but competition between producers for the favours of consumers. Indeed, are not educators, social theorists, ideologues and others doing to individual agents exactly what producers of consumer goods do? The fact that individuals are not so easily duped is attested to by the failure of 'money illusion', noted above.

A further liberal argument defends the role of calculation and individual rationality itself. To depict man as an assiduous calculator of means to ends is to incorporate all his consumption behaviour into a coherent (personal) plan. Thus the purchase of many household goods does not indicate an instability of tastes, an ephemeral and transient set of desires dictated by producers, but a rational allocation of resources. Thus, for example, as people's incomes rise they will value *time* more highly, since this is spent more profitably on work, and therefore will invest heavily in time-saving devices, such as washing-machines, in the home.[46] This does not, of course, prove that *ultimately* all wants stem from autonomous agents, but it does suggest that much of what might be thought irrational or arbitrary behaviour can be incorporated into the liberal 'minimalist' concept of man.

This has been, perhaps, a slightly less than relevant, and admittedly inconclusive diversion from the main theme of this chapter. However, the significance of the critique of the 'individual as mere consumer' for the main ideological structure of the consensus should not be under-estimated. Its importance lies not simply in the justification it gave for controls and regulations over production and, especially, advertising, but also in the fact that the whole structure of state (i.e. compulsory) welfare rests upon a view of man that denies the capacity of individuals to plan their consumption habits rationally. The assumptions that lie behind social-democratic welfare systems are not solely concerned with equality and social justice (those could be approached through income redistribution rather than by the direct provision of welfare services), but include, implicitly, one that casts doubt on the ability of individuals to allocate their resources so as to satisfy their 'true' long-term desires. It is often held that individuals will prefer to spend their incomes on consumer goods, at the behest of producers, rather than insure against sickness, unemployment and old age. It is a fundamental belief of liberal political economy that individuals rather than governments are the best judges of an appropriate welfare provision.

Notes and References

1. For an excellent general introduction to classical liberal political thought, see J. Gray, *Liberalism* (Open University, Milton Keynes, 1986). For a more specialised treatment of the various philosophical foundations of liberalism, see N.P. Barry, *On classical liberalism and libertarianism* (Macmillan, London, 1986).

2. A splendid and provocative statement of extreme libertarianism (anarcho-capitalism) can be found in M. Rothbard, *For a new liberty* (Collier-Macmillan, New York, 1973).

3. S. Brittan, *Left or right: the bogus dilemma* (Secker and Warburg, London, 1968).

4. For a lucid description see J. Burton, 'Positively Milton Friedman' in J. Shackleton and G. Locksley (eds), *Twelve contemporary economists* (Macmillan, London, 1981), pp. 53–71.

5. M. Friedman, *Capitalism and freedom* (University of Chicago Press, Chicago, 1962). Also, see M. & R. Friedman, *Free to choose*, (Penguin, Harmondsworth, 1979) and *The tyranny of the status quo* (Penguin, Harmondsworth, 1985).

6. Mises's political thought is admirably summarised in his *Liberalism: a socio-economic exposition* (Sheed Andrew and McMeel, Kansas, 1978; 1st English edition, 1962).

7. For Hayek's politial and economic philosophy, see his *The road to serfdom* (Routledge and Kegan Paul, London, 1944); *The constitution of liberty* (Routledge and Kegan Paul, London, 1960); *Law, legislation and liberty* (Routledge and Kegan Paul, London, 1973, 1976 and 1979) 3 volumes. For commentaries see N.P. Barry, *Hayek's social and economic philosophy* (Macmillan, London, 1979); and J. Gray, *Hayek on liberty*, (Blackwell, Oxford, 1984).

8. J. Buchanan and G. Tullock's major joint work is *The calculus of consent* (Ann Arbor, Michigan, 1962).

9. See M. Olson, *The logic of collective action* (Yale University Press, New Haven, 1965); and *The rise and decline of nations* (Yale University Press, New Haven, 1982).

10. R. Nozick, *Anarchy, state and utopia* (Blackwell, Oxford, 1974).

11. Ibid., p. 32–3.

12. For a comprehensive account of the 'calculation debate' in the history of economic thought, see D. Lavoie, *Rivalry and central planning* (Cambridge University Press, Cambridge, 1985). Also, see N.P. Barry, 'The philosophy and economics of socialism', *Il Politico*, vol. XLIX (1984), pp. 573–92.

13. See Hume's *Essays: moral, political and literary*, Eugene Miller (ed.) (Liberty Classics, Indianapolis, 1985). See also, N.P. Barry, 'The tradition of spontaneous order', *Literature of Liberty*, vol. V (1984), pp. 7–58.

14. Adam Smith, *The theory of moral sentiments*, D.D. Raphael and A. Macfie (eds) (Clarendon Press, (eds) 1976); and *An enquiry into the nature and causes of the wealth of nations*, R. Campbell and A. Skinner (eds) (Clarendon Press, Oxford, 1976).

15. Smith, *The wealth of nations*, p. 456.

16. See F.A. Hayek, 'The division of knowledge in society' in his *Individualism and economic order* (Routledge and Kegan Paul, London, 1948) p. 23.

17 M. Polanyi, *The study of man*, (University of Chicago Press, Chicago, 1959), p. 59.

18. See 'Individualism: true and false' in *Individualism and economic order*, p. 23.

19. See *Rules and order*, vol. 1 of *Law, legislation and liberty* (see note 7).

20. See O. Lange, 'On the economic theory of socialism, *Review of Economic*

Studies, vol. 3 (1936–7), pp. 53–71.

21. See F. Hahn, *On the notion of equilibrium in economics*, (Cambridge University Press, Cambridge, 1973).

22. For a critique of the equilibrium model, see N.P. Barry, 'In defence of the invisible hand', *The Cato Journal*, vol. 5 (1985), pp. 133–48.

23. For an analysis of market process theory, see S.C. Littlechild, 'Equilibrium and the market process', in I. Kirzner (ed.), *Method, process and Austrian economics* (D.C. Heath, Lexington, 1982), pp. 85–102.

24. S.C. Littlechild, 'Misleading calculations of the social costs of monopoly power', *Economic Journal*, vol. 91 (1981), p. 348–63.

25. Lange, 'On the Economic Theory of Socialism'.

26. For an account of successive British governments' failed interventions, see J. Burton, *Picking losers . . . ?* (Institute of Economic Affairs, London, 1983).

27. I. Kirzner, *Competition and entrepreneurship* (University of Chicago Press, Chicago, 1973); and *Perception, opportunity and profit* (University of Chicago Press, Chicago, 1979).

28. See L. Von Mises, *Bureaucracy* (Arlington House, New York, 1969), chapter III.

29. A. Alchian, 'Uncertainty, evolution and economic theory' in his *Economic forces at work*, (Liberty Press, Indianapolis, 1977), pp. 15–35.

30. In 'The princples of a liberal social order' in Hayek's *Studies in philosophy, politics and economics*, (London: Routledge and Kegan Paul, London, 1967), p. 173.

31. The technical objection to macro-economics rests on the claim that economic 'aggregates' display only a kind of statistical regularity whereas micro-economics is concerned with *causal* laws.

32. See M. Friedman, *Unemployment versus inflation?* (Institute of Economic Affairs, London, 1975).

33. An easily comprehensible account of the quantity theory is in *The counter-revolution in monetary theory* (Institute of Economic Affairs, London, 1970).

34. See A.W. Phillips, 'The relation between unemployment and the rate of change of money wages in the United Kingdom, 1861–1957', *Economica*, vol. 25 (1958),pp.283–99.

35. See Friedman, *Unemployment versus inflation?* for a refutation of the Phillips curve hypothesis.

36. For a standard account of Keynesian economic policy, see M. Stewart, *Keynes and after* (Penguin, Harmondsworth, 1968).

37. See M. Friedman and A. Schwartz, *A monetary history of the United States, 1867–1960* (Princeton University Press, Princeton, 1963).

38. See F.A. Hayek, *Prices and production* (Routledge and Kegan Paul, London, 1931), pp. 160–2.

39. F.A. Hayek, 'The pretence of knowledge' in his *Full Employment at Any Price?* (Institute of Economic Affairs, London, 1975), p. 33.

40. Of contemporary macro-economists, R. Mundell is notable in advocating a return to a form of the Gold Standard: see his 'Inflation from an international point of view' in D. Meiselman and A. Laffer, (eds), *The phenomenon of world-wide inflation* (American Enterprise Institute, Washington, DC, 1975) pp. 141–52.

41. See *Capitalism and freedom*, chapter III, for Friedman's recommendation

of a monetary rule.

42. See F.A. Hayek, *The denationalisation of money* (Institute of Economic Affairs, London, 1978).

43. Hayek's advocacy of fixed exchange-rates dates back to 1937: see his *Monetary nationalism and international stability* (Longman, London).

44. See J.K. Galbraith, *The affluent society* (Hamish Hamilton, London, 1958).

45. F.A. Hayek, 'The non sequitur of the "dependence effect" ' in his *Studies in philosophy, politics and economics* (Routledge and Kegan Paul, London, 1967), p. 314.

46. See G. Becker, *The economic approach to human behaviour* (University of Chicago Press, Chicago, 1967).

3

The Liberal Alternative — Politics

I

Contemporary classical liberalism is as much a political theory as an economic theory. Unlike any other social doctrine or ideology, however, liberalism preserves a close and intimate theoretical connection between economics and politics. Indeed, liberalism has been described by one of its leading twentieth-century exponents, L. von Mises, as simply 'applied economics'.[1] Other classical liberals have found it hard to resist the temptation to convert all political problems into economic ones. It is easy to see why: the application of the 'economic calculus' to familiar social problems has yielded such good predictions, mostly concerned with mistaken government policy, that it is not surprising that liberals have tended to regard social theory as being exhausted by applied economics.

An additional reason why this view should be taken is that applied economics seems, superficially at least, to be 'value-free' — concerned more with tracing a causal connection between means and ends than pronouncing upon the value of the ends themselves. In fact, classical liberals of the positivist strain tend to assume a virtual unanimity in society about ends. These are taken to be full employment, prosperity and the advancement of individual liberty. However, in the contemporary world this is perhaps an optimistic assumption. Certainly the value of equality as a *substantive* ideal, and the concomitant obligation laid upon governments to promote it, has become a major feature in the social democrats' programme; and because it conflicts with much of liberal individualism, political argument has to a greater extent than before been about intrinsic desirability of the various ends of social life. The inequality of resource endowment and of factor earnings seems to be so much an accepted part of market society that it has rendered capitalism unattractive to people despite its acknowledged efficiency.

There are two additional reasons why the reduction of politics to economics is an unsatisfactory response to the problems of the contemporary world. The first concerns the need for a theoretical explanation of the contemporary malaise of Western democracies. The seemingly unstoppable growth in public spending, sustained bouts of inflation and the gradual erosion of legal and institutional structures have all deeply concerned classical liberals. However, they have not been content merely to record these events, least of all to resign themselves merely to diverting or delaying, in a conservative manner, what might be thought to be an inevitable process. Instead they have constructed general theories to explain why these events have occurred and drawn from them certain normative lessons for the arrest of such undesirable processes, and for the prevention of their re-occurrence. Although these explanatory theories of social and political behaviour do very largely draw upon the model of man as the rational and self-interested calculator familiar to classical liberal economics, the application of this to *unfamiliar* areas has led to the development of a distinctive liberal political theory. This approach does not, as critics maintain, represent the reduction of politics to economics, but rather the explanation of political phenomena in terms of powerful analytical tools. From this has emerged a new way of looking at the appropriate demarcation line between political and economic decision making. Previous liberal political economists had tended to look upon political institutions as exogenous 'givens' and upon political behaviour as inaccessible to scientific analysis; but the incorporation of an explanation of them into a general social theory has been a major innovation in the liberal credo.

The second reason for the inadequacy of a purely economic approach to human affairs involves the problem of 'self-interest'. Since Adam Smith the assumption of individual self-interest has not only been highly serviceable as a descriptive account of human behaviour, but also it has been shown on analysis to be a socially beneficial motivational concept. Thus, although the orthodox Western moral tradition has persistently devalued self-interest and defined appropriate ethical behaviour in terms of the deliberate suppression of egoism and the promotion of the public good, 'underground' liberal moralists (beginning perhaps with Bernard Mandeville[2]) have always pointed to the coincidence of public benefit and private or self-regarding action. This conjunction, however, is successful only when self-interest is constrained by general social rules — as in a free-enterprise economy subject to the rule of law. Self-interest is extremely damaging in the modern world, characterised as it is by the organisation of individuals into groups, each of which is striving for a benefit from government or an exemption from the operation of an impartial rule of law. While such action is potentially self-destructive to individuals as members of society, no one person has an incentive to abstain from such action as a member of a group. Thus there is something of a paradox in the fact that although the contemporary liberal complains of the all-powerful nature of the modern state, that very state is implicitly berated for its inability to resist political pressures from well-organised minorities. This is perhaps the most serious of practical and ethical problems for contemporary classical liberalism and it will be considered in some detail later in this chapter.

II

The most important question for liberal political theory is the role of the state in economic and social life (for the sake of convenience, and at the cost of some analytical rigour, I shall use the terms 'state' and 'government' interchangeably[3]). It is here that a rationalistic element in liberalism does perhaps become apparent, for the state has no *a priori* entitlement to reverence, as it does in most varieties of conservative political thought. Its activities are subject to critical analysis and its range limited by general principles. Furthermore, some of the most sophisticated techniques of contemporary social science have been used to explain the (to the liberal) unwelcome growth in the size of the state in all Western democracies throughout this century. This growth has become especially serious in the post-war years. Before these points can be explored further, however, a distinction must be made, and elementary though this is, it is of paramount importance to the classical liberal theory of political society.

The crucial distinction is between *state* and *law*, for although all liberals[4] accept the necessity of the state (as an essential instrument of coercion), they maintain that it does not in any way follow from this that all law must emanate from state institutions or that the state cannot itself be bound by rules. All political actors should be restricted by rules *not of their own making*. At its most elementary level political liberalism is constitutionalism — though this simple assertion leaves entirely open the content of constitutional rules, how they are to be enforced and so on. What it does, however, is to turn the question of forms of government in a different direction from that which is conventional in political theory. Thus the question of the substantive form a government may take, such as constitutional monarchy or democracy, is less important than the nature of the rules that bind it. Unlimited democracy would therefore be as unwelcome as unlimited monarchy. Indeed, the liberal complaint is that the honorific overtones that the word democracy has acquired in the twentieth century have distracted attention away from serious analysis of the nature and forms of political rule.

The argument for the logical independence of law from the state derives from the classical liberal theory that predictability and regularity in social arrangements can exist without central direction and control. If this is so then state can be seen as a form of *organisation* (i.e. a product of deliberation and design) charged with specific functions — normally, services that for technical reasons cannot be provided efficiently (if they can be provided at all) by the market. Its value therefore depends upon its efficiency in providing these functions.

The attempt to find a theoretical limit to the activity of the state contrasts clearly with the Hobbesian tradition in political thought. The liberal emphasis is on a natural harmony in society, not in economic matters alone but also in law and other social institutions. There is an optimistic assumption that if individuals are left alone they will to a very great extent spontaneously develop appropriate institutional frameworks: the necessity for a body (the state) to *design* social order is accordingly reduced. In fact, there is an element of Hobbesianism in some forms of traditional conservatism. Pessimistic conservatism, with its belief in the ultimate depravity of man, naturally leads to an elevated view of the state as the only possible guarantor of order: without centralised authority the 'state of nature' is always likely to emerge. Thus, for many conservatives the distinction between law and state is smothered by a Hobbesian belief in the necessity for a sovereign to exist for order to be possible.

Classical liberals do differ on the question of how this conceptual difference between law and state is to be cashed out in practical terms. Historically, the common law has developed a body of legal rules in a spontaneous manner quite independently of the sovereign's command (through formal legislation). For this reason many liberals have detected an analogy between the progressive development of law in a case-by-case manner and the market itself.

The key point is that in both phenomena the resulting outcome or 'pattern' is not the intended result of one mind but the unintended consequence of the activities of innumerable individuals. Again, the justification for this seemingly haphazard legal process derives from the liberal's belief in the ever-present fact of ignorance. It follows from this that legislation could not possibly be designed which could cover all cases that might occur in an unknowable future; and to the charge that common law is unpredictable because its development depends entirely on judicial interpretation, the liberal reply is that this is preferable to the caprice regularly displayed by legislatures. This point is especially pertinent in the modern democratic world where most legislation emanates from shifting and transient coalitions of interests. The greater predictability of the common-law system is said to arise from the fact that judicial interpretation and innovation are confined to difficult cases that arise within a general system of rules.[5]

Of course, the common law is always subordinate to statute and that intricate network of rules which has grown up over the centuries could be overturned at any moment by sovereign parliaments. Nevertheless, according to liberal political theory, its virtue lies in the fact that it deals with *individual* claims and disputes and coheres with a private-property system. Thus Marxists are in a clear sense right when they maintain that the common law protects a bourgeois property-owning regime — though they obviously cannot accept that such a system has any permanent value. Common-law liberals also claim that since this legal order permits an individual to do anything which is not actually forbidden, it in principle allows a greater range of 'rights' to develop than would be the case if such rights were specifically delineated in formal statutes. This again is a consequence of the liberal theory that society is a spontaneous process characterised by ignorance.

What the common-law liberal is after is a recognition of a clear distinction between legal and political decisions. In a legal process there is in principle a 'right' answer to a dispute and this answer will be independent of any end of purpose of society at large. Indeed, the classical liberal doubts that there are genuine purposes or ends of society which are not resolvable into individual actions. However, the rise of the administrative state has steadily eroded the common law so that people's lives are more governed by statutes which specify particular social plans than by common-law rules. This is particularly so in the area of welfare where individual decision-making, via insurance, has to a large extent been replaced by collective action. Since administrative law confers wide discretionary powers on ministers, the liberal argues that large areas of social life become almost irredeemably 'politicised'. Of course, administrative law and welfare legislation are not the only examples of this politicisation. They are, however, a striking feature of modern British society and will be considered in more detail below. In general, the classical liberal draws a parallel between the process of the politicisation of economic life, through the nationalisation, subsidisation and regulation of industry, and that of social life, through the replacement of the insurance principle by the welfare principle.

It is, however, because of the vulnerability of the common law to statute that has led to the demands by many liberals for written 'bills of rights', with demarcation lines drawn between individual and collective action. Once again, the British situation is germane to the argument since our largely 'unwritten' constitution has proved to be an ineffective barrier to the encroachment of the state on economic and social life.[6] All other countries that followed the postwar consensus have written constitutions of some kind or other. The interesting question for liberal political theory is how it is that the existence of 'constitutionalism' has not prevented the partial disintegration of the liberal society.

Of more local interest is whether Britain's social and political dilemma is resolvable by the adoption of more formal guarantees to individualism than those provided by the common law. Certainly, those common-law liberals[7] who are sceptical of the value of a written constitution for Britain have a point when they say that the US Constitution has been singularly ineffective in preventing the systematic undermining of economic liberty in that country over the past 50 years or so. They would also point out that the institution of a written set of rights, necessarily subject to judicial interpretation, would not solidify the necessary distinction between law and politics: in fact, it would make it worse since judges would be directly involved in what would undoubtedly become controversial political decisions. Nevertheless, all liberals believe that there must be some constraints on political action if the liberal ideal of constitutionalism is to be realised. What form such constraints should take is the most difficult of the problems of contemporary liberalism. There may be no one answer to it but only separate answers for separate countries, appropriate to their own particular traditions. Although this approach would attenuate the *generality* of liberalism, and therefore acknowledge the potency of a kind of conservatism, it may very well be unavoidable.

The liberal ideal of law is that it should be a general body of rules which enables individuals to pursue their own ends. The limits of legal regulation are determined by the requirement that no one person or group's purposes should override those of other persons or groups. Thus liberal society has no end itself and its rules are 'purpose-independent'; if any end can be attributed to it at all it is merely that it should maintain the framework for a variety of ends to be pursued. This is essentially the doctrine of John Stuart Mill's *On Liberty*[8] or Herbert Spencer's 'equal liberty', as expounded in his *Social Statics.* [9] It is indeed the essence of pluralism — though not that version described in political-science textbooks which understands social harmony as a kind of equilibrium between competing interest groups.

In effect, the liberal asks that society be organised under the principle of the 'rule of law'. In itself the principle is not very helpful and does little to distinguish the liberal system of values from other ones — notably, some varieties of conservatism. Indeed, there is no doubt that the collectivist policies of the consensus could be regarded as sanctioned by the principle of the rule of law if that is interpreted to mean merely 'lawfulness'. Thus, from a legal positivist[10] standpoint, any act or law must be regarded as technically valid if it emanates from a procedure which is recognised as legitimate. However, the principle of the rule of law in liberal doctrine is not merely a principle of technical legitimacy: it is a method of evaluating legislation that may well be formally valid.[11] Thus a statute emanating from the British sovereign Parliament may well be, in a non-positivist sense of legitimacy, 'invalid' if it fails to meet with the criterion specified by the rule of law. These criteria vary a little from one version of the doctrine to another, but they normally stipulate that statutes must be non-discriminatory, equal in application, should not exempt (named) individuals or groups from law, or be retrospective — in other words, 'law' should be 'blind' in its effect on the citizenry: only then can it provide a predictable framework of rules to enable individuals to pursue their ends in reasonable security. It is also a feature of the rule of law that legislatures should be bound by general rules, usually in the form of a written constitution. It is for this reason that the principle of parliamentary sovereignty, which imposes no external constraints on what a legislature may do, is in breach of the principle of the rule of law.

The kind of legislation that liberals have typically criticised as being objectionable on the above grounds includes trade-union law currently operative in Western social democracies, and tax laws. In a number of these countries, unions are specifically exempt from the law of tort in industrial disputes. The inability of people to sue unions for damages caused by unions in the course of their activities tilts the balance against employers in industrial disputes and has had an adverse effect on economic growth in social democracies.[12] The steep rates of progressive income tax in these countries not only have a disincentive effect but also arbitrarily discriminate in favour of low earners as against high earners. The only tax rule that would be consistent with the rule of law would be a proportionate tax, i.e. a uniform tax-rate paid by all wage-earners.

It is to be noted that in these two examples the liberal objections are based on utilitarian *and* 'meta-legal' considerations. The utilitarian criticisms of trade-union privilege and progressive taxation are self-explanatory. The 'meta-legal' principle of the rule of law, however, is held by many liberals to be more decisive since it encapsulates the individualist principle of *justice* in the law. Thus, if the utilitarian considerations were indecisive, or even if they did not hold at all, the rule-of-law doctrine would still tell against legislation or acts of government that were arbitrary and partial. In fact, liberals would claim that the major aims of feminists and opponents of racial discrimination are already encompassed within the principle of the rule of law since this explicitly 'invalidates' legislation or acts of policy which discriminate on grounds of sex or colour of skin.

Nevertheless there are problems within the rule-of-law doctrine. The major issue is whether it is to be interpreted in a *substantive* or *procedural* sense: in other words, does it put a specific limitation on what legislatures may do or merely demand that what ever it is that they do should meet with certain procedural, albeit highly restrictive, requirements? The latter is normally favoured by liberals on the grounds that there is less likely to be agreement on substantive issues than on procedural forms. Unfortunately, as has often been pointed out,[13] it would be possible to pass discriminatory legislation that still met the rule-of-law criteria outlined above if it were worded carefully enough. A group could be arbitrarily treated by a law without being named *if* the terms of that law could only possibly apply to it. It is for this reason that many liberals favour written constitutions that specify the rights and duties of citizens in substantive terms.

Given the fact that liberalism denies the right of the state or society to impose collective ends on individual choosers, it is

necessary that it should recommend a considerable loosening of the
bonds that coercive law has confined individual conduct involving
private choices in moral matters. Hence, liberals actively supported
the repeal of oppressive legislation in the field of personal morality,
in homosexuality, abortion and in political, literary and artistic
expression, which was such an important feature of consensus social
policy. This was one thing that united liberalism and social
democracy. However, what divided the two ideologies was the
former's insistence that the liberalising of society must include
economic affairs as well as personal morality. This was required for
the broadly utilitarian reasons outlined in the previous chapter. In
addition, however, liberals stressed that a belief in the *principle* of
liberty dictated that any line drawn between freedom in morality
and economic freedom was arbitrary and unsustainable. A genuine
'permissive society' requires capitalism.[14] Furthermore, it is argued
that in practical terms it is impossible for personal liberties, especially
freedom of expression, to be effective in the absence of economic
liberty.[15] The formal guarantee of, say, a free press, would be
useless if no private publishing were allowed. If presses, paper and
so on, were to be allocated by some collective institutions, then
restrictions could be placed on freedom of expression without in
any way abrogating a formal right. This utilitarian argument for
economic liberty would then hold independently of any moral claim
to individual ownership (which liberals make anyway).

III

In classical liberal theory there is a role for the state in economic
and social life, despite the emphasis on spontaneity and the efficiency properties of private enterprise. There has, however, always
been an 'underground' anarchistic wing of *laissez-faire* political
economy, which is undergoing something of a revival in the USA
at the moment, which claims that any wanted good or service can
be provided by the market.[16] Ingenious though some of the
'anarcho-capitalist' arguments are their remoteness from the world
of power-politics has meant that their practical significance has been
virtually in inverse relation to their intellectual elegance. Most
classical liberals have come to accept the inevitability of the state
and have searched for coherent principles which would limit its
activities rather than pressing for its elimination — to 'roll back'
the frontiers of governmental activity instead of demanding its

instant abolition.

Nevertheless, there is more than a lingering affection for the sentiment expressed in Bastiat's delightfully sententious definition of the state as that 'fictitious entity by which everybody tries to live at the expense of everybody else'. What Bastiat meant, although he was no anarcho-capitalist, was that the institutions of government were no more than artificial devices for transferring income from one group to another whilst the illusion was maintained by statists that the state was some kind of natural entity with a life, and indeed an income, of its own.[17] That it is, and does, is a view which persists today, fallacious though it is.

The most disturbing fact for the classical liberal is the inexorable growth of the size of the state, in terms of people employed and its expenditure as a proportion of GNP.[18] These facts, as we will see later, are common to all countries governed by the principles of the consensus. It seems as if the state is something a civilised society cannot do without but which it has had great difficulty in controlling. The activities of the state cannot be determined by evolution, chance or custom since these factors seem to have produced the contemporary bloated social-democratic state. In other words, the state requires a *rationale* for its existence and an appropriate *agenda* of its permissible activities. From Adam Smith, through Bentham and John Stuart Mill, to the present day, this has been a major task of liberal theory. More than any other social philosophy, liberalism has to show how the demand for the reduction of coercion to the absolute minimum (a demand made on either utilitarian or ethical grounds) can be made consistent with the necessity for some organised force in society. In contemporary liberal thought the most important contributions to the analysis of the state have come from the 'Virginia School' of public choice economics (its foremost spokesmen being James Buchanan and Gordon Tullock), Milton Friedman and the Chicago economists and the Austrian tradition of von Mises and Hayek. However, it must be understood that the liberal theory of the state derives from a long tradition in orthodox welfare economics[19] — a subject which, although it has the same individualistic basis of micro-economics, is not to be identified with the liberal ideology.

The liberal account of the state depends very largely on the theory of 'public goods' elaborated by welfare economics.[20] Public goods are those such as defence, law and order, clean air and so on, which for technical reasons cannot be provided by the market. Although they have to be supplied collectively, this form of provision is not thought to be antithetical to individualism since the goods in question are held to be desired by individual maximisers; it is simply the case that the market 'fails' in certain areas. The aim of the liberal idea of the state is to justify some collective action without any recourse to the notion that the state embodies ends or purposes which are superior to individual ends or purposes. Even apart from the technical difficulties involved in the supply of public goods, the liberal approach is likely to generate serious problems. This is especially so in the area of personal conduct involving things such as drug addiction: should the state take a purely 'want-regarding'[21] view and permit trade in substances known to be harmful to individuals? In fact, a purely liberal approach does necessitate that individuals must not be prevented by a paternalist state from harming themselves — a radical view which is in many respects at odds with conventional morality.

At this stage it is more important to concentrate on the theory of public goods. A public good is normally defined in terms of *non-excludability* and *non-rivalness*. The non-excludability property means that once the good (or service) has been provided it is impossible to prevent others (who have not paid for it) from consuming it. This is the well-known 'free-rider' problem. If a good is non-rival it means that, in clear contrast to private goods, one person's consumption of it does not reduce the amount available to others. Thus, for example, the information transmitted by a light-house is available for everybody at zero price once it is supplied — though there are severe doubts that a light-house, once thought to be the paradigm case of a public good, really is one.[22]

These two properties taken together have led to the conclusion that public goods will be under-supplied, or not supplied at all, by the market: in some crucially important respects, people will be made worse off by market arrangements. Put more technically, the argument is that an exchange economy does not generate 'Pareto-optimal' outcomes: a Pareto-optimum is a situation in which no improvement can be made without (at least) one person being made worse off.[23] It should be noted that since Paretian welfare economics is silent about the initial distribution of property rights from which exchange begins, it has no necessary connection with a particular economic ideology, although it would appear to be compatible with some important features of liberalism.[24]

The market fails not only in the under-production (or non-production) of public goods; it also fails in the sense of generating 'negative externalities'. These are the costs imposed on the neighbourhood by the activities of private producers, thus generating a difference between marginal private and marginal social costs. The familiar example is the producer using the least-cost methods of production causing pollution to the atmosphere. The logic of public-good and externality theory is identical in both cases and the phenomena provide a justification for state (i.e. coercive) activity.

For the liberal, however, what differentiates his rationale for such coercion from that of other social doctrines is that it purports to rest upon purely individualistic foundations. The state provides only those services that individuals want but which cannot be provided in any other way: although it acts coercively it is nevertheless a curious kind of 'voluntary' coercion. The difficulty, of course, is that in the absence of a market, it is almost impossible to determine accurately what it is that people want. Furthermore, once coercive power has been granted to the state, what machinery can be constructed to prevent its expansion beyond theoretically prescribed limits? Certainly, the growth of the size of the state in the post-war period has not been in the production of what the liberal would call public goods. This expansion has come about through inadequate constitutional mechanisms that have allowed the state to become burdened with tasks which would not be permitted by orthodox liberal public-good theory.

Even with the theory itself, however, there are few clear limits to the expansion of state activity. There is no real limit on what can count as 'external effects' and collectivists have been quick to use the argument to justify a wide expansion of the state: for example, education is said to confer benefits on the community at large and not just to the recipient of the service.[25] If education were treated as a form of investment in training for employment (or indeed personal pleasure), it could be treated as a form of purely private consumption to be paid for individually. However, even such a convinced liberal as Milton Friedman[26] concedes that it has public-good features in that it transmits those cultural attitudes that are necessary for a free society: some public support for education is therefore justifiable.

The contemporary liberal is obviously concerned to limit the expansion of the state under the anodyne rubric of public-good theory. The most fruitful advances have been made in the field of property rights. The phenomena of negative externalities, pollution and the like, have conventionally been solved in welfare economics, by collection action, at least since the pioneering work of A.C. Pigou.[27] The gap between private and social costs is closed (a

'Pareto-optimum' is generated) by appropriate taxes, regulation, prohibition or nationalisation of particular activities. However, it is now maintained that if property rights are specified. external harms can be eliminated by *legal* action[28] — that is, victims of the accidental harmful actions of others should be able to sue in the courts for damages, and evidence from the common law is adduced to support this view. Of course, it is readily conceded that transaction costs (especially where large numbers of people are affected) may be extremely high, but in principle it would be possible to reduce the ambit of the state and thence 'internalise' the externalities generated by the market.

The preference for market solutions over collective solutions stems from the liberal's distrust of unconstrained activity of any kind. There is no guarantee that public officials will of necessity promote the public interest: government failure is as prevalent as market failure. If public officials are treated as utility-maximisers, then even though they are not motivated by profit, their actions can still be explained in terms of the individualistic calculus. They are just as likely to maximise the size of their bureaux as they are the public interest. The increased size of public-sector employment experienced in consensus countries since the War seems to owe little to genuine public-good theory and much more to political activity as such.

Liberal social theory has been particularly effective at locating crucial difficulties in the whole idea of public or collective owner-ship. The trouble is that, given certain contingent (but scarcely alterable) features of the human condition, common right to prop-erty is certain to lead to inefficiency in comparison with private ownership: most particularly it will lead to over-use, or exploita-tion, of resources. David Hume first noticed this phenomenon, which is now known as the 'tragedy of the commons'.[29] Thus if a piece of land is held in 'common' with no private rules restricting its use, then it is certain to be over-used, leading to a much greater deple-tion of stock and other resources than would otherwise be the case. Yet although no individual would have desired this outcome, no one would have any incentive to prevent it. This is simply another example of the familiar public-good problem mentioned earlier.

It has, however, an important implication for the analysis of the public sector, for here there are no real incentives for political actors to economise on the use of resources. Not only that but interest groups make demands on the public purse, as if it were common land, even though the long-run effect of this is to make the member of each interest group worse off than he otherwise would be. The liberal theory blames much of this on a tradition of social theorising which treats public officials (elected or not) as if they were altruists, concerned only to implement the public interest. However, if officials canot be relied upon to do this spontaneously, once again constitutional procedures will have to be designed to divert their natural self-interest into less harmful channels. Government activity itself has become a kind of negative externality, but given the nature of democratic politics, individuals have little or no incentive to allay its effects.

Liberals have differing views as to how this might be done. Ideally, they would like to limit government activity to the supply of genuine public goods and to solve the problem of externalities by re-defined property rights and legal rules that enable individuals to negotiate settlements between themselves. Obvious candidates for public goods are defence (internal and external) and the supply of legal services. Even welfare may be included in the category: individuals may experience a loss of utility knowing that some members of the community are in considerable distress, so that the alleviation of this would in fact make *everybody* (including the rich) better off.[30] Reliance on charity may well lead to the under-supply of welfare since the difference the contribution of *each* individual donor makes to the problem is so small that it may not seem worth his while. Hence, a measure of compulsion could be justified on purely liberal grounds.

There is, however, a difficulty in categorically specifying a range of public goods and enjoining governments to produce them, since there is an element of subjectivity in determining what is and what is not an activity appropriate for collective delivery.[31] Most liberals would argue that this should be a matter of political decision, emanating from a voting process. However, the voting rule should be more than a bare majority, since this rather undemanding condition has been, it is claimed, a major cause of the expansion of the state. The particular solutions to the problem will be considered in the context of a more detailed explication of the liberal critique of interest group activity.

IV

As we shall see in succeeding chapters, there has been a dramatic expansion in state activity in just those countries where constitutional rules, in the form of democratic-choice methods, have been operative. Yet those countries have experienced what has come to be known as the 'fiscal crisis of the state': a phenomenon general enough to demand some theoretical explanation. The phrase (which has a Marxist ring to it) refers to the fact of the increasing burdens being imposed on the state — burdens which are heavy enough to drive some commentators to the conclusion that the welfare-capitalist state (the 'consensus' in the terminology of this study) may well be facing 'contradictions' within its structure which, although not of a Marxist kind, may be severe enough to destroy the system.[32] The most important of these burdens is the welfare system (see below), mainly because it creates expectations in people (and imposes 'obligations' on government) which can only be fulfilled if economic growth continues indefinitely. The slow-down in economic growth, which began in the mid-1970s, exposed Western countries to the crisis.

The major argument of liberal theory is that the operation of simple majority-rule democratic procedures prevents the emergence of the public interest. The public interest may be conveniently defined as the interest each individual has as a member of the public, as distinct from his interests as a member of a group *smaller than* the public.[33] Things that are said to be in the public interest for the liberal must include a stable monetary system, a predictable legal order, and so on. Indeed, the utilitarian benefits, in terms of freedom and prosperity, of a free-market system may be said to be in the public interest since they are enjoyed by anonymous individuals rather than named groups. Public-interest theory is simply another version of the problem of public goods: indeed, the whole structure of the liberal political economic order may be said to display public-good features.

Now in some traditional democratic theories, the rather heroic assumption is made that individual citizens will vote for the public interest: that, unlike monarchy or aristocracy, democracy will generate the interests of the community rather than those of private persons or groups. Indeed, individual 'rationality' was sometimes identified with the pursuit of 'objective' community ends rather than with the calculation of the means necessary for the successful realisation of subjectively chosen ends. Yet there is no reason at all, given the liberal's somewhat unflattering but surely realistic concept of man, why the traditional theory should be at all persuasive. Even if the individual citizen were to have the appropriate motivation for non-selfish action, it would be a costly business for him to determine whether policies of competing political parties were consistent with the demands of the public interest. Since the single vote cast by one person is likely to have very little effect on the result of an election, it would be quite *irrational* for him to become informed of all the complexities of alternative public policies.[34] In fact, the picture of an ill-informed, prejudiced and volatile voter painted in sociological voting studies is an unwitting tribute to his rationality (in the liberal economist's sense of the word).

The trouble is that rational self-interest will drive the citizen to vote for his immediate group interests rather than for the public interest. This is because the benefits that accrue from policies sanctioned by this principle are remote and long-term in their effect and thinly spread across the members of the community. However, the benefits from the securing of a particular group-privilege are immediate and tangible. What liberals have in mind here are privileges to politically favoured groups in taxation (e.g. tax relief on mortgages), exemption from general rules of law (trade-union immunities are the prime example here), and the protection of politically significant industries from the natural forces of the market. Taken individually these will have a small effect on the functioning of a free society, but in the aggregate they constitute a corrosive force on the structure of the market. There is, however, nothing in the liberal theory of self-interest to prevent individuals in a democracy voting for such policies. This has the disturbing implication, of course, that the liberal will have to appeal to something other than self-interest if there is to be an escape from the dilemmas of modern democracy.

The problem is that if party leaders are assumed (quite plausibly) to maximise their votes to win office, there is no guarantee that this strategy will generate even 'moderate' policies, i.e. those favoured by voters in the centre of the political spectrum (though these are not necessarily policies in the public interest). Since the vagaries of Western electoral systems permit a party to form a government with less than a majority, this makes it relatively easy for winning *coalitions of interests* to be formed by offering 'bribes' to various groups spread across the political spectrum. The results of elections may then be indeterminate; they will depend on the skill of political entrepreneurs in putting together winning policy packages.[35]

Thus there is a kind of 'political market', a competition for votes (an insight originally associated with Joseph Schumpeter)[36] that may be said to be analogous to economic competition. However, there are crucially important differences between economic and political markets — differences which prevent a benign 'invisible hand' operating in politics as it does in economics. The decisive point is that there is no *immediate* budget constraint in politics acting so as to contain the ambitions of politicians as there is for entrepreneurs in private markets. This means that politicians can offer bribes to the electorate for which they do not have to pay in the immediate time-period. If electorally attractive policies had to be paid for in taxes, then that itself would be a constraint since heavy taxation is a vote loser. Indeed, it is this that has motivated many classical liberals in the US to demand a constitutional amendment embodying a 'balanced-budget' requirement (see chapter 6). However, in present circumstances governments in social democracies can finance their vote-winning strategies by borrowing and/or inflation — thus ensuring that the costs can be pushed on to different people, sometimes in the distant future. A spectacular example of this process is the practice of introducing 'unfunded' state pensions, the cost of which is borne by unknown, and necessarily unconsulted, future generations — a dubious scheme validated by a spurious 'contract' between the generations.

Thus there is a tendency for government deficits and inflation to be built into the system of competitive democracy. There is therefore a need to make a slight but important modification to the familiar classical liberal's claim that inflation is always and everywhere a 'monetary phenomenon'. What is known as the economic analysis of democracy pushes the *causal* explanation of inflation a stage further back in the social process than is normally the case in monetarist economics. It shows why it is the case that governments are regularly driven to finance deficits by inflation (or by borrowing that eventuates in inflation): this is the fact that such action is the best immediate strategy dictated by the short time-horizons (the length of the period between elections) of political actors.

A particularly intriguing application of the economic approach to social life is the analysis of the political economy of Keynesianism in practice. It is undoubtedly the case that the emergence of regular budget deficits coincided with the adoption of Keynesian demand-management politics in the post-war period. In the work of James Buchanan and Richard Wagner[37] the emphasis is not on the internal logic or theoretical adequacy of Keynes's economic theory but on the behaviour of political actors implementing Keynesian policies. The conclusion reached is that even if the theory were true, there are good public-choice reasons why it is likely to fail as a policy under *conditions of competitive party-democracy*.

The argument is as follows. Keynesian policies for full employment require that the government regulate the economy at the
macro-level. In a depression the economy must be stimulated by
fiscal policy (i.e. a government running a deficit so as to raise
demand), but in the boom a government should run a surplus to
prevent the boom turning into runaway inflation. Keynesian theory
(and common sense) tells us that the government budget must
balance through the course of the business cycle. The role of macro-
economic policy is to iron out the bumps in an economic cycle, for
which, it is alleged, the market itself provides no automatic corrective mechanism.

We have already noted the fact that governments do not have
the information that is required to 'fine-tune' the economy; however,
the achievement of Buchanan and Wagner was to show that even
if they had, certain crucial facts of political economy prevent them
from acting upon it. Given the theory of group politics outlined earlier,
it is theoretically predictable that government will continually run
deficits. If democratic politics is understood as a vote-maximising
process, it is easy to show how economic managers will respond to
the demands of electoral politics rather than the prescriptions of
Keynesian economic rationality. The electoral timetable will dictate
that political entrepreneurs pursue lax monetary and fiscal policies
so as to secure favourable, but temporary, economic conditions,
especially increases in employment. However, this has no necessary
relationship with some hypothetical macro-economic timetable. Once
again it is the absence of a budget constraint that ultimately causes
the profligacy of governments. For there will always be more interest
groups demanding political action that culminates in government
expansions than those demanding financial probity. The liberal asks
the question: 'who is to speak for the "public", the main beneficiaries
of financial rectitude, when people are organised into groups considerably smaller, but more effectively organised, than the public?'

The liberal objection to Keynesianism then does not just concern its content as an economic theory; it is also addressed to the
absence of any consideration of the *institutional* context in which the
practical implementation of that theory must take place. Keynes
himself was in some senses a 'philosopher king'[38] who would (and
did) act disinterestedly for the public interest, and his theory does
presuppose the existence of an omniscient and benevolent elite
insulated from normal political, social and economic pressures. It
would indeed achieve its full fruition in a non-democratic age. It
is no coincidence that the rise of Keynesianism should have been

accompanied by the gradual disintegration of those shackles on government action, the Gold Standard, balanced budgets and *effective* constitutions (of either a formal or informal kind), which had been a product not of an unaided reason but of tradition and experience. As liberal political economy has shown, however, these constraints were not replaced by omniscient and benevolent dictators but by vote-maximising politicians, themselves shackled by the demands of their client groups.

V

The importance of interest-group analysis for the contemporary classical liberal cannot be over-estimated: it is perhaps the most significant of the innnovations that have taken place in traditional individualist thought in the post-war years. What the critique of pressure-group politics does is to challenge a prevailing theme of consensus political thought — namely, that politics is a benign activity and that social stability is secured by permitting a *plurality* of groups to operate in an almost unconstrained manner in the political system. In Britain this view was argued forcefully by Bernard Crick and his definition of politics nicely encapsulates the political sociology of pluralism:

> Politics . . . can be simply defined as the activity by which differing interests within a given unit of rule are conciliated by giving them a share of power in proportion to their importance to the welfare and survival of the whole community . . . a political system is that type of government where politics proves successful in ensuring reasonable stability and order.[39]

It should be obvious that the above is not merely a neutral definition of politics as a particular form of decision-making. It is a *persuasive* definition designed to elicit from the reader a favourable attitude towards politics. Decisions that result from the interplay of groups, mediated perhaps through the electoral process, are in a normative sense superior to those that emanate from command (coercion) or from the market. A similar view appears in the work of the American political scientist, Robert Dahl, whose *A Preface to Democratic Theory*[40] endeavoured to show that competition between minority groups, later to be called 'polyarchy', prevented the occurrence of the 'tyranny of the majority' — a fear that has haunted traditonal democratic theory. However, what these writers failed to appreciate was the possibility (now a probability) that pluralism would produce a new tyranny of minorities or a form of social stagnation or immobility.

It was Mancur Olson, an economist, who first alerted the social sciences to the dangers that lurk behind the anodyne theory of pluralism. In his *The Logic of Collective Action* he put the matter succinctly with the following observation:

> It does not follow that the results of pressure group activity would be harmless, much less desirable, even if the balance of power equilibrium resulting from the multiplicity of pressure groups kept any one pressure group from getting out of line. Even if such a pressure group system worked with perfect fairness to every group it would still tend to work inefficiently.[41]

It is easy to show how treating each group 'fairly' would result in inefficiency. Imagine every producer group in a country getting an equal amount of protection from foreign competition: this of course would be to act impartially towards each group, but it would result in a massive misallocation of resources and the consequent fall in income for everyone (including the members of the producer groups who are also consumers). Yet this would be eminently 'politic' by Crickian standards. Although such an extreme 'political' approach to economic affairs has not been attempted in the consensus countries, a movement in that direction is easily detectable in post-war Britain and the US.

Olson makes some further salient observations on the nature of group activity. The most important is the argument that certain groups can only remain viable by coercion (or by providing some direct incentives to their members). This is because interest groups provide quasi-public goods to their members, normally in the form of exemptions from the rule of law and government-sponsored privileges. Since, as we know, public goods are available to people whether they pay for them or not, there is a free-rider problem for entities smaller than the state. In small groups there may be informal social pressures to secure compliance from members but this becomes less effective the larger a group becomes; direct sanctions have to be used in large groups to prevent their disintegration. This is why trade unions have to use the 'closed shop' and other coercive tactics to keep their members in line.

In his more recent work, *The Rise and Decline of Nations*,[42] Olson tackles directly the argument that politics is an especially virtuous activity and shows how that *stability* which is a product of Crickian pluralism is itself a cause of the current malaise of consensus countries. Olson argues that so far from group bargaining being a source of *benign* order, it is in fact corrosive of a genuine public interest. Pluralism encourages an investment in politics and other redistributive activities rather than production: pressure groups behave like 'wrestlers struggling over the contents of a china shop'.[43]

Olson argues, with supreme irony, that it is conditions of stability and political tranquility that encourage this corrosive process. These favour the solidification and entrenchment of group privilege and the stultification of the economic system through the attenuation of competitive market-processes; they lead to the slowing-up of economic growth. Casual observation seems to bear this out. Britain has a notoriously stable political system yet seems to suffer most from what might be termed 'group sclerosis'. Again the east coast states of America, whose legislatures have gone some way down the British road, have experienced a similar phenomenon.

Yet those countries that have suffered political upheavals in the last 50 or so years, such as Japan, France and West Germany, have experienced much more rapid economic growth; and this must be in part be due to the fact that these political traumas helped to breakup entrenched groups. West Germany is a particularly instructive example, since its 'social market economy' (see chapter 7) was founded upon a wrecked collectivist economic system and a bankrupt political order. Groups that have remained strong and powerful in Britain were simply eliminated in West Germany. Within the US itself, Olson argues that the difference between the growth rates of the far western and southern areas (the so-called 'sun-belt' states) and those of the north-eastern seaboard is explained by the fact that interest groups have been less successful in the former than the latter. In a federal system the right of 'exit' to areas where the political, economic and social system is less prone to the enervating effects of group activity goes some way towards preserving the conditions for a liberal and open economy.

The upshot of the liberal economics of politics school is that the continual politicisation of consensus society has produced a certain kind of *immobility* and a gradual atrophying of its productive forces. Whether this will eventually result in the disintegration of the market economy is a much debated point amongst contemporary liberals.

A common theme, first espoused by Hayek in 1944,[44] is that the first serious steps towards intervention would set in train a process that would almost inevitably culminate in 'serfdom', even though this was not the intention of the original interveners. However, it should be stressed that the causal explanation of this, given in Hayek's early analysis, was the influence of mistaken *ideas* about social and economic policy. Today the emphasis is on group pressures which operate in an almost mechanical fashion — the implication being that ideas are relatively impotent.

Yet almost all contemporary liberals, including Olson, claim that only a massive change in ideas can halt the process, let alone reverse the trend, towards complete immobility and ultimate collectivisation. One seemingly insuperable obstacle is the size of public-sector bureaucracies which now constitute significant voting blocs in contemporary social democracies. The public sector, insulated as it is from the corrective forces of the market, is an Olsonian group in its own right. The tendency for it to generate internal mechanisms of expansion is reinforced by the phenomenon of 'rent-seeking'.[45] To put this point simply in this context, economic rent is the difference between income earned by a factor of production in the public sector and its best return in the private sector. Given the protection against the market that public-sector officials enjoy, the amount of economic rent earned is likely to be quite high. It is in cases such as this that the appeal to self-interest is clearly self-destructive. What effect can the coherence and persuasiveness of the ideas of liberal political economy have on people certain to be adversely affected by their implementation, in the short run at least, if not permanently?

Contemporary history may well be seen not as a battle between vested interests but between ideas and vested interests — for it is certainly the case that the last 20 years has witnessed a renaissance in liberal ideas, if not much success in breaking up the coalitions of groups that have, for the individualist, constituted formidable barriers to progress.

VI

One important feature of the consensus which contemporary classical liberalism has criticised at considerable length is the remarkable extension of welfare services that has been such a significant part of the seemingly inexorable growth in the size of the state. The criticism has taken a number of forms but they can perhaps be reduced to two categories: those stemming from efficiency considerations and those that emanate from the often understated liberal view of morality. Before proceeding to discuss these issues, however, it is advisable to make one or two general observations on the liberal view of welfare.

It is not true that the idea of some collective provision is alien to the individualist view of the world. It is true that anarchocapitalists and extreme *laissez-faire* liberals do maintain that pensions, unemployment protection, health and education should be provided privately, largely through insurance schemes, and that those unable to attain an adequate level of well-being must rely on private charity (the supply of which, those thinkers insist is unnecessarily reduced by the existence of state welfare and excessive taxation). It is also the case that almost all classical liberals believe that much of the welfare state would gradually 'wither away' with increasing prosperity, were it not for the existence of large welfare bureaucracies which, they claim, generate internal mechanisms that perpetuate the system largely for the benefit of the officials who operate it. They also claim that the supply of welfare at virtually zero price simply increases the demand: in other words, the demand curve for the welfare service is 'negatively sloped', like the demand curve for normal goods and services. Nevertheless, most liberals would claim that there is a case for *some* collective provision of welfare for the genuine indigent and that the compulsion necessarily involved in the process can be justified on liberal principles.

This is because although welfare is not technically a public good since it is clearly not non-rival in consumption and does not satisfy the non-excludability criterion, it does, as mentioned earlier, resemble public goods in some important ways. On the assumption that people are not egoists, yet only imperfectly altruistic, we can assume that they would prefer a social state in which no individuals were left in distress, especially in an economic environment of general prosperity. Most people would, in fact, feel better off themselves if the poverty of others were eliminated. However, private charity may not be able to generate this level of general utility since the difference anyone person's contribution makes to the poverty problem is so infinitesimal that it might appear to him not worthwhile making it. Thus, the problem may only be soluble by compulsion. However, on this analysis, people would approve of such compulsion rather in the way that they approve of the compulsion required to produce internal and external defence. There is also the more cynical consideration that even a small minority of poor and alienated people could pose a serious threat to the stability of the liberal order. None of this, however, would convince the liberal of the need for a welfare *state*, i.e. an administrative order in which large areas of individual decision-making are made the responsibility of centralised authority.

The objections to the welfare state on grounds of efficiency are almost self-explanatory, or at least easily deducible from the foregoing exposition of liberal principles. The existence of guaranteed levels of welfare reduces the incentive to work. Since all economic decisions are taken at the margin, the decision to seek employment or not will depend on just what a person gains in employment compared with his position if remaining unemployed. In all consensus countries, evidence indicates that these can be very small indeed. The loss of welfare benefits through taking work, and the drawing of lowly paid people into the tax system, can produce effective tax rates of over 100 per cent.

The phenomenon of the 'poverty trap' is a well-documented feature of welfare systems. Again the provision of public-sector housing invariably at below free-market rents, which must be considered as a welfare provision even though it is not (except in some cases) at zero price, further reduces the incentive to work since work may only be on offer in places where cheap housing is unavailable.

Irrespective of these criticisms of the welfare state, which relate to wider economic issues, there is the crucially important question of the efficiency of the welfare system itself. In consensus countries the majority of welfare redistribution is in *kind* rather than cash (though there is some redistribution through the tax and social-security system). According to liberal economists, this has produced a vast and complex system of qualifications and entitlements, many of which are not dependent on income. This ensures, it is claimed, that not only do benefits *not* reach those in genuine need but also the maintenance of a wasteful bureaucracy. As we will see in succeeding chapters, a constant complaint of contemporary liberals is that the *form* of existing welfare states is actually beneficial to the middle classes.[46]

The general solution proposed is that the whole welfare system should be dismantled and replaced by a simple income-transfer system from rich to poor. Following Milton Friedman, this is known as the negative income tax.[47] This would be automatically paid to families whose incomes fell below a certain level: they would be free to spend it on what services they wished (in fact, the logic implies that they would not have to spend it on the typical welfare services anyway). This method is claimed to have two essential virtues: it eliminates the waste of organised bureaucracy and preserves freedom of choice for welfare recipients.

Appealing though this doctrine is to liberals, it is not without its difficulties. One obvious problem is the level at which the negative income tax is fixed; and there is no 'scientific' way of deciding this. If it is too high then it will obviously provide a strong disincentive to work — a disincentive compounded by the fact of the *ease* with which it is received. It is because of this that some liberals prefer the present system *because* it is complex and incomprehensible to would-be claimants.[48] They argue that this acts as a deterrent and so reduces the take-up rate. A negative income tax would by definition, have a 100 per cent take-up rate and could therefore be extremely costly. As will be seen in chapter 6, experiments with this form of welfare in America have produced disappointing results.

The other problem relates to the rigorous anti-paternalism of the above proposal. Are liberals prepared to permit the negative income tax to be spent on anything — drink and horses rather than education and pensions? In fact, a policy proposal often espoused concurrently with income redistribution reveals that liberals do impose some conditions on how welfare benefits may be spent. This is the suggestion that 'education vouchers' should replace bureaucratic determination of schooling.[49] Under the scheme, parents would be issued with vouchers which could be 'spent' at any school of their choice: supply and demand would determine which schools (and the type of education offered) would prevail. It is easy to show that this could be combined with a policy of redistribution since the *value* of the voucher could be varied according to income. The assumption behind all this is that education is a social good that must be made compulsory. However, this is only a minute concession to paternalism since it is provided for the benefit of children rather than parents. Nevertheless, it is easy to see how the technique could be used in other areas such as housing and health, inevitably leading to paternalism.

As a matter of fact, some theorists, who could be broadly called 'liberal', have justified some 'paternalism' in welfare provision that involves redistribution. It is argued that since some people are being coerced to pay for the well-being of others, they ought to have some say in how their money is spent. Thus, they would be made worse off if cash transfers were 'wasted' on pure consumption goods rather than spent on desirable welfare services. This would indeed justify the delivery of at least some welfare services in kind rather than in cash.[50] This is an argument that derives from Paretian welfare economics rather than liberalism but it is not difficult to see how it could be used to justify *specific* forms of welfare expenditure by the state. Nevertheless, most classical liberals maintain that welfare payments should be in cash, and freedom of choice of the recipients preserved, since they argue that not only do individuals know their own interests best, and can be relied upon to make 'rational choices', but that any alternative increases the power of the state over men's lives.

On the question of the morality of welfare the liberal philosophy is vague and less clear-cut. However, individualists are united on at least two themes. The first is relatively trivial but is still worth mentioning. Liberals do not 'blame' in some moral sense people who exploit the welfare system rather than working. It is not merely the fact that they respond in a rational manner to a distorted (from a liberal 'efficiency' point of view) set of signals, but also the point that ethical words such as 'good' or 'bad', 'just' or 'unjust' are quite inapplicable to individual behaviour in a welfare system. Nevertheless, liberals do point out that such systems do tend to inculcate habits and dispositions of *dependency*, and the attenuation of personal *responsibility* for action, which can have deleterious effects on the structure of a free order. It is doubtful that welfarism produces 'servility' on the part of citizens so that they become docile and submissive, but it is likely to be the case that excessive reliance on the state reduces the capacity for genuine free action on the part of individuals.

Perhaps a more important issue is the problem of the connection between welfare and justice, for it is a crucially important argument in classical liberal thought that welfare is not owed to individuals as a matter of *justice*; they do not have a right to it in the strict sense of that word. Governments may be said to have a duty to relieve obvious cases of indigency, and may even be criticised for not doing so, but whether they ought so to act will depend on particular circumstances: no person has a universal claim to welfare benefits in the way he has such a claim to free speech, free movement and so on.[51]

The social philosophy of the consensus did make the claim to welfare a claim of justice, or rather *social* justice. The concept of social justice is a collectivist term since it affirms that questions about justice are questions not about individual conduct but about society as a whole: a social order can be evaluated by reference to some external values. Thus its distribution of income, wealth, power, status and so on can be criticised if it does not accord with desert, merit or need. Indeed, on this view it would be morally permissible, if not obligatory, for it to be re-arranged by coercive law, so as to secure a more socially just 'outcome' or 'end-state'. Thus individuals are not treated as natural owners of whatever property, resources, or even talents, that they have: instead, these are regarded as elements in a kind of social pool which can then be redistributed in some ethically desirable fashion. Of course, this does not entail an egalitarian distribution of income and wealth, since there may be other reasons, mainly utilitarian ones, why some inequality should persist; but it does mean that there is a *presumption* in favour of equality, departures from which have to be rationally justified. The kind of targets social-justice theorists have in mind are the 'undeserved' income of entrepreneurs, speculators, film stars, and vast fortunes inherited by virtue of birth. In this view, incomes policies should not be used as devices to counter inflation but as 'objective' measures of the socially just wage.[52]

For the liberal, it is illegitimate (and, some would say, meaningless) to evaluate 'society' as a whole for its justice or injustice. It is claimed that justice is a property of individual conduct under general rules and since society is not a person it cannot be so evaluated. Of course, particular rules may be evaluated for their justice or injustice: they must be fair and impartial, favour no particular person or group and impose no arbitrary burdens. They should also recognise the right to private property and enforce rules for its legitimate transfer and exchange. Justice is not to do with the imposition of any kind of 'end-state' on a spontaneously developing process.

If it were possible to characterise the classical liberal approach to politics in one proposition it would be that liberalism sees political and economic systems in terms of processes and procedures.[53] As long as procedures meet with certain standards of fairness, it matters not what the outcome of the social process is. In this, liberalism contrasts both with collectivism and certain types of conservatism. All these doctrines have a vision or conception of what an ideal society should resemble. A consequence of this is that such doctrines show little detailed concern with how ideals should be implemented: the ultimate logic of this would be that desirable outcomes could be imposed dictatorially. However, it is the liberal's distrust of any sort of unconstrained power that drives him to constitutionalism. He is therefore, as far as is possible, 'neutral' about outcomes but not about procedures.

Notes and References

1. Although a great liberal economist who wrote extensively on politics, Mises never established an independent theory of law and state: see N.P. Barry, *On classical liberalism and libertarianism* (Macmillan, London, 1986), chapter 4.

2. His notorious *Fable of the bees* was first published in 1705. See W. Block, *Defending the undefendable* (Fleet Press, New York, 1975), for an amusing and penetrating demonstration of how various selfish and immoral actions produce virtuous outcomes.

3. See N.P. Barry, *An introduction to modern political theory* (Macmillan, London, 1981), chapter 4.

4. Extreme libertarians, anarcho-capitalists, do not accept the need for the state, although they do insist on the necessity of legal rules. See M. Rothbard, *Power and market* (Institute for Humane Studies, Menloe Park, 1970).

5. Critics of the common law tend to ignore the fact that human actions are constantly being co-ordinated by its rules without the need for adjudication.

6. See N. Johnson, *In search of the constitution*(London: Methuen, 1980).

7. Shirley Letwin has argued cogently that individual liberty would not be enhanced in Britain by a written constitution. See her 'A case study of the United Kingdom' in *1982 General Meeting papers, The Mont Pelerin Society* (Institut für Wirtschafts politik an der Universitat zu Koln).

8. For the interpretation of John Stuart Mill as a liberal individualist, see J. Gray, *Mill on liberty: a defence* (Routledge and Kegan Paul, London, 1983).

9. H. Spencer, *Social statics* (Gregg, Farnborough, 1970), first published in 1851.

10. See H.L.A. Hart, 'Positivism and the separation of law and morals' in his *Essays in jurisprudence and philosophy*, (Oxford University Press, London, 1983), pp. 49–87.

11. See F.A. Hayek, *The constitution of liberty* (Routledge and Kegan Paul, London, 1960), chapter XIV.

12. See J. Addison and J. Burton, *Trade unions and society* (Frazer Institute, Vancouver, 1983).

13.R. Hamowy has made extensive criticismns of the rule of law as a purely procedural doctrine: see his 'Freedom and the rule of law in F.A. Hayek', *Il Politico*, vol. 36 (1971), pp.347–77.

14. See S. Brittan, *Capitalism and the permissive society* (Macmillan, London, 1973).

15. See chapter 6 for Friedman's views on the indivisibility of freedom.,

16. Milton Friedman's son, David, is a prominent *laissez-faire*, anarchist: see his *The machinery of freedom* (Arlington, New York, 1973).

17. See F. Bastiat, *Economic harmonies* (Foundation for Economic Education, New York, 1964), originally published in 1850.

18. Information on the size of governments can be found in the *OECD*

economic outlook (Organisation for Economic Co-operation and Development, Paris, 1984).,

19. For an introduction to orthodox welfare economics, see W.J. Baumol, *Welfare economics and the theory of the state*, 2nd edn (Harvard University Press, Cambridge, 1967).

20. See J. Buchanan, *The demand and supply of public goods* (Rand Macnally, Chicago, 1968).

21. For an explanation of want-regarding principles, see B. Barry, *Political argument* (Routledge and Kegan Paul, London, 1965), chapter 1.

22. See A. Peacock, 'The limitations of public goods theory: the lighthouse revisited' in his *Economic analysis of government* (Martin Robertson, Oxford, 1979), pp. 127–36.

23. For a critical discussion of the Pareto-criterion, see C. Rowley and A. Peacock, *Liberal economics: a liberal restatement* (Martin Robertson, London, 1975).

24. There is a subtle argument that attempts to show the incompatibility of Paretianism and liberalism. See A. Sen, 'The impossibility of a Paretian Liberal', *Journal of Political Economy* vol. 78 (1970), pp. 152–7.

25. Services that exhibit these features are sometimes called 'merit goods'.

26. See M. Friedman, *Capitalism and freedom* (Chicago University Press, Chicago, 1962), chapter VI.

27. A.C. Pigou, *The economics of welfare* (Macmillan, London, 1932).

28. See R. Coase, 'The problem of social cost', *Journal of Law and Economics*, vol. 3 (1960), pp. 1–44.

29. This is known as 'the tragedy of the commons'.

30. The relief of welfare has public-good features, since the relief of poverty gives satisfaction to the rich: it is therefore a Pareto-improvement. For a critique, see R. Sugden, *Who cares?* (Institute of Economic Affairs, London, 1983).

31. Extreme libertarians deny that there can be any such phenomena as public goods on the grounds that the 'public' is an abstraction that cannot be meaningfully said to have 'wants'. See M. Rothbard, *Toward a reconstruction of utility and welfare economics* (Centre for Libertarian Studies, New York, 1977), p. 34.

32. The 'collapse' of the liberal state has been predicted by many liberals if certain trends continue. For a clear discussion see J. Burton, 'The instability of the ''middle way'' ' in N.P. Barry *et al.*, *Hayek's serfdom revisited* (Institute of Economic Affairs, London, 1984), pp. 89–115.

33. See B. Barry, *Political argument*, pp. 190–2 for a definition of the public interest.

34. The pioneering work in this area is A. Downs, *The economic theory of democracy* (Harper and Row, New York, 1957).

35. See Barry, *An introduction to modern political theory*, chapter 9, for an account of recent work in the political economy of democracy.

36. See J.S. Schumpeter, *Capitalism, socialism and democracy* (Allen and Unwin, London, 1943).

37. See J. Buchanan and R. Wagner, *Democracy in deficit* (Academic Press, New York, 1977).

38. For Keynes as a 'philosopher-king', see N.P. Barry, *Hayek's social and economic philosophy* (Macmillan, London, 1979), pp. 171–2.

39. B. Crick, *In defence of politics* (Penguin, Harmondsworth, 1964), p. 21.

40. See R.A. Dahl, *A preface to democratic theory* (University of Chicago Press, Chicago, 1956).

41. M. Olson, *The logic of collective action* (Yale University Press, New Haven, 1965), p. 124.

42. M. Olson, *The rise and decline of nations* (Yale University Press, New Haven, 1982).

43. Ibid. p. 44.

44. F.A. Hayek, *The road to serfdom* (Routledge and Kegan Paul, London, 1944).

45. See J. Buchanan and R. Tollison, *Toward a theory of the rent-seeking society* (A & M University Press, Texas, 1980).

46. The gains to the middle classes from state-provided welfare are well described in J. Le Grand, *The strategy of equality* (Allen and Unwin, London, 1982).

47. Friedman, *Capitalism and freedom*, chapter XII.

48. The accidental advantages of a complex and incomprehensible welfare system are commended in M. Rothbard, *For a new liberty*, pp. 167–9.

49. See A. Seldon, *The riddle of the voucher* (Institute of Economic Affairs, London, 1986).

50. See H. Hochman and J. Rogers, 'Pareto-optimal redistribution', *American Economic Review*, vol. 59 (1969), pp. 542–57.

51. M. Cranston, *What are human rights?* (Bodley Head, London, 1973).

52. See B. Wootton, *The social foundation of wages policy*, (Allen and Unwin, London, 1955).

53. For an account of procedural justice, see Barry, *An introduction to modern political theory*, pp. 119–23.

4

Conservatism

The main concern of this book is with the classical liberal response to the collapse of the consensus. Nevertheless, some discussion of traditional conservatism is essential, for although most of the intellectual running of the new Right has been made by non-partisan free-market individualists, it is undeniable that there is some connection between these views and orthodox conservatism. Just what this connection is, however, remains a matter of some dispute. The connection is deeper than the fact that free-market philosophies have been partially adopted by nominally conservative governments in Western countries in recent years, for many conservatives would claim that this has not been a pragmatic response to failed collectivist policies but a reassertion of traditional anti-socialist values.

Many classical liberals, however, are anxious to distance themselves from conservatism. In a famous appendix to his *The Constitution of Liberty* entitled 'Why I am not a Conservative',[1] Hayek made a distinction between liberalism and conservatism which has been almost unquestionably accepted by most individualist social thinkers. The main thrust of Hayek's argument is that conservatives lack a commitment to *principles* and that this refusal to indulge in theoretical speculation about the nature of society leads to pragmatism and straightforward political opportunism. It is this flaccid unprincipled 'ideology', which, it is claimed, has led conservatives to accept, sometimes willingly, those institutions and policies that are ultimately destructive of a free society. In some ways, however, the liberal description of conservatism has been something of a caricature; and the desire to differentiate liberalism from conservatism has had the unfortunate consequence of masking some important similarities between the two doctrines. These similarities do not derive merely from the shared hostility to a common enemy, socialism, but from a common attitude to politics, society, property, justice and, albeit to a lesser extent, the state.

The conventional liberal likes to differentiate his doctrine from conservatism on the superficially plausible grounds that the typical conservative eschews abstract principles and refuses to connect policy proposals to some over-arching theory of man and society. In this view conservative thought is *dispositional* rather than substantive; consisting of a favourable (and perhaps non-rational) attitude towards the established order, whatever that may be, rather than a reasoned demonstration of the virtues of some particular order. From this it follows that there are conservatives in the Soviet Union, and (more plausibly) that extreme Right-wing nationalist movements in twentieth-century Europe are not conservative. More important, it supports the argument that in the US, conservatives are generally liberal-individualist since this has been the prevailing political and economic tradition of that country. Indeed, non-liberal conservative doctrine there seems little more than a pale, sometimes comic reflection of European reactionary thought.

There is no doubt much to be recommended in this description but it clearly does not capture the richness of genuine conservative political thought — for to reject the relevance of general principles to political life, to prefer the concrete to the abstract and look for knowledge of the *particular* rather than indulge in *a priori* speculation, is not the same thing as discrediting entirely the role of reason in politics. Conservatives do have general principles, even if they are rooted in specific political experience, and they have a critical attitude towards many of those policies and institutions that have, as a matter of fact, become established in Western democracies.

It is here that some similarities between liberalism and conservatism emerge. It is only that heavily rationalistic liberalism that is clearly discordant with sophisticated contemporary conservatism. This liberalism has taken two forms: abstract natural rights individualism and Benthamite utilitarianism. It is clear that conservatism cannot accept a pure individualist conception of rights[2] that divorces them from experience and tradition any more than it can tolerate a utilitarianism that subjects every institution and policy to some rational 'test' of social happiness. However, as we have seen from our discussion of classical liberal aims, the contemporary version of this doctrine is not necessarily couched in these terms either. The current emphasis in liberalism is on *spontaneity*; that there are natural tendencies to growth and progress in complex societies which operate more effectively the less the state intervenes. This sceptical doctrine, which casts doubt on the efficacy of political action, is in fact an old conservative idea — an idea that has perhaps been lost by those contemporary conservatives too willing to accept the post-war collectivist legacy.

There is then a coherent set of conservative ideas which can be constructed out of the great variety of doctrines that has appeared under the name; and this is much more than a blind acceptance of the *status quo*. I shall confine my brief account of this to English sources,[3] largely because they provide what is most distinctive in the substantive conservative doctrine. Also, it would be more helpful to concentrate on the main themes rather than exegeses of particular thinkers: nevertheless, I shall briefly discuss two slightly contrasting contemporary conservatives, Michael Oakeshott and Roger Scruton, later in this chapter.

II

Perhaps the first point to stress in a description of contemporary conservatism is its *secular* nature. This may sound slightly odd since traditionally, conservatism has been associated with religion, either as a source of natural law, political morality or as a sociological requisite for a stable society. It is true that some recent statements of conservatism, notably that of Lord Hailsham,[4] have founded the politics of traditionalism on a natural law that ultimately derives from God, but it is a significant achievement of the modern doctrine that it has become almost entirely independent of religion.

The most important secular feature of conservative thought is its *scepticism*. This is the claim that because of our ignorance about the consequences of various forms of action there is an implicit commitment to the preservation of traditional practices and procedures. This is an argument that has something in common with certain forms of liberalism — indeed in this respect both liberals and conservatives can claim David Hume as an intellectual forebear. However, the conservative tends to take scepticism to extremes, denying, for example, that the logic of the free market has any necessary priority over tradition. Thus some conservatives would regard *laissez-faire* economics as just another form of political rationalism which has no claim on our intellects unless rooted in some specific experience. Oakeshott put this claim graphically in his observation on Hayek's *Road to Serfdom*; 'A plan to resist all planning may be better than its opposite, but it belongs to the same style of politics.'[5]

From this, it does not in any way follow that conservatives do not value the market, but only that market principles and the logic of individual choice should not be the only criteria for evaluation in politics. The *wholesale* substitution of market arrangements for social activities that hitherto had been subject to centralised (or localised) political control would be just as objectionable to a sceptical conservative as a substantial shift to socialism. The principles that are used for the allocation of the respective spheres of individual state action cannot be universal and timeless but derived from particular traditions, the reason being that a tradition will embody more wisdom than an unaided reason.

By the same token the claims of politics are treated sceptically by conservatives. Thus, the desire to create human well-being by political action alone is an illusion and, worse, an illusion likely to have deleterious consequences. This partly reflects an aesthetic judgement (i.e. there are more important things in life than politics), and partly the more serious point that in a general utilitarian sense, happiness is more likely to be realised through private, voluntary action than by state control. The importance of associations smaller than the state is constantly stressed by conservative thinkers.

This anti-political strain in conservative thinking largely derives from an abiding belief in the *imperfectibility*[6] of man. Revolutionaries and utopians are mistaken in supposing that reconstructed laws and institutions can bring about a change in the human personality — a change that will eliminate poverty, suffering and injustice. These are thought to be inevitable features of the human condition; and to the (limited) extent that they can be alleviated, this is more likely to come about by spontaneous initiatives rather than political action. It follows for a conservative that to entrust too much power to the state, and therefore subject large areas of social life to politics, is to make that intrinsic imperfectibility in man a force for evil.

There is, however, a certain ambiguity in conservatism over the role of the state. On the one hand, a pessimistic, Hobbesian streak compels a strong, powerful state, as both a source of law and morality. Without a strong central authority, imperfect men will not co-operate spontaneously but will tend towards anarchy. On the other hand, a too-powerful state is distrusted precisely because of this imperfectibility: necessarily imperfect men will do great damage if allowed too much power. From Burke, the conservative tradition in political thought has wanted to entrust to the state only that which is appropriate to it. However, what is appropriate to it is itself controversial and a certain over-zealous anti-rationalism in some conservatives has led to the damaging conclusion that there are no theoretical principles available to determine the respective spheres of compulsory and voluntary action.

Underpinning conservative traditionalism is the understanding of society in terms of *organic*[7] growth. A society is not an artifice, the structural features of which can be designed and redesigned at will, but a naturally evolving entity which contains its own self-generating properties. This again has something in common with liberal individualism, but with the important proviso that conservatives tend to use the organic analogy to buttress the argument for an acceptance of *natural authority*. Whereas liberals are eager to evaluate the claims of political authority on 'critical-rational' grounds, conservatives would claim that to question the validity of naturally evolving institutions is to undermine their authority and consequently the stability of a society. There are, then, no universally desirable political institutions but only those which are appropriate to the natural evolution of particular societies.

There are two areas in which conservatism speaks in louder and more substantive tones: justice and property.[8] On both these subjects we can find similar conclusions to liberal individualism, albeit reached by different routes. With regard to the former, conservatives reject equality or social justice as a substantive aim of social policy. Although, unlike liberals, they might argue that desert or merit should sometimes modify that 'arbitrary' income distribution determined by the market,[9] this in itself should not license the imposition of an egalitarian pattern of income and wealth on a society of *naturally unequal* people. For the conservative there is a natural hierarchy in society (and not one merely based on wealth), and to disrupt this by constant governmental intervention disturbs the necessary stability which that hierarchy provides. It is to be noticed here that the conservative is less worried by the violation of an individual property entitlement, an issue that is the pre-eminent concern of the contemporary classical liberal, than by the threat to social and collective order that constant redistribution imposes.

One important reason why conservatives should reject egalitarian economic policies is the effect which they believe such measures have on the family. It is a fundamental conservative dogma that the autonomy and independence of this institution are essential for social stability. Naturally, the family is a source of inequality and to attempt to rectify this would be to destroy the institution. For a conservative, the family has value not merely because it is a natural phenomenon but also because if it is undermined, it transforms an integrated society into a mere 'collection' of anomic and alienated individuals without secure values. Furthermore, it is argued that easily available welfare encourages the break-up of the family and makes vast numbers of people dependent upon the state.

Closely linked to anti-egalitarianism and the defence of the family is the importance conservatives attach to private property and inheritance. The most obvious justification for private property is that it provides centres of independence from the state. For a conservative, the state is not the sole source of legitimacy, and the customary and common-law rights of property that have grown up have an independent validity. Again, in contrast to classical liberals, the claims of property are not primarily based on an individualistic theory of ownership but on the contribution that private property makes to social equilibrium. There is a conservative cliché — 'property has duties as well as rights' — which nicely illustrates this point. A property right is not an unlimited right to do what one will with what is rightfully one's own: it is a right limited by the needs of the community. Thus, the owners of lands and estates are understood to be carriers of a tradition; they have positive duties to maintain that tradition. The 'duties' of property are never precisely defined in conservatism (perhaps they never can be), but they would include charitable obligations, public service and the exercise of the political arts on behalf of the general good rather than for specific interest groups.

As we have already noted, the most complex problem of conservative thinking is the question of the state. In most conservative thought the state is venerated: without a centralised system of power and authority a stable society would be impossible. Indeed, in some extreme views, paradoxically, morality itself would be impossible without it. The state is not, as in much classical liberal thinking, a mechanism for the production of public goods, but the embodiment and summation of law, politics and morality, in the absence of which individuality is meaningless. It might well be asked, then, how can the other conservative aim of independence from the state be achieved? It is this, of course, which makes liberal individualists so sceptical of the claim that a limited state is possible under traditional conservative doctrine.

The problem stems from the reluctance of conservatives to make the crucial conceptual distinction between law and state.[10] It is true that conservatives tend to prefer common law to statute and to see permanence and stability in judicial decision-making rather than in unpredictable and capricious legislatures, but the tendency is to define the apparatus of the state so as to include legal institutions and processes. This leads to the anti-liberal view that law has no validity apart from the state and thence the (possible) attribution of great power to the centralised authority. Given the reluctance of conservatives to concede the relevance of natural rights (or any other purported universal principles) to the evaluation of political conduct, it is not surprising that liberals accuse conservatives of a more than incipient statism.

From this cursory summary of these 'principles' it is clear that conservatism is not merely a dispositional creed, one that automatically evinces a favourable attitude towards the *status quo*, for it is possible to criticise rationally any *status quo* with these ideas. To take one example, consider the structure of the welfare state (in both Britain and the USA). This is a form of social organisation which has a reasonably long history (in Britain especially): it has developed in a partially spontaneous manner, and to attempt to revolutionise it according to abstract, *laissez-faire* principles would be to disappoint legitimate expectations (expectations validated by custom and tradition). It is this type of reasoning that has led many contemporary conservatives to accept the welfare state almost without question. Yet an equally plausible traditionalist response would hold that the universal provision of welfare has no basis in custom and convention but is entirely a product of party and interest-group politics. Its creation of a state apparatus of supposedly virtuous officials depends on a bogus perfectionist view of political man, and its encouragement of a 'dependent' attitude on the part of vast numbers of citizens is destructive of that notion of personal responsibility on which a stable order depends. Such a critique might entail a fundamental restructuring of the welfare services, on lines more consonant with a more pessimistic view of human nature, rather than the simple and uncritical view that it is only possible to check their *growth*[11] — a view common to active conservative politicians. On economic policy, too many contemporary conservatives display a passive acceptance of modernity compared with their more robust predecessors. It has been a feature of traditional conservative dogma that one of the functions of the state is to maintain a sound currency. Indeed, the affection for the Gold Standard was not simply a matter of economic logic (as it is, perhaps, for some classical liberals), but it also involved the belief that monetary profligacy threatened social morality and civil order. To depart from Gold would be a step into the unknown. Yet the Keynesian 'revolution' in economic policy which, intended or not, has caused the post-war inflations, has been welcomed by many conservative economic thinkers.[12] This is perhaps the best example there is of conservative political opportunism triumphing over conservative principle.

III

Almost all contemporary conservative thinkers claim to be intellectual ancestors of the eighteenth-century thinker, Edmund Burke (1729–1797). He is the one writer whose general principles have always been considered applicable to present circumstances, occupying as they do a convenient middle ground between abstract metaphysics and causal empiricism. Most important is the fact that conservatives anxious to distance themselves from classical liberalism and *laissez-faire* political economy have been as eager to seek a Burkean validation of their views as those concerned to reject a rationalistic socialism.

It is certainly true that there is much of the contemporary conservative message which is Burkean in spirit. I have concentrated on secular conservatism and although Burke is in some important senses clearly a Christian thinker, it is not the case that his (ultimately) divinely based natural law has any *direct* implication for his theory of political conduct — for this theory is based on a scepticism and anti-rationalism which is a common feature of contemporary secular traditionalism. It is to be found primarily in his *Reflections on the Revolution in France*[13] and *An Appeal from the New Whigs to the Old*.[14]

This is not the place for even a brief exposition of Burke's thought. Suffice it to say that his belief in the superiority of collective wisdom over individual reason, his faith in 'prejudice' over an excessive rationality and his paean to the virtue of experience ('The science of constructing a commonwealth, or renovating it, or reforming it, is, like every other experimental science, not to be taught *a priori*. Nor is it a short experience that can instruct us in that practical science . . .'[15]) have all combined to form an almost sceptical conservative ideology. In addition, his rejection of natural rights in favour of prescription (i.e. rights that emanate from a known tradition) has delighted those contemporary conservatives who eschew an abstract liberal individualism.

Nevertheless, if Burkean ideas are to have any direct contemporary application, it is much more plausible to suggest that they validate a more free-market oriented conservatism. Despite his well-known sneer at 'sophisters, calculators and economists', his political economy (on his own admission) was little different from that of Adam Smith. In *Thoughts and Details on Scarcity* (1795)[16] he expounded a market philosophy that can hardly appeal to that Tory activism that has become dominant in the twentieth century. The state is given a very limited role and Burke stresses that, to the extent that it tries to do that which is inappropriate to it (i.e. the close regula-tion of economic life), it will fail in its primary duty, which is to preserve the conditions of freedom and order: governors *'cannot* do the lower duty, and in proportion as they try it, they will certainly fail in the higher'.[17] Furthermore, despite the traditional conser-vative view that the state had a positive obligation (however minimal) to provide a measure of welfare, this was not the view of Burke: the moral duty of charity rests on private individuals, not the state.

The truth is that Burke has been used as an ideological flag of convenience by many contemporary conservatives: his real intellec-tual descendants are the Hayekian 'Old Whig' individualists who founded their theory of a limited state and private economy on his specific anti-rationalism. Nothing could be more alien to the spirit of his thinking than those doctrines of 'managed capitalism' and the benevolent, paternalist state which have dominated conservative thinking in the post-war consensus.

IV

Two contemporary British conservative social theorists are well worth a brief consideration in the light of general conservative principles. These are Michael Oakeshott and Roger Scruton. Neither is associated with the Conservative Party although both have been linked with the emergence of the new Right. In the case of Oakeshott especially, such a connection is quite erroneous: indeed the trend of almost all official conservative thinking in the post-war period would be alien to his thought.

Oakeshott is primarily a philosopher who would deny that there are any *direct* political implications of his metaphysics.[18] Never-theless, he has contributed some acerbic essays on politics which form a coherent attitude (though not an ideology).[19] I shall con-sider these in some detail in the next chapter but it will be appro-priate here to outline his general principles of political action (or inaction).

Oakeshott's political stance or attitude shows some affinity with a Burkean view of the world (though its philosophical roots are quite different). It is sceptical, anti-rationalist and highly critical of the view that human well-being can be improved by deliberate political action. It shows a marked hostility to 'doctrine', to the prevailing tendency of attempting to capture our knowledge of political reality in some ideology and to license the imposition of a grand scheme on a social system which has its own ordering mechanisms. Such doctrines or dogmas as Marxism or Benthamite utilitarianism make bogus claims to universal knowledge when, in fact, we can only have genuine knowledge of particular political traditions. Such knowledge can never be *a priori* but must be grounded in some specific historical experience. In his words, rationalists 'pass a futile and feverish existence endeavouring to make their random desires and capricious hopes conform to some pre-conceived system of general maxims'.[20]

The theoretical force of this argument depends on a subtle distinction between two forms of knowledge, *technical* and *practical*.[21] Technical knowledge can be precisely formulated; it is knowledge of those mechanisms and procedures required precisely to bring about certain ends: 'engineering' knowledge, one could say. Practical knowledge, on the other hand, cannot be so formulated because it is knowledge of *how to do things*, knowledge acquired by practice and experience and therefore incapable of being reproduced in textbooks and manuals. 'Governing' requires this sort of knowledge and it is an activity better carried on by an elite which has that kind of political experience appropriate for the maintenance of a general system of rules and practices.

None of this excludes the legitimacy of political change: Oakeshott's conservatism is not therefore a reactionary doctrine that wishes to re-create some past era of aristocratic order (as is the case with the European 'Old Right'). Such a political aim would be yet another example of 'dogma' or 'doctrine'. Correct political action is the 'pursuit of intimations', i.e. striving for the understanding of those procedures that sustain a political tradition and which may occasionally require modification or adjustment. In a famous phrase he described politics as 'the activity of attending to the general arrangements of a set of people whom chance or choice have brought together'.[22]

Thus there can be no legitimate appeal to abstract principles such as 'social justice' or 'natural rights' in the evaluation of political conduct. Criteria for political activity is always internal to a set of arrangements and the appropriate political change should always be towards rendering some 'incoherence' coherent in the prevailing set of arrangements. To put it crudely, political wisdom is the detection and elimination of untidiness in a particular set of procedural rules. There is in Oakeshott's thought, then, a rejection of the whole idea of political 'argument', with policies justified in terms of principles.

Superficially, all this might suggest a sharp distinction between Oakeshottian conservatism and new-Right classical liberalism: the latter is, at least in some representations, a 'doctrine'. The approach also has possibly bizarre anti-market implications: would it, for example, sanction the wholesale institution of economic protectionism if the majority of industries in a given community were already protected? Would not the liberal's demand for free trade than be condemned as dogma or a political 'crib'?

However, such a judgement would be premature for there is within Oakeshott's thought important common ground with the classical liberal individualist political philosophy. This is apparent in Oakeshott's more recent writings.[23] The crucial point is the stress on procedures and rules and the rejection of the imposition of outcomes or 'end-states' on ongoing orders. For Oakeshott, politics is a secondary activity which should be limited to the facilitating of those procedures within which individuals may pursue their own plans. What is required, in other words, is *predictability*. This can only be provided by something like the common law. This is brought out in Oakeshott's brilliant essay, 'The Rule of Law',[24] in which appropriate rules of just conduct are described as 'adverbial': they tell us *how* we ought to go about doing something, but they do not tell us *what* it is we ought to do.

This lies at the heart of Oakeshott's important distinction between a 'civil association' and an 'enterprise association'[25] (see chapter 5). A civil association is an order of predictability based on general rules of just conduct; it does not have a specific purpose or any collective goal to be realised. It is consonant with freedom precisely because, although its rules prohibit specific courses of individual action, it does not direct persons towards pre-conceived, abstract goals. It celebrates the primacy of private over public law. In contrast, an enterprise association is a contrived order that directs people to maximise, say, economic growth, social welfare, or full employment. In Oakeshott's view, certain aspects of the welfare state are implicitly totalitarian precisely because they compel the movement of individuals in directions they would not have taken under 'adverbial' legal arrangements.

The similarities between all this and classical liberalism, especially the Hayekian variety, should be obvious. What is lacking from an individualist point of view is any indication of what the substantive content of the rules of a 'civil association' should be. Such rules could be quite restrictive of individual action without necessarily imposing some collective purpose on a community. Presumably, speculation on the ideal form of procedural rules would be precluded by Oakeshott's scepticism: we can only work within a given set and seek improvement by eliminating its internal inconsistencies. Hence there is no real discussion of, say, federalism or constitutionalism as positive doctrines in Oakeshott's political thought. Issues such as these are, of course, distinctive features of the liberal's political programme. Indeed, in his essay 'The Rule of Law', there is an implicit commitment to a Hobbesian sovereignty from Oakeshott, at least in the sense that any 'civil association' requires some final authority for its validation.

In Roger Scruton's *The Meaning of Conservatism*[26] we find a more robust conservatism, a more overt expression of those anti-individualistic tendencies that have always been at work in traditionalist thought. On the author's own admission, the book is a work of 'dogmatics', a full-blooded expression of doctrine (though most certainly not of the party-political type). Though there are implications that the conservative order is a kind of 'civil association', the book is suffused with a kind of muted authoritarianism which has disturbed liberals. Indeed, much of the argument of *The Meaning of Conservatism* is directed at what may be called the liberal-individualist cosmology. Liberalism is described as 'the principal enemy of conservatism' with 'all its attendant trappings of individual autonomy and the "natural" rights of man'.[27]

What seems to be objectionable about liberalism is its apparent belief that an order can be constructed out of the concept of a person which is itself devoid of those social attributes (and consequential social obligations) which make that order possible. Thus, for Scruton, abstractions such as 'freedom' and 'rights' cannot be torn from particular traditions and made to function as moral benchmarks against which we can assess the legitimacy of given political orders. The idea that there are abstract individuals held together only by contract, and whose social duties can only be derived from their autonomous choices, is unacceptable to Scruton. The bonds of society transcend individual choice: 'we cannot derive the ends of conduct from choice alone'.[28] It ought to be pointed out here that the liberal does not hold this view either. Choice is always constrained — by law, general rules, and by the ethical demand that the individual chooser does not violate the right to choice *equally* possessed by others. In Scruton, however, there is an *essential* political order, organically defined, which itself evinces a set of rules and conventions which are not mere contrivances or artifices constructed by utility-maximising individuals to advance their subjective ends.

Although on many occasions in the book Scruton refers to the need to deflate the pretensions of government and to arrest its intrusions into private worlds, it lacks that relative indifference to ends and purposes which more liberal versions of the concept of civil association (including, I believe, Oakeshott's) express. What it specifically denies is that a constitution can, or ought to be, *neutral* towards competing ends and purposes. A constitution is an *essence*: it is not understood merely as a set of articulated rules and procedures but also in terms of customs, habits and assumptions that defy an uncontroversial exposition. It is really this notion of law and constitutionalism which permits (theoretically) the intrusion of the state into what might be thought of as protected areas: 'Thus it is inescapable that there should be family law, planning laws, laws which regulate the days and times when men may work, drink or seek recreation, even laws which control the nature of permitted intoxicants.'[29] It is legitimate then for power to be used to maintain the customs and conventions of a community in the face of the demands of a liberal individualism.

Yet, undoubtedly Scruton is unhappy about the over-weaning power of government in modern society. His critique of the obsession with social justice, his defence of the rule of law against numerous socialist interventions and his claim that there is no overriding purpose in political life beyond the maintenance of government itself, all combine to make him a particularly eloquent spokesman for certain anti-consensus views. What clearly puts him into the anti-liberal camp is his organic conception of society which resists any dissolution into individual choice and his doubts that, in the absence of power, spontaneous social forces can generate order and stability. For him, a body of legal rules is not analytically separate from the state itself. This means that because state institutions of coercion are not limited to certain prescribed tasks, as in the 'public-good' theory of liberal political thought, there is little in the way of theoretical limitation on what a state may do to preserve a not uncontroversial conception of order and tradition.

A further liberal objection to Scruton's conservatism would focus directly on his organic and specifically non-individualist explanation of social institutions. The liberal argues that even though the state as an idea may represent values of a permanance and historical significance that cannot be resolved into individual actions and volitions, an understanding of its behaviour still requires us to start from the fact that it is *manned* by individuals. Therefore, the explanation of the expansion of state activity in the post-war years, which Scruton regrets, must be one in terms of individualistic motivations — the kind of motivations which liberal public choice theorists have concentrated on to great effect in their accounts of the growth of the state. In their view, the attribution of a kind of moral grandeur to state institutions deflects critical attention away from a realistic analysis of the behaviour of state officials. The liberal solution to the problem of the expansionary state is to subject more of its activities to the market, in fact to 'privatise' large areas of the public sector, especially education and welfare — a solution made easier by the fact that no special moral significance is attached to the state. In a conservative position which attaches great significance to the state, it is not clear what rational criteria are available to determine its legitimate role and what institutional recommendations could be made for keeping it in the place prescribed by that conservatism.

V

As I have suggested earlier in this chapter, classical liberals, and especially libertarians, like to distinguish themselves from conservatives. The briefest overview of conservative thought does lend credence to this distinction. In the contemporary world liberals criticise those conservatives who favour a free market in economic matters (normally on pragmatic grounds) but reject the demands of liberty in other areas. It is true that conventional conservatives show little interest in advancing freedom in personal moral matters. The importance of the family, and the pre-eminence of the state as the source and protection of traditional moral standards, seems to make conservatives critical of permissiveness in matters of sexual conduct and artistic expression. Further still, some traditional notions of hierarchy and order seem not to gell with the liberal claim that openness and innovation are essential features of a progressive social philosophy. Certainly, the conservative attachment to the agricultural interest in the nineteenth century put traditionalists at odds with the new commercial politics and economics.

Furthermore, a paternalism that seems endemic to modern

conservatism extends to the field of welfare. Indeed, historically in Western societies, much modern welfare provision and anti-market economic regulation by the state was originated by conservative governments. To a conservative, that element of rationalism that lingers in liberal thought leads to the prescription of extreme individualist values which are destructive of an ordered society. This qualification of the claims of liberalism applies both to questions of personal morals and social welfare.

There is a difference, though, between what may be called 'old' conservatism and the newer, more pragmatic, variety that has emerged in the twentieth century. The older version, perhaps represented in contemporary times by Oakeshott, was sceptical and distrustful of the power of the state. It had *principles* of a limited kind, sound money and the rule of law being the two most important. It rejected Keynesianism, mild planning and the post-war welfare state, all of which have been embraced by moderate, pragmatic conservatism, either because of some theory of the depravity of man or because of a more sophisticated conception of the limits of human knowledge. This sceptical tradition is not that distinct from the cautious liberalism of Hayek. Indeed, they share a common intellectual ancestry in Burke. So far from accepting the post-war consensus as inevitable and unalterable, they might well maintain that it was erected on insecure foundations and would not survive. To reject Keynesian economic policy, then, would not be to opt for some doctrinaire classical liberalism but to revive traditional well-tried economic principles.

From this perspective, the pragmatic conservatism of recent times appears as something of an aberration. I shall suggest in the following chapter that in Britain at least, the kind of corporatist, 'managerial' conservatism introduced (albeit in embryonic form) by Harold Macmillan and carried to excess by the 1970–74 government is just such an aberration.

Nevertheless, there is one respect in which almost all branches of conservative thought are vulnerable to liberal strictures: this is their relative indifference to public-choice theory and the dangers of group politics. Despite the conservative fear of an all-powerful state, conservatives are prepared to invest great authority in it, and they are little influenced by liberal social theories which rely on the individualistic assumptions of micro-economics: these explain why, in a democracy, state activity rises inexorably. Not dissimilar observations can be made about groups in society. Although many conservative thinkers, especially Burke, have stressed the importance of voluntary associations for a free and stable order, they have been less cognisant of the tendency for them to seek governmental and legislative privileges — privileges that would be prohibited by a rigorous classical liberalism. Conservatives have been particularly vulnerable to the influence (which persists to this day in the EEC) of the agricultural interest. The protection of farmers from foreign competition is the issue that has historically divided conservatives and liberals. To many traditional conservatives, free trade is simply a classical liberal dogma that subverts the 'true' interests of society.

Notes and References

1. F.A. Hayek, *The constitution of liberty* (Routledge and Kegan Paul, London, 1960), pp. 397–411.
2. Nozick and Rothbard are pre-eminently Lockean-rights theorists.
3. There are numerous histories of conservative thought. I have profited from A. Quinton, *The politics of imperfection* (Faber and Faber, London, 1978); and W.H. Greenleaf, *The British political tradition: vol. ii: The ideological heritage* (Methuen, London 1983).
4. Lord Hailsham, *The conservative case* (Penguin, Harmondsworth, 1959).
5. M. Oakeshott, 'Rationalism in politics' in his *Rationalism in politics and other essays*, (Methuen, London, 1962); p. 21.
6. Quinton, *The politics of imperfection*, pp. 17–18.
7. Ibid., pp. 16–17.
8. See Lord Hailsham, *The conservative case*, p. 99.
9. Though this has never been given any explicit philosophical analysis.
10. The liberal's distinction stems largely from the conception of the state as merely a 'mechanism' for generating public goods — a view unacceptable to almost all conservatives.
11. Greenleaf, *The ideological heritage*, pp. 254–62.
12. Ibid, pp. 254–60.
13. (Dent, London, 1912), first published in 1790.
14. (Indianapolis, New York, 1962), first published in 1791.
15. *Reflections on the revolution in France*, p. 58.
16. Volume 7 of Burke's *Works* (Rivington, London, 1815–27).
17. Quoted in R. Nisbet, *Conservatism* (Open University, Milton Keynes, 1986), p. 37.
18. In addition to *Rationalism in politics*, two other important sources for Oakeshott's politics are *On human conduct* (Oxford University Press, London, 1975); and *On history* (Blackwell, Oxford, 1983).
19. See especially 'The political economy of freedom' in *Rationalism in politics*, pp. 37–58.
20. *Experience and its modes* (Cambridge University Press, Cambridge, 1933), p. 300.
21. See Oakeshott, 'Rationalism in politics', pp. 7–13.
22. 'Political education' in *Rationalism in politics*, p. 112.

23. See 'The character of a modern European state' in *On human conduct*, pp. 185–326.

24. See 'The rule of law' in *On history*, pp. 119–64.

25. See 'On the civil condition' in *On human conduct*, pp. 111–21.

26. See P. Scouton, *The meaning of conservatism* (Penguin, Harmondsworth, 1981).

27. Ibid. p. 16.

28. Ibid. p. 72.

29. Ibid. p. 80.

5

Britain

Outside the US, Britain is the most significant source of anti-consensus political and economic ideas, of both orthodox conservative and classical liberal persuasions. The intellectual history of Britain in the last 20 years has witnessed, if not a revolution, at least a significant 'new Right Enlightenment'. Of course, many of the sources of contemporary British individualistic thinking are foreign, most notable here being the American schools of free-market economics and liberal political economy (Chicago and Virginia) and the 'Austrian' tradition represented by F.A von Hayek (although he became a naturalised British subject in 1938). What is interesting about British individualist thinking is not so much the innovations that its leading protagonists have made, but the fact that some traditional liberal social theories were given new significance and vitality through their application to the special circumstances of post-war Britain.

Outside the Scandinavian countries, Britain exhibited most spectacularly the defining features of the economic and political practice of consensus. After 1945, successive British governments deliberately took upon themselves the responsibility of guaranteeing full employment through Keynesian macro-economic policies (in other words, there was an implicit acceptance of the argument that an undisturbed market would regularly produce under-employment). Furthermore, the welfare state, the foundations of which were laid in the early part of the century, was extended: health care, pensions and so on were in large part 'nationalised' and educational opportunity was widened (culminating in the Robbins Report of 1960 on the expansion of higher education). At the more directly economic level, industries were nationalised and organised in a complex, and ultimately quite unsatisfactory, mixture of commercial freedoms and political controls. There were also efforts to plan the economy 'as a whole', although these proceeded more by exhortation (and indeed hectoring) than by direct physical controls.[1] In sum, the post-war Labour Government's strategy involved for the first time in British history (excluding wartime conditions) a sustained attempt, albeit for a short period, to direct and steer society towards a pre-determined end — different from that which would have obtained if individuals were left to order their lives as they saw fit subject only to general rules of just conduct (as exemplified in the common law). It was a perfect example of the construction of what Michael Oakeshott was later to call an 'enterprise state' i.e. a political organisation with a specific purpose.

What is significant here is not the historical detail of the 1945–51 Labour Governments (although it is significant that some of their aims were revived under a Conservative administration in the 1960s) but the fact that this experience provoked brands of political and economic thought, of both a conservative and liberal kind, which although they went into eclipse in the 1950s and 1960s, were to be revived in a particularly sophisticated form in the 1970s and 1980s. What was perhaps not appreciated by the early conservative and liberal critics of 'planning' in Britain was the problem of the British 'constitution', the laxity of that permitted highly speculative experiments in social engineering which appeared to have considerably less then overwhelming popular support. The great achievement of contemporary anti-consensus thought — and this comes from its liberal rather than its conservative manifestation — has been to incorporate some highly plausible scientific explanations of the political process into a coherent set of political values.

It is important, nevertheless, to consider some of the reactions to socialist planning in Britain, not merely because these provided the foundations for the later and more well-known British attack on collectivism, but also because they have some considerable intrinsic intellectual value and have been unjustly neglected. One notable feature of the *immediate* post-war criticism of collectivism is that it concentrated on the more robust aspects of socialism than on the modified form of collectivism inspired by Keynes and welfarist thinkers that was to dominate the period of consensus politics. Nevertheless, the style of criticism employed was to anticipate much of today's anti-collectivist ideology.

II

The two books by economic liberals that dominated anti-collectivist thought in the late 1940s were Hayek's *The Road to Serfdom*[2] and John Jewkes, *Ordeal by Planning*[3], but mention should also be made of some acerbic and caustic essays by the conservative philosopher, Michael Oakeshott, published in *Cambridge Opinion*. Although all of these works seem to be addressed to the particular problems of the moment, they are couched in a universal conceptual language and can be interpreted just as much as crucial contributions to a style of political thinking as they can answers to contemporary questions. In fact, Hayek's *Road to Serfdom* was published in 1944 and was therefore not concerned with specific post-war British economic and social policy. However, Jewkes's work was published in 1948 and is a fine example of the critique of socialist planning.

There was however, one important claim of both *The Road to Serfdom* and *Ordeal by Planning*: this is the argument that systematic attempts at economic planning must eventuate in consequences unanticipated by the planners — namely, the destruction of personal liberty. Hayek and Jewkes were here stressing the indivisibility of liberty; that it was not possible to attenuate the traditional economic liberties without at the same time seriously undermining the whole structure of freedom. Jewkes put the point emphatically with his argument for the 'logical incompatibility of a planned economy and freedom of the individual'.[4] It was a major claim of the political thought of the consensus that this was empirically false, that traditional civil liberties were compatible with a considerable degree of centralised economic control. Indeed, Jewkes's work was frequently cited as an unduly pessimistic prognosis of the likely course of events under economic planning. It is certainly true that the increasing progress towards centralised economic control (albeit of a fairly mild kind that has occurred in Britain) has not produced tyranny (as a matter of fact, during the Labour Governments of the 1960s personal liberty was widened in certain areas, such as the relaxation of censorship and the liberalisation of the laws concerning abortion, homosexuality and divorce). Nevertheless, Jewkes's *Ordeal by Planning* is a brilliant and unjustly neglected analysis of the economic and social implications of the more aggressive form of economic interventionism employed by the first post-war Labour Government.

Ordeal by Planning was published in 1948 and recounts a two-year period of rationing, controls and almost frenetic activity by the

Labour Government in the setting of production targets and the attempted organisation of the economy. Although much of the latter proceeded by exhortation, and the attempted creation of a kind of communal moral fervour, rather than by command, Jewkes was convinced that such methods would certainly fail and that if the planning were to continue, it would inevitably result in the use of direct *physical* controls. The pertinent issue here is the direction of labour, for it was stressed repeatedly at the time by Government ministers that the experiment in economic planning would not involve peacetime conscription of labour. Jewkes (and other economic liberals) constantly pointed to the theoretical anomaly in a comprehensive 'rational' plan that included the direction of all factors of production *except* labour. In fact, legal controls over the movement of labour between occupations were introduced in 1947, though not enforced. Despite Jewkes's concentration on the day-to-day complexities (and absurdities) produced by planning, his work invokes *general* considerations and principles which are highly pertinent of the theory of an individualist market society. It is worth picking out those issues discussed by Jewkes which have had continuing relevance to anticonsensus social thought.

Jewkes understood the fashion for planning as an example of misplaced modernism: the belief that the conscious control of economic events, the overriding goal of all anti-market economic philosophies, somehow represented a peculiarly scientific and rational enterprise. It is of course a common objection to socialist planners that they misunderstand the nature of an economic and social system: they see it as a mechanical system which can be subjected to prediction and control in the way that physical systems are thought to be so controllable. Closely allied to this view is the planner's obsession with size — the contention that large-scale organisations are necessarily more efficient, and more appropriate to a scientifically organised society than small ones. Part of the argument here seemed to be derived from the view that the historical course of capitalism was itself a movement towards larger, and ultimately monopolistic, industrial units. The collectivist seemed to be saying that since the competitive process was being eroded anyway, the state, armed with scientific 'knowledge' about society, was better equipped to direct the course of economic events.

Jewkes effectively disposed of the arguments that bigness was an inevitable feature of a capitalist economy, and also that it was an economic virtue. A typical market system is a complex web of inter-related parts which is held together by the price system: it is 'efficient' because competition weeds out those producers less successful at meeting consumer demands. Thus any emergence of large industrial units that display monopolistic tendencies is checked by *impersonal* competitive processes. Jewkes argues that the claim that the market spontaneously produces monopoly is sustained by superstition and irrational economic 'fashions' rather than by hard evidence.

A large part of this fashion, a movement of opinion that pre-dates and post-dates *Ordeal by Planning*, is the contempt for the 'businessman'.[5] What is important here is the distinction between the 'producer' and the merchant or trader. Jewkes stresses the fact that the planners seem to believe that the satisfaction of consumer wants is brought about by physical production alone, that there is no need for the 'middle-man' or entrepreneur. The down-grading of the business ethic is a recurring feature of socialist thought. One point which Jewkes constantly stressed in this context was the unfortunate inability of the business 'class' to produce a 'theory' to explain the role of business or entrepreneurial activity in a complex, decentralised market economy. The planners' arguments had a certain plausibility, or speciousness, precisely because they were expressed in a technical, often mathematical jargon. In contrast, the businessman's political economy was hardly articulated at all. Jewkes made the rather prosaic observation that businessmen are too busy to theorise about what it is that they actually do.[6] In fact, his rather robust common sense concealed a subtle theory that was to be elaborated by later philosophers of market society, notably Hayek and Michael Polanyi. This is the idea that the type of knowledge involved in market activity is 'tacit' or unarticulated knowledge. It is specialised knowledge of time and place, the 'know how' that is essential to the operation of the price system. It is that 'alertness' to price discrepancies which entrepreneurs display in their daily activities which enables a market to move imperceptibly towards an efficient allocation of resources. None of this type of knowledge can be expressed in the diagrams and equations of the economic planner.

Thus, part of the *appeal* of planning to intellectuals lies in the fact that it depends on the type of knowledge they are most familiar with, i.e. 'scientific' or 'objective' knowledge, and part of its *success* in popular debate is a consequence of the fact that its alleged emancipation from the profit motive seems to accord well with a popular morality which condemns self-interest. However, as Jewkes stressed, without the pursuit of profit there can be no co-ordination of market activities. The experience of 1945-7 with the obsession with physical production simply led to the manufacture of unwanted goods. Furthermore, in an argument made more sophisticated by later classical liberals, Jewkes showed that the central planner is not immune from the promptings of self-interest — though this manifested itself in the aggrandisement of *power* rather than in the acummulation of wealth.

A particularly important point stressed by Jewkes was the incoherence of central economic planning. So far from being a rigorous commitment to a rational pre-determined set of goals, planning showed itself to be a series of desperate responses to ever-changing circumstances: 'each new plan was clearly obsolete, over-run by the speed of events as soon as published'.[7] Thus, the aims, purposes and content of the plans change rapidly in a grim tribute to the incessant flux of economic society. Of course, the only way economic planning could achieve any permanence would be if *all* aspects of life were to be controlled, including the movement of labour; but this was not seriously contemplated by the 1945 Labour Government.

Jewkes was particularly effective in rebutting the charge that economic planning represented the high point of rationality and scientific endeavour; for planning did not involve the objective weighing of evidence and the impartial pursuit of truth, but rather the arbitrary declaration of ends and goals in a haphazard manner. Most important of all was his exposure of the fallacy that economics was a *predictive* science. He emphasised the fact that the social world was too complex for precise forecasting of events. Indeed, in the early post-war period the Government was repeatedly caught unawares by crises, largely of its own making. The most spectacular of these was the fuel crisis of 1947, which resulted precisely from the Government's refusal to let the price system allocate resources.

It is not just the meticulous documentation of the mistakes in economic management that makes *Ordeal by Planning* such an impressive book; it is the careful drawing of the connection between economic and political liberty that is its more permanent message. As he points out, the increasing bureaucratisation of society that inevitably accompanies economic planning also attenuates personal liberty, for without the traditional economic freedoms of consumption and occupation, other liberties are worthless. Furthermore he rejected that trade-off between efficiency and liberty, even before it became the fashion of pluralist political thinking in the 1960s.[8] We cannot sacrifice little bits of liberty for increases in efficiency (prosperity, economic growth and so on) since efficiency is unattainable without liberty.

What was also important in *Ordeal by Planning* was the implicit rejection of 'economism'. Although Jewkes was mainly concerned with a critique of economic planning on grounds of its demonstrable inefficiency, a large part of his study was concerned with the limits of economics: economic activities should be considered merely as a means towards the realisation of more elevated ends and purposes. It was the collectivists, so Jewkes argued, who made production the sole purpose of human life; and in so doing they turned a society of freely choosing individuals into an *organisation* committed to the pursuit of pre-ordained economic goals.

Although I have dealt with the political thought of Michael Oakeshott in the previous chapter, it is worth discussing here an important essay. 'The Political Economy of Freedom',[9] first published in 1949, which nicely complements *Ordeal by Planning*, although it was written from a conservative (and philosophical) standpoint rather than from that of an economist. Oakeshott does not specifically refer to the 1945 Labour Government in this essay though it is clear that much of his intellectual aggression is addressed to that administration's attempt to create a new form of society. In his view, this was an enterprise alien to the traditional politics of Britain. Thus, although in this essay Oakeshott expounds a broadly liberal-individualist view, it is a liberalism that is nurtured in a particular pattern of political behaviour rather than one deduced from general and abstract principles.

In 'The Political Economy of Freedom', Oakeshott was concerned to delineate the features and conditions of a free society and to indicate certain tendencies in modern politics which were undermining what he, approvingly, called the liberal order. Undoubtedly, these tendencies were the very phenomena that Jewkes had been so effectively dissecting in *Ordeal by Planning*. It is to be noted that Oakeshott's account of a free order was couched in traditionalist language: there were customary ways of doing things which were themselves the sources of those liberties which we come, on reflection, to value. In other words, British economic and civil liberties were a product of the peculiarly British form of political association.[10] Nevertheless, in view of the conventional classification of Oakeshott's thought as a kind of arcane, metaphysical conservatism, it is surprising to find a vigorous individualism in his less philosophical essays.

The tradition of liberty requires pre-eminently an absence of a concentration of power:[11] the British are free because no one group or body is able to coerce others. It is a fundamental obligation of government to maintain this diverse and fragmented social order and it should be invested with just sufficient power to prevent its corruption by any one potential group. It is significant that Oakeshott, unlike the *a priori* classical liberals, is as concerned about the dangerous potentialities for inordinate power exercised by private economic groups, such as large-scale business enterprises, as he is about any others.

The greatest single protection of freedom is the maintenance of the *rule of law*.[12] This is no more than a body of abstract and impartial rules which is required for the guaranteeing of those expectations which a tradition of behaviour has validated. A society regulated by the rule of law requires two essential conditions if it is to remain a free society: these two pre-requisites for liberty under the law are freedom of association and the freedom to acquire and retain private property. Within such an institutional framework there would be only a small role for government since the market would integrate human action more effectively than political direction. In an implicit reference to the actions of government in the post-war years, Oakeshott protests that the 'partnership' of the generations had been dissolved and that a free association of individuals was being replaced by an attempt to implement a 'managed' society.[13]

The major institutional threats to freedom under the law are *collectivism* and *syndicalism*, precisely because they both operate through the concentration rather than the diffusion of power. In a highly perceptive anticipation of the development of consensus politics under semi-collectivised regimes, Oakeshott comments critically on the lavish use of discretionary authority and the necessary accommodation of interest groups which all forms of collectivism necessitate. Syndicalism is of course the ideology of unionism, and Oakeshott sees the rise of compulsory unionisation of the labour force as the biggest source of the concentration of power and therefore the single most important threat to freedom under the law. While never denying the need for some regulation of competition, his major concern was to stress the difference between regulation through the rule of law, which is consistent with freedom, and regulation through discretionary directives, an approach which can only lead to the dissolution of liberty. It is also worth mentioning the fact that Oakeshott sees the maintenance of a stable currency as an essential element in a free order — an obligation of government which was to be neglected by many conservative thinkers during the period of the consensus.

III

The relevance of this discussion of the 'right-wing' critique of post-war British planning lies in the fact that so much of what was said then became important in the later restating and restructuring of anti-collectivist thought. Although no further experiments in *direct* economic planning were made after 1950, the main thrust of anti-collectivist thought has been to show how societies can ineluctibly slip into forms of authoritarian organisation neither envisaged nor intended by the authors of even mild types of planning, such as Keynesian demand-management policies. The temporary demise of the type of liberal-conservative thinking represented by Jewkes and Oakeshott was no doubt partly a consequence of the fact that Britain did not experience a collapse into authoritarianism as a result of those welfarist and macro-economic policies that were continued with after the period of controls, rationing and more direct regulation of the economy was discontinued.

Nevertheless, the prevailing ideology of both the Conservative and Labour Parties in the 1960s was anti-market in various degrees. Although the Conservative Governments of the 1950s restored the workings of the market to some extent, they did not repudiate very much of the inheritance of the quasi-socialist revolution of 1945-51. The welfare institutions remained and the obligation of the government to maintain full employment was accepted. Furthermore, the industries nationalised in the 1945-51 period, with the exception of steel, remained in public ownership.[14] The Conservative Party, under the influence of R.A. Butler, seemed anxious to shed as much of its association with *laissez-faire* as possible (although the strength of the latter has been very much overrated) and to act as merely a moderating force against the growth of interventionism. Throughout the 1950s (and beyond) 'Butskellism', a political logo used to describe the economic and social consensus, and derived from the names of Butler and Hugh Gaitskell, the Labour Chancellor of the Exchequer, reigned supreme.

The apparent economic success of consensus politics in Britain, notably in keeping unemployment down to levels way below those of the 1930s, reinforced the intellectual case for Butskellism. Although an inexorable rise in public expenditure was of course noted, it was not thought to portend any dramatic effect on political freedom or efficiency; and neither was the systematic extension of the welfare state. The low rates of inflation, at least by contemporary standards, were thought to be ample refutation of the claim by anti-Keynesians that macro-economic management of the economy through 'fine-tuning' would lead to the eventual collapse of the currency. However, what was scarcely appreciated, if at all, was the fact that the obligation imposed by the Bretton Woods[15] agreement to maintain the external value of the pound was a significant restraint on any government's freedom to manipulate the money supply in pursuit of economic goals.

Nevertheless, such 'moderate' collectivist economic policies were not thought sufficient to remedy the alleged defects of the market. The desire to direct the economy in a more active manner reasserted itself in the 1960s, this time by both Labour and Conservative Governments. The major reason for the renewed potency of the planning ideal seemed to be that Britain's economic growth rate was markedly slower than those of her European competitors, especially France and West Germany. The mention of these two countries is particularly illuminating since it was the French idea of national economic planning that was most influential in the 1960s; yet West Germany had experienced a spectacular economic revival since 1950 by pursuing broadly classical liberal non-interventionist economic policies. Not only was direct planning eschewed in that country but also Keynesian macro-economic management policies were rejected (at least until the late 1960s). It was not until the mid-1970s, however, that British economic and political commentators began to take seriously the philosophy that inspired West Germany's achievements.

The fact that is most illustrative of the all-encompasing nature of the ideological orthodoxy is the Conservative Government's initiation in 1961 of the planning movement of the 1960s. Although it was by no means as direct a form as that of the 1945-51 experience, it was nevertheless predicated on the assumption that central-governmental institutions could 'know' more than decentralised markets — hence, the establishment by successive governments of growth targets, which were products of politically motivated ambitions rather than economic rationality. In terms of aspirations, and indeed machinery, there was precious little to choose between Conservative and Labour Governments of the 1960s.

The plans produced in the 1960s had little or no effect on Britain's economic performance at the time. What was important, however, was the emergence of a 'corporatist' mentality — a predilection in favour of centralisation over decentralisation, of the public over the private: for what was to become a prominent feature of British political life in the 1970s — the all-pervading influence of powerful organised groups, labour organisations and large business enterprises — first came to prominence in the 1960s. The beginnings of the movement towards corporatism go back a long way but the establishment of the National Economic Development Council in 1961 was a significant event; and the close involvement of trade unions and business in government, even at an advisory level, was a portend for the future. It indicated an important stage in the movement away from Britain as a society of loosely co-ordinating individuals, via general rules, to an organisation with centrally prescribed ends and purposes. This was to continue, along with the inexorable growth in public spending, an increase in public-sector employment and an ever-widening welfare net, throughout the 1970s.

In many ways it was a trend that had been (implicitly) forecast in the critique of syndicalism. The consensus held that both major parties should accept that government is responsible for the management of the economy as if it were a large firm, and this responsibility entailed that if dictatorship were to be avoided, the major groups in society should be consulted on all important issues. This meant that large areas of social and economic life became 'politicised', i.e. subject to categorical decisions binding on the community as a whole, rather than left to spontaneous processes. However, what was significant in the development of the British policy was that this politicisation did not come through an increase in parliamentary activity alone (although the contemporary increase in statute law was itself a remarkable phenomenon) but from the influence of pressure groups, operating outside the legislature, on government decision-making. It was this practical circumstance that was to provoke some of the most creative responses from anti-collectivist political thought, for it was claimed that the entrenchment of powerful groups in the interstices of British and economic and political life had much to do with that country's relative economic decline. In fact, it was plausible to argue that the mild and essentially non-coercive planning that Britain has experimented with produced not tyranny, as suggested by Hayek and Jewkes, but *stagnation*.[16]

In fact, the half-hearted planning of the 1960s consisted of attempts to direct and control the economy by fiscal and monetary methods at the macro-level and by politically inspired and unsystematic interventions at the micro-level. As in earlier experiments, the ideology of planning remained invulnerable to evidence and impervious to scientific refutation. Recurrent sterling crises, culminating in the devaluation of 1967, were always used as an excuse for the failures of an interventionism; it was not considered by the apologists of planning that the opinions of the holders of sterling might be a better guide to the performance of the economy than planners themselves.

However, it is worth stressing that towards the end of the sixties, when the Labour Government of 1966-70 had more or less abandoned any real attempt at directing the economy, a period of comparative tranquillity ensued. Indeed the budget deficit was eliminated and inflation was under control. However it must be stressed that the comparative inactivity of government was effectively the product of an *external* constraint, namely, the necessity of maintaining the value of the pound in accordance with Britain's obligations under the Bretton Woods international monetary arrangements. It was only after the break-up of Bretton Woods and Britain's decision to float the pound[17] that full vent was given to Keynesian macro-economic policies — which amounted in fact to no more than a series of attempts by governments to spend their way out of recessions.

Thus despite Edward Heath winning the 1970 election on a remarkably free-market programme, it was his administration that inaugurated that inflation which was to be the hallmark of the decade and which, amongst other things, inspired the revival of 'new Right' political and economic thinking. The experience of the 1970–4 Heath Government is particularly instructive. Its experiment with the use of markets was quickly abandoned; in fact it had only a small theoretical foothold in the Cabinet, and the movement towards the creation of a 'managed', state-capitalist economy quickened. The Conservative Government became heavily involved in industry, very largely in *resisting* the spontaneous forces of the market in allocating resources efficiently: it also implicitly encouraged 'tripartism' — the directing of the economy by decisions of government, unions and business. After the failure to reform trade unions via the ill-fated Industrial Relations Act of 1971, labour organisations became even more heavily involved in the activity of government. Indeed, it was assumed almost *a priori* that their consent (an extra-parliamentary form of decision-making) was required for all important economic matters: that union power was invincible.[18]

This, together with the apparently inexorable rise in the rate of inflation and the continuing growth of public spending as a proportion of GNP, led to severe disquiet about the state of the British polity. It also resulted in the popularisation of the phrase 'the British disease', a term of opprobrium referring to the phenomena of low growth, high public spending and excessive union power. Although this is not of course a precise description of the British, or any other, social system and its ailments, its general acceptance by informed commentators indicates the extent of the disquiet felt about consensus politics.

The experience of the Labour Governments between 1974 and 1979 did not bring about any qualitative change in social and economic policy, although a quantitative worsening of the fabric of political life in Britain was clearly discernible. Most noticeable was the further rise of union power (helped by legislation which significantly extended the legal immunities of trade unions),[19] continued inflation and further growth of the public sector. At the same time, a quiet revolution was taking place in British political thought. Although Mrs Thatcher's election victory in 1979 is thought to be the first direct political expression of the new anti-consensus ideas, it should be stressed as a matter of historical fact that the Callaghan Labour Government, albeit under pressure from the International Monetary Fund, made the first tentative moves towards the breakup of the old economic and social order. Towards the end of the 1970s the *growth* in public spending was restrained and the dangers of inflation recognised. Indeed, it was James Callaghan (in 1976) who first publicly pronounced the death of the crude Keynesianism that had been practised throughout the previous decades, with his admission that governments could no longer (if they ever could) *spend* their way out of depressions.[20] What was perhaps different about the Wilson-Callaghan era, however, was that it provoked intense political debate, not merely over economic issues but also about the fundamental nature of British society — more particularly, the disruptive action of minority groups and the apparent inability of the Constitution to contain them.

The scene was then set for a substantial revision of accepted political and social values in Britain. It is undeniably the case that contemporary classical liberals have made most of the running in this area and this is so for a number of reasons. Firstly, conservatives have tended to retreat from abstract, ideological debate: hunch, instinct, faith in the immanent wisdom of an inarticulated tradition have always been preferred to the dissolving powers of human reason. Closely allied to this is the fact that there is a tradition of anti-individualism in conservative political thought. Secondly, conservatives were deeply implicated in the consensus — indeed, 'progressive' conservative spokesmen were assiduous in their claim to have incorporated elements of social-democratic thought into their doctrines. Thirdly, much of the criticism came from 'foreign' sources. The objection here was partly intellectual, that it was inappropriate to attempt to apply alien ideas to the specific conditions of Britain; and partly emotional, expressive of an insular distaste for outside influences. It is, of course, true that the most persuasive criticisms of post-war Britain emanated from American and European sources.

Both contemporary conservative and liberal economic and political thought have been decisively influenced by individualist ideas and perspectives. Although it is true that these often came from 'foreign' sources, much of the restructuring of British social thought was based on indigenous principles, many of which, as we have seen, were thoroughly aired in the post-1945 period. The current individualist trend of *some* conservative thinking is part of an attempt to recapture that lost intellectual ground. I will consider first, then, those general liberal principles that have been most influential. I shall try to present these ideas in the context of the British experience.

IV

It is important to stress that classical liberal ideas are not associated with any political party in Britain (certainly not the Liberal Party) though their influence has in contemporary times been felt most strongly in Conservative ranks. The aim of liberals has been to convert intellectual opinion to a particular view of the social world. The main organisational protagonist of individualist economic thought, the Institute of Economic Affairs,[21] is specifically non-political and the major single exponent of the market philosophy, Samuel Brittan of the *Financial Times*, at one time worked for a Labour Government, and has consistently dissociated his ideas from the Conservative Party's tradition. Undoubtedly the most important single influence has been the Austrian-born liberal thinker, Hayek; indeed, Samuel Brittan is to be credited as the first British writer to bring his work back into the public eye. What makes it appropriate to classify him as a British political thinker is not merely his British citizenship (acquired in 1938) but the fact that much of his social philosophy is addressed to the twentieth-century experience of his adopted country. In many ways Hayek's political work is a supremely sophisticated and philosophical critique of those trends in British society identified in a more empirical way by John Jewkes.

As mentioned earlier, Hayek's *Road to Serfdom* was a notorious attempt to demonstrate the totalitarian tendencies in even the mildest forms of state intervention, and although it was addressed to the collectivism of fascism, its individualistic message was obviously equally appropriate to a critique of socialism. The broad outlines of its doctrines have received more elaborate and complex attention in *The Constitution of Liberty and Law, Legislation and Liberty* and numerous other books, essays and pamphlets.[22] The influence of Hayek on British intellectual life can be summarised in the following areas: anti-rationalism and the theory of spontaneous order, the theory of the market order, the doctrine of the rule of law, the fallacy of 'social' justice, and the disintegration of democratic society under the weight of special interest groups. All of these topics have direct relevance to the British experience.

Hayek's general political philosophy is a kind of utilitarianism[23] in which it is claimed that human progress depends not upon the conscious direction of events according to a rational plan but upon *spontaneity*.[24] This means that people when left to themselves to act within general rules of just conduct, will generate a more complex and efficient social order than that planned centrally. Unlike some extreme libertarians who would structure a free society around a natural right to individual liberty, Hayek's theory of freedom is largely instrumental. The case for liberty 'rests chiefly on the inevitable ignorance concerning a great many of the factors on which the achievement of our ends and welfare depends'.[25] Although his famous dispute with Keynes in the 1930s was over technical issues in monetary theory and the theory of the trade cycle, his post-war social philosophy has been addressed to that *act-utilitarianism* that is inherent in Keynesianism. This is the belief that we can assess immediately the pains and benefits of alternative social policies and therefore steer society in some desirable direction. Traditional rules and constitutional and moral principles, if they have no immediate rational justification, are regarded in this approach as an impediment to the artificial production of happiness.

For Hayek, however, this illustrates all too well the hubris of reason. He insists that we can never *know* the consequences of all our actions. The future is unknowable and therefore the following of traditional rules and practices, which have survived a process of evolution, is likely to be more beneficial in terms of progress than the design of abstract schemes of social improvement. In fact, nations improve themselves not by the implementation of such abstract schemes but by 'imitating' the more successful ones.[26] Obviously, the market process is the supreme example of the results of evolution improving on reason but Hayek, more controversially, extends the idea to other social institutions, especially the law. It is this emphasis on tradition that has endeared Hayek to conservative thinkers as well as classical liberals, since a commitment to the immanent wisdom of tradition can easily be used to invalidate more extreme and rationalistic *laissez-faire* proposals. Nevertheless, the various attempts at rational planning of the economy that did occur in Britain were obviously vulnerable to Hayek's strictures since a market economy is the paradigm case of a spontaneously evolving social order.

In later works, notably volume III of *Law, Legislation and Liberty*, Hayek makes much use of the contemporary theory of group politics, and it is this which has had most relevance for contemporary British political thought: for what has prevented the automatically adjusting processes of the market working effectively in Britain is the influence of minority groups on the making of policy. Thus, even if it were possible to devise a rational social and economic plan in a world of ceaseless change and uncertainty, its implementation would require some form of dictatorship which would be immune from the influence of pressure groups. Indeed, Keynesian demand-management policies presuppose the existence of an omniscient and benevolent elite insulated from the normal pressures of political life: but the point of 'Invisible Hand' theory, as described by Hayek, is that there are mechanisms in a more or less free economy that render harmonious the impulses of *individual* self-interest with the demands of public interest. What prevents this harmony emerging in modern society is the fact that individuals have an incentive to seek group privileges which disrupt the market process — that process of individual interaction which unintentionally generates the public interest.

The major pressure groups in British society that have this disequilibriating effect are, of course, the trade unions, but mention should also be made of farmers, an interest group closely associated with conservatism yet historically favoured by all governments of whatever ideological persuasion. Throughout British history the ability of farmers, through price-support schemes, tariffs and other impediments to the free importation of cheap foreign food, to exempt themselves from market forces has been a familiar source of frustration to classical liberals. The success of farmers' groups is entirely due to their curious capacity to influence government: indeed, in Britain, the Ministry of Agriculture is virtually a spokesman for the National Farmer's Union.

Hayek has spent more time criticising trade unions, and this is partly because they have been the most successful of all pressure groups in influencing governments in a variety of directions. For the classical liberal this has had the disastrous effect of mixing politics with economics, diverting the natural course of economic development towards ends determined by political agents. Thus, a major objection to prices-and-incomes policies is not merely that they fail to control inflation (though all classical liberals would stress that this is true), but that in order to get trade unions to agree to such policies, political inducements have to be offered. These will include such policies as nationalisation, exemptions for some industries from competition, government support for certain industries, and granting to the unions an important voice in taxation and welfare policy. This happened to a remarkable extent in Britain during the period of the 'social contract', 1976–9. What tends to happen is that these exemptions from competitive forces remain *after* the prices-and-income policies are abandoned because in a nominally free society the trade unions cannot *enforce* their side of the deal.

The failure of the social contract could have been predicted from certain developments in liberal social theory. These relate to the problem of providing public goods on the assumption that the members of a society are entirely motivated by self-interest. Since a public good benefits everybody whether they have paid for it or not, the likelihood that it will be provided by spontaneous market forces is remote even though self-interested maximisers desire the public good. This is the primary justification for the coercive state in liberal theory. This is no more than a political application of the 'prisoner's dilemma' of modern game theory: a 'prisoner's dilemma' occurs whenever individual rational self-interest leads to undesirable collective outcomes.

Irrespective of the economic logic of prices-and-incomes policies, in a nominally free society they are bound to come up against 'prisoner's dilemmas'. In the social contract between the Labour Government and the trade unions, the latter had to accept a five per cent wage-increase as being in the common interests of their members. The policy required that all trade unions should *voluntarily* agree to bargain with their employers for no more than five per cent. However, since no one trade union could be sure that all the others would abide by the agreement, the possibility of defection was very great. This in fact happened in 1978 when the Ford workers negotiated a pay deal with their employers which was in excess of the five per cent norm. Despite very strong government pressures, this deal went through and therefore breached the social contract. Predictably, other unions, especially those in the public sector, followed suit. This led to the strikes and disruptive industrial action of 1978/9 ('the winter of discontent') which ultimately brought down the Labour Government.

Of course, governments could always use coercion to enforce wage agreements but this would not be corporatism, which is supposed to rest on consent, but authoritarianism and the abandonment of the trade union movement's traditional role in the economy. The lesson of the 1970s was not that governments cannot govern without the co-operation of the trade unions (which is the opinion of many commentators on British politics), but that they cannot govern with it.

This brings us straight to the heart of Hayek's liberal political philosophy: the concept of the rule of law.[27] What a free-market economic system requires is *predictability*. Thus while it is accepted that prices and costs in a capitalist system will change in an unpredictable manner (indeed, this is one crucially important reason why a planned economy is doomed to failure), the rules under which transactors operate must know in advance how the law will affect them. In Hayek's view, a predictable legal order is better guaranteed under the spontaneously evolving common-law system than statute. Statutes emanate from legislatures — institutions which are characterised in a modern world by caprice and arbitrariness rather than predictability. *Legislation*, as opposed to 'law', is likely to advance the interests of particular groups rather than those of the general public.

Whereas some liberals have justified the resistance to encroachments by the state on individual liberty by references to natural rights, Hayek, in common with many conservative thinkers, has rejected such a notion as dangerously abstract and rationalistic. Indeed, he believes that liberty is advanced more effectively by the existence of perfectly general and impartial laws. Such laws constitute boundaries within which human action takes place. Somewhat controversially, Hayek maintains that liberty is *not* infringed by general rules, but only when individuals are directed to perform specific tasks by coercive authorities, as would be the case with the direction of labour in a socialist command economy. Under a Hayekian 'rule-of-law' regime, everybody, including governments, would be bound by laws not of their own making. By this criterion, a political system such as that of Great Britain, which has a legislature with unlimited law-making powers, would be unacceptable to liberals. Sovereignty is alien to the rule of law, even though the legal rules of a sovereign legislature are 'lawful' in a formal sense. One particular inference from all this is that the freedoms protected by the common law are constantly vulnerable to statute. The vast increase in *public* law in Britain, in the twentieth century, especially in relation to welfare and housing has gradually eroded individual liberty and the property rights that flow from this.

Following on from the rule-of-law doctrine is Hayek's critique of social justice.[28] For a classical liberal, justice is satisfied by the principles of legality; if a law is abstract, non-discriminatory and favours no named individuals or groups, it is a *just* law. This theory of fair rules and practices, however has nothing to do with the distribution of income and wealth that emerges from the following of such rules. The consensus, however, held that the state could not be neutral about the outcomes of social processes but had an obligation to create some 'fair' or 'socially just' distribution , through progressive taxation and the collective delivery of many welfare services. Hayek's objection to this is not merely the familiar one that redistributive tax measures misallocate resources in a market economy, but also that the whole concept of social justice is meaningless: it is a 'mirage'. However, the pursuit of this illusion has had dire consequences for the economic well-being of social democracies. It has led to an investment in redistributive rather than productive activities by individuals and groups. The state has ceased to be an impartial umpire and has become instead the active distributor of benefits.

It is this influence of groups in democracies (characterised by unlimited legislatures and competitive party-systems) which has concerned Hayek most in recent years: for the sum of interests of pressure groups does not equal the public interest. Although individual self-interest does produce benign outcomes for society, this cannot be the case with the pursuit of group interests, for this is invariably directed towards the exemption of groups from general rules of just conduct.

The British writer most responsible for the dissemination of Hayek's ideas in Britain is Samuel Brittan.[29] Known mainly as an economic commentator, a 'monetarist' and an early advocate of freely floating exchange rates, he has nevertheless set his practical economics in a political philosphy that is broadly classical liberal. He has never been a supporter of the Conservative Party, even though some of his ideals have been taken up, if not implemented by leading Conservative politicians.

Indeed, Brittan has objected strongly to what he maintains are conservative features of Hayek's thought. His critique here echoes that of the more extreme libertarians who argue that Hayek's stress on the evolutionary growth of social institutions and his anti-rationalist philosophy disables him from a necesssary attack on those inherited forms of organisation which, although they may be inimical to a free society, have neverthless survived. Certainly in Hayek's later writings [30] there is some tension between a kind of rationalistic classical liberalism (which recommends, amongst other things, a free market in money) and a deep-seated traditionalism which drives him to accept rules and practices which may be of an authoritarian kind.

Brittan suggests a more *direct* version of utilitarianism than Hayek's rather convoluted consequentialism. This is related to his original advocacy of the 'permissive society' and his belief that capitalist economic arrangements were more compatible with the movement for the relaxation of legal controls over personal conduct than socialist ones. This was in itself a significant intellectual breakthrough since permissive social policies in Britain have traditionally been associated with collectivist economic policies. In Brittan's liberal utilitarianism, happiness is maximised if individual choice is widened across all areas, subject to the necessary constraints imposed by the rule of law. We should look to the evaluation of prospective laws and policies in this light rather than in terms of social evolution and the slow growth of institutions.

Brittan is also more radical in respect of property,[31] for he does not believe that a market economy is incompatible with some redistribution of initial property titles. As he argued many times, the classical liberal theory of income distribution by the market says nothing about the starting point of each transactor: there is no reason, he thinks, why this should be left to chance, history or social evolution. Brittan would therefore argue that some redistribution would be justified, perhaps through interitance taxes or, more interestingly, by the 'return' of publicly owned assets such as North Sea oil to the people. Nevertheless, he is no egalitarian in the *conventional* sense: he argues that a reallocation of factor earnings away from the impersonal decision of the market would not only abrogate personal liberty but also reduce prosperity. Nevertheless it has to be conceded that it is difficult to see what use such possibly pro-market redistributive devices such as a 'wealth' tax would be to a more egalitarian liberal political economist in contemporary Britain. Even a heavy tax on the really wealthy would not yield a large amount for redistribition, and if that yield were to be increased this could only be done by taxing the much less wealthy in society. [32] In fact, as Brittan himself has said, the best way to pursue an egalitarian goal would be to remove government privilege and widen the range of social and economic activities subject to the market.

Of course, it is the role of government in the economy that has greatly concerned Brittan. It should be stressed that he is no liber-tarian or *laissez-faire* extremist. He does accept a role for government in a market society — a role that is not limited to the provision of the traditional public goods (defence, law and order, and so on), but which extends to the supply of welfare services. In Britain, however, he claims that government has come to be seen as a pro-vider of unlimited benefits irrespective of economic considerations. He calls this the 'Wenceslas myth': the idea that government can provide prosperity costlessly and that it is only ill-will or ideological prejudice that prevents it from so doing. This is a genuinely Hayekian theme in Brittan's political economy: government, instead of being the enforcer of general rules of just conduct, becomes an active participant in social and economic processes. Its role here is inevitably redistributive. Brittan does not object to government having a redistributive role: however, in modern social democracies this redistribution does not operate according to some fixed rule but is determined by pressure groups.

Also, it is the case that the welfare state has ceased to be a safety-net for those in need but a complex redistributive organisation which actually favours the middle classes.[33] Brittan has been consistently critical of middle-class privilege, especially the system of tax relief on mortgage interest. Not only is this a breach of the rule-of-law doctrine, but it also encourages over-investment in housing, under-occupation and a redistribution of income from private and coun-cil tenants to owner-occupiers. Also, this phenomenon, together with rent control has produced in Britain the paradox of rising homelessness in the context of an increasing supply of housing units and a stagnant population.

It is the all-pervasive influence of interest groups in British Society that Brittan has identified as the major cause of the 'British disease'. In a seminal paper first published in 1975,[34] he applied American political economy and public-choice theory to the peculiar problems of Britain. By that time this country had almost become a test case for the analysis of the general problems of social democracy. The classical liberal argument was that the prevailing institutional arrangements in Britain prevented the emergence of policy outputs that reflected the public interest.

Most classical liberals, from Jewkes onwards, agreed on the main features of the 'British disease' — low productivity, a strike-prone workforce, over-powerful trade unions, and insatiable demands on government leading inexorably to high public spending — but Brittan was probably the first commentator to trace their root cause to a certain kind of *constitutional* malaise. Thus, although he is primarily an economist, his work implies the primacy of the *political*; that the offering of technical economic advice was of little practical value in the absence of a theory of the political process. Indeed, most post-war classical liberals, including Hayek, have accepted Keynes's view that the causal factors in social affairs are ideas rather than interests.[35] They held to the somewhat optimistic view that all that is required to inaugurate a new era of economic policy is to change the ideas of the ruling elite.

Brittan, building on ideas first fomulated by Joseph Schumpeter, Antony Downs and the Virginia School economists, James Buchanan and Gordon Tullock,[36] argues that there are parallels between the political market and the economic market, but that a democratic political system does not contain those automatic stabilising devices present in a market economy. In private economic markets, transactors are under budget constraints which operate almost immediately to curb their potential extravagance. Competition between firms for the favour of the consumer is controlled by the threat of bankruptcy posed to those enterprises that misjudge the market. Consumers, faced with the problem of allocating their incomes between a variety of goods and services, have every incentive to be informed of the real costs of their choices.

The political market, however, is substantially different. Parties do compete for the favours of voters (who may be treated as consumers), but the constraints that operate on them (i.e. government budget deficits and the costs imposed by inflation) are all long-term and remote. Since the aim of a political party is to win the next election, the temptation is to offer 'bribes' to the electorate which do not have to be immediately paid for in terms of increased taxation. Indeed, since taxation is a vote-loser, it is almost certain that attractive policies will not be genuinely costed. Of course, without a constraint on the government's power of money-creation, the temptation is to pay for the increased public services that are offered by inflation, the pains of which are experienced later. Hence, party programmes are constructed which appeal to interest groups, house-owners, trade unionists, recipients of welfare benefits and employees of declining industries dependent on public support.

Conventional majority-rule democracy fails because it gives each individual no incentive to reverse this ultimately socially destruc-tive process, for the voter will inevitably vote for a party that max-imises his sectional interests, since he can be sure that others will do likewise. The public interest is defined by classical liberals as zero inflation, the strict enforcement of the rule of law and the absence of group privilege; but no person has any incentive to vote for it since the benefits of these policies are all long-term and thinly spread across the whole population.

This is the true explanation and description of the 'British disease' which appeared to be rampant throughout the 1970s. Indeed, successive governments, Labour and Conservative, appeared to give official sanction to group politics with policies seemingly deliberately designed to accommodate important sectional groups, often to the detriment of the authority of Parliament. Similarly, government spending increased under all governments largely as a consequence of the need to buy electoral support. The ultimate cause of all this, from a liberal point of view, was an electoral and political system which imposed so few constraints on government action.

Thus, it is mistaken to blame the British political system for pro-ducing 'adversary politics' — i.e. a form of politics in which each side takes a confrontational stance on every issue and each govern-ment rapidly reverses the policies of its predecessor. What characterised the period of the 1970s was a consensus over incomes policy, government aid to industry and related matters, despite a superficially adversarial attitude of the major parties. It was only in the late 1970s, with a change in the ideological nature of both British socialism and conservatism, that adversarial politics became the pattern of British economic and social life.

This type of analysis is perhaps the most important advance on the traditional classical liberal approach to public policy. It reveals a superficially paradoxical appraisal of the modern state — for on the one hand, it contains a critique of the state's extensive activities and power over the lives of ordinary citizens, yet on the other, the state appears as a weak and pliable institution, unable to resist the incessant demands of pressure groups. Furthermore, instead of government being (in Hayek's phrase) a 'maintenance squad'[37] charged with the duty of servicing an otherwise self-correcting economic and social system, in Britain especially, it has become, through its officials, part of the system itself. Witness, for example, the increase in heavily unionised public-sector employment.

The classical liberal analysis of *why* government intervention increases in a competitive party democracy yields its own solution: that government should be bound by strict rules. There is a parallel here between debates over constitutionalism and debates over monetary policy. For classical liberal 'hard-money theorists have favoured strict monetary rules precisely because they have distrusted the granting of *discretionary* power to centralised authorities. In a similar way they have preferred written constitutions because they do not accept that governments generate an *objective* public interest. At one time there might have been some plausibility in the suggestion that governors in Britain may have been restrained by 'internalised' rules, even in the context of a flexible constitution, but this attitude could not survive in an age of competitive party democracy. The classical liberal therefore has a Hobbesian view of political activity — with the proviso that the 'war of all against all' characteristic of the Hobbesian state of nature is more descriptive of the interaction between *groups* in a democratically organised society.[38]

Although Samuel Brittan is the foremost exponent of a popular (but nevertheless extremely sophisticated) classical liberalism, he is but one of many writers who have pressed the intellectual case for individualism in Britain. Outside formal academic treatises on political philosophy, those thinkers have mainly been concerned with devising schemes for the return of many government activities to individual choice. Most notable here is the work of the Institutue of Economic Affairs, a non-party political organisation dedicated to the transmission of radical free-market ideas. Of particular importance has been their popularisation of the 'voucher' scheme for maximising parental choice in education.[39]

This is particularly important since it focuses directly on the issue of public versus private choice, so that the ideological question of the distribution of income and wealth can be neatly avoided. In state schools, a kind of *syndicalism* operates: what is to be taught, and how it is to be taught, is largely determined by teachers and educational activists in local government rather than by the consumers of the service. This has led to increasing dissatisfaction. What the voucher scheme entails is that parents should have the right to express that dissatisfaction by removing their children from inadequate schools and 'spending' their vouchers elsewhere. To work effectively the scheme requires that manifestly unpopular schools be closed down and incompetent teachers dismissed. Any objections based on the grounds that there is inequality of access to what would be, in effect, privatised schools could be met by varying the value of the voucher according to parental income.

The intellectual interest of this scheme lies not only in the fact that it shows how market choice can be extended to superficially unpromising areas, but also because it illustrates the 'classlessness' of classical liberal thought — for there is no reason at all why a socialist should oppose what is in effect an exercise in 'people's power'. The opposition in Britain has come mainly (but not exclusively) from Labour, largely because that party has come to represent *producer* groups (in this case teachers and public-sector employees). In his earlier work Brittan was concerned to show that the Left/Right dichotomy was a misleading description of political attitudes. He also stressed that the classical liberal should not ally himself to a rigid party dogma, but should propagate ideas that have an appeal across conventional party lines. The debate about vouchers amply bears this out.

The political thought of contemporary classical liberalism in Britain is broadly utilitarian; in fact in many ways it is simply applied political economy. Thus, it is at its most potent in the analysis of public policy and in the description of the most efficient *means* towards the realisation of uncontroversial *ends* — namely, freedom and prosperity. Surprisingly, classical liberals are positivist in their attitude to ends; that is, they assume that reason is incompetent to adjudicate between rival forms of social and political life. They believe that the impasse in political debate that this might imply is largely illusory. This is because they assume that there is very much less disagreement about ends than is commonly supposed.

This in no way commits the classical liberal to the consensus: the consensus about politics and economics that ruled throughout so much of the post-war period was really about means. It denied that the market was an efficient mechanism to ensure economic well-being, it claimed that a satisfactory welfare system could not be generated from individual choice, and maintained that political *discretion*, subject only to the constraints of the democratic system, would produce superior outcomes to those that flow from the adherence to abstract rules (such as a balanced-budget rule or a 'monetary constitution').

Hence, the classical liberal's intellectual programme has largely consisted of piecemeal attacks on the prevailing consensus-orientated institutions in Britain. Of course, of particular importance has been the critique of the welfare state. Very few British classical liberals have rejected the idea that some of the wealth created by capitalist society should be redistributed to those who are unable to secure a satisfactory income within the market. However, the argument has always been that such redistribution should be in cash rather than through the compulsory consumption of state services in such areas as health, education, unemployment and pensions.[40] Not only is such a method inefficient (a special problem in Britain has been the creation of a heavily unionised, rent-seeking band of state employees), but the effect is also to reduce individual choice substantially. A further disadvantage is that a state welfare system generates, through the vote-maximising mechanism, virtually irresistible demands for increased public spending. A spectacular example of this is in the field of pensions. Here, the consensus produced perhaps its final gesture in 1975 with the establishment of *earnings-related* pensions, financed not by a 'fund' but by direct transfers in a 'pay as you go' system.[41] This promised to build up massive financial obligations for *future* generations (although the system was modified in 1986), indicating that the taxation of the present generation had reached exhaustion point.

If all these services were privatised on grounds of efficiency, however, it still might be claimed that there was a disagreement about ends since it could still leave a degree of inequality of wealth and income which would be unacceptable to non-liberals. We have already noted that Samuel Brittan has raised this problem. The normal liberal response is to draw a crucially important distinction between a welfare and redistribution programme that raises the well-being of the worst-off (a programme that can be justified on Rawlsian grounds) and one which merely maximises equality. As liberals have consistently pointed out, the latter policy, theoretically and empirically, does not do anything for the worst-off. Nevertheless, rather than discuss the intrinsic values of equality and inequality, some liberals have tended to recommend a trade-off between equality and efficiency.

However, there is a tradition within English liberal thought that is as much concerned with the *moral* features of a free society as its efficiency. On this view individuals have *rights* (not derived from the state or law) and state intervention violates those rights. It is

therefore morally condemnable irrespective of any utilitarian
objections that might be advanced against it. This is a position that
derives in English political thought from Locke, and it has erupted
periodically in the history of English liberal theory. What
distinguishes liberal rights theorists from others is their stress on
the inviolability of legitimately acquired property. Most of the
demands in Britain for a written constitution embodying a 'bill of
rights' have demanded liberty of expression and association, and
protection against police and government, rather than explicit
guarantees of private property.

In contemporary English political thought this brand of individualism is less influential in policy debate, although, in certain areas
involving rent control, compulsory purchase and planning law,
objections to state action are often couched in rights terms. However,
it is in American liberal political thought that rights-based
arguments have more immediate potency. Nevertheless, at the
fringes of the general classical liberal intellectual tradition there is
a growing movement towards the establishment of an individualism
that derives its rationale entirely from propositions about the moral
autonomy of the person.

There is one aspect of British political life in which the consensus still reigns supreme: this is in the area of constitutional reform.
Here the present Conservative leadership is wedded to a constitutional *ancien régime* which sanctions parliamentary sovereignty,
unlimited government and an unfair electoral system that grossly
distorts the people's choice. It is this institutional structure which
classical liberals have identified as the causal factor in the rise of
statism, public spending and the dominance of group interests over
the public interest. It is in an important sense only by chance that
a government was elected in 1979 (and re-elected in 1983 with a
reduced share of the popular vote) which had a commitment to
turning back the tide of collectivism and socialism. Those institutions of state that have been used (albeit gingerly) to re-establish
the market economy can so easily be used by future governments
to reinstate the main features of the consensus, even though this
may not have popular support.

Although some Conservatives have favoured a new constitutional
settlement that would end the formal sovereignty of Parliament and
entrench individual rights, including property rights, traditionalists,
including Mrs. Thatcher, have showed no inclination whatsoever
to tinker with Britain's existing political institutions. If there is any
intellectual justification for this it must depend on the idea that

ultimately it is 'ideas' that are the causal factors in social change. It also assumes that the masses are in a modern democracy more or less inert. Therefore on this view the strategy should always be to change the ideas of elites rather than design institutions appropriate for the protection of individualism.

This was indeed at one time the view of classical liberals, but in recent years the concentration on institutional reform indicates that there is a growing belief amongst individualists that ideas are much less influential in the determination of events than the pressure of group interests. If this is the case then clearly constitutional reform is imperative for the preservation of a free society. In Britain there is a growing demand from classical liberals for not just a written constitution of the traditional type, but for an *economic* constitution to protect individual economic rights against the encroachment of the collectivist state. Such a constitution would include, *inter alia* a 'monetary rule' which would limit the power of money creation on the part of government, and a 'balanced-budget rule' which would compel government to pay for its expenditure by taxation rather than by running never-ending deficits. Most classical liberals would also favour a constitutional constraint on the amount of tax that governments could levy on individuals. However, as long as the sovereignty of Parliament remains as the cornerstone of the British Constitution (and as long as this is supported by the major political parties), such a statutory innovation will be precarious.

V

When we look at the conservative response to the collapse of the consensus, we are faced with a number of problems. As was noted in chapter 4, there is the perennial difficulty of reproducing a coherent conservative political ideology. Indeed, the very search for 'coherence' (in the sense of a logically consistent set of policies derived from principles) is alien to much of conservative thinking. This is *dispositional* rather than rational. Furthermore, a distinctive brand of English conservatism was bound up with the post-war consensus, either because its main features were thought to be intrinsically right or because in a more pessimistic strain, it was thought to be impossible to undo certain features of British society.

Of course, a distinction should be drawn between conservatism and the Conservative Party. There are important conservative thinkers who hold to a body of political beliefs which have a validity ndependent of party dogma. Indeed these thinkers often claim that Conservative governments frequently betray these beliefs. Nevertheless, conservatism is accurately associated with political power and the art of government in the way that classical liberalism is not. Despite a certain kind of anti-rationalism that lurks at the heart of individualistic political philosophy, classical liberalism is obsessively concerned with the logical analysis and critique of policy. An important strand of conservative thinking, as we have seen, deliberately eschews the application of *principles* to political life — either from a kind of elegant despair, the immediate injunction of which is merely to resist any change as far as is possible, or from a sincere belief in the superiority of 'hunch', intuition or prejudice over reason. This latter view is by no means irrational and is quite effective as a critical response to socialism. Indeed, Oakeshott's attack on post-war socialist planning was based on a highly sophisticated version of this. Most important of all, it evinces a profound scepticism of the ability of 'politics' to produce human wellbeing: an end, it is thought, more likely to be brought about by less tangible social forces.

Yet the post-war years saw something of a divergence between conservative sceptical thought and conservative political practice, for Oakeshott's message was not heeded and the Conservative Party developed a kind of muted interventionism and, fatally, a version of corporatism that was scarcely distinguishable from that of the more moderate wings of the Labour Party. The mixed economy, most of the 1945–51 nationalisation (steel being the exception) and the welfare state were accepted as irreversible, if not actually welcomed, by active Conservatives up until about the mid–1970s.

There was an ideological justification for this, and one that did not rest merely on the unalterability of a received set of institutions and policies. This justification stems from a traditional conservative distrust of untrammelled markets and the corollary that the state had a duty to intervene to produce those desirable social outcomes which the market did not produce. The title of a book written by Harold Macmillan in the 1930s, *The Middle Way*,[42] illustrates this position perfectly. Although this book was in some ways a response to the Great Depresssion it represents a general position in conservative ideology: indeed, the pursuit of the 'middle way' has been a persistent activity of Conservative Governments in Britain throughout the latter half of the twentieth century. It is worth dwelling on its pre–1939 origins since they had an oblique influence on the thought of those conservatives who embraced the consensus.

In a series of publications in the 1930s, Macmillan and his associates published a variety of articles, pamphlets and books which set the agenda for an activist state. The content of the agenda was based on the assumption that *laissez-faire* and free trade had somehow failed. Although private property and capitalism must remain, these should be 'managed' and made to conform to guide lines laid down by centralised political authorities. The state's welfare role should not be limited to providing a minimum outside the market for the few unable to sustain themselves by their own actions, but should be involved *inside* the market in providing aid and encouragement to depressed areas. Trade unions were not to be concerned solely with bargaining with employers but should be directly involved in the management of industries. Instead of trusting in the market co-ordinating the actions of decentralised transactors, Macmillan proposed a plethora of councils, supervisory boards and investment and development agencies. Not even nationalisation of key sectors (energy and transport) was excluded.

In all this, there was clear anticipation of the 'corporatism' that was to dominate social and political thought in the 1960s and 1970s: it was a doctrine that was to infect almost all brands of conservatism. Corporatism rests on foundations diametrically opposed to liberal individualism. It rejects the idea of a society as a 'civil association' of individuals held together by general rules; as we have seen from a brief examination of Michael Oakeshott's political thought, this is a quintessentially conservative idea. Instead the corporatist presupposes that such an association will mutate into a system of power blocks which will confront each other in a socially destructive manner unless their behaviour is not co-ordinated *artificially*. However, what distinguishes corporatism from out-and-out *dirigisme* is the fact that such co-ordination is not to be a product (it is hoped) of commands from an all-powerful state but a function of all those blocks co-operating *with* the state in a collective enterprise.

We have noted earlier in this chapter that it was during Macmillan's premiership (1957–63) that the foundations of the corporatist state were laid, with the creation of the National Economic Development Council and the introduction of prices-and-incomes policies. After a brief flirtation with the market, the Heath Government of 1970–4 carried those policies even further, with the addition of an inflationary monetary policy. This latter addition is a further crucially important break with old conservatism, for a fundamental feature of that was the obligation of the state to provide a sound currency — an obligation stressed in Oakeshott's post-war polemical writings. It is worth observing that even in Roger Scruton's *The Meaning of Conservatism*, a book which in some ways belongs to the pre-corporatist tradition of political thought, this traditional benchmark of conservative financial probity is not stressed.

To borrow another enlightening phrase from Oakeshott, this whole ideological movement is aimed consciously at turning the state into an 'enterprise association': government is charged with the specific task of bringing about desirable states of affairs — 'economic growth', a 'welfare' society, managed capitalism and so on. This was spectacularly illustrated during the Heath era when the whole of the British economy was treated as a mechanistic enterprise which could be pushed in some desired direction by a series of piecemeal and *ad hoc* interventions, such as prices-and-incomes policies, monetary injection and nationalisation.

Although interventions of this type are often said to be consistent with traditional conservatism (indeed, their derivation from an earlier 'Tory paternalism' is claimed), it is doubtful whether these arguments can be sustained. It may be more plausible to argue that the Macmillan-Heath pattern is itself an aberrant style of conservative politics, consistent neither with old-style paternalism nor with the *laissez-faire* strand of conservative thought. Firstly it breaks with that conviction of the 'imperfectibility' of man that informs so much of conservatism. It is because man is so imperfect and so potentially venal that conservatives have claimed that government should refrain from too active an involvement in economic and social affairs. Furthermore, the involvement of groups in the political process outside the framework of Parliament undermines the authority of the state. Of course, the very idea of a wide economic role for the state is alien to the old conservative tradition, largely because it was felt that this would make it the plaything of organised interests.

In many ways the Thatcher 'revolution' can be seen not as a simple-minded and crude reproduction of *laissez-faire* economic principles but a reversion to a traditional conservatism that had been almost obliterated by the semi-collectivism of which Macmillan and post-Macmillan Conservatives had been the main architects. Of course, there has always been a libertarian or *laissez-faire* strand in conservative thinking, a strand that became especially important at the end of the nineteenth century as the Liberals (traditionally the home of free trade and capitalist philosophy) became increasingly collectivist. Indeed, it can easily be shown that 'Thatcherite ideas' owe very little in practice to the formal properties of strict classical liberalism and *laissez-faire*.

The re-thinking of official Conservative policy began, of course, before 1979. Throughout the 1970s, Sir Keith Joseph was active in disseminating what was essentially classical liberalism:[43] and he also took full intellectual and moral responsibility for the mistaken policies of the Heath Government of which he was a senior member. Perhaps his most important contribution was the speech at Preston in 1975 in which he specifically rejected the Keynesian orthodoxy and repudiated the obligation of governments to use macro-economic policy to promote full employment. The defeat of inflation became the sole priority. The election of Mrs Thatcher as leader in 1975 signalled the end of the policies associated with Edward Heath, even though a number of his supporters remained Conservative spokesmen and could not be excluded from Mrs Thatcher's first Cabinet.

The policy that was formulated in this period, and which to a small extent was carried out in Mrs Thatcher's administrations, bore a resemblance to classical liberalism only in certain aspects of *economic* management and in its general utilitarianism. There was less concern with *personal* liberty or with the dangers of group privilege (except in the case of trade unions) that has pre-occupied much anti-statist political thinking.

At the macro-economic level the influence of Samuel Brittan was most evident. He had argued extensively throughout the 1970s that attempts to get unemployment below the 'natural rate' (or as he prefers to call it, the 'non-accelerating inflation rate of unemployment') must inevitably result in both higher inflation and higher unemployment. The 'natural rate' is determined by structural features in the economy that prevent the labour market adjusting to changing conditions. The most important of these is the housing market where the occupation of cheap public housing (and the inability of council tenants to exchange 'leases' on their properties) discourages people from moving to areas where jobs become available. This, together with a welfare system that *at the margin* makes the benefits of paid employment relatively low, has rendered large numbers of the workforce in Britain immobile.

Of course, strict monetarist theory does not say that high public spending necessarily causes inflation. If it is financed by taxation then its inflationary effect is nil: the only adverse economic consequences result from the nature of public spending and taxation. Normally, however, the vote maximising strategy of competitive party politics impels governments to run *deficits*: if these are financed by printing money then inflation will result, but if they are financed by government borrowing then this will force up interest rates and 'crowd out' private (and economically more viable) investment. Either way, then, deficits cannot be good for the economy.

The new Conservative strategy was therefore to cut both inflation and public spending. Although it is undoubtedly the case that some of the converts were naïve enough to believe that merely by reducing inflation, full employment and prosperity would ensue almost painlessly, there is nothing in monetarist theory to suggest this. It is regrettable that the new conservatism concentrated entirely on the defeat of inflation to the neglect of those micro-economic reforms that are essential, according to strict classical liberal doctrine for the efficient functioning of the market economy. Thus the 'consensus' view amongst classical liberals was that the only real achievement of the first years of Mrs Thatcher's administration was the defeat of inflation. The fact that public spending had increased (from 46 per cent of GNP under Labour to over 50 per cent under the Conservatives) and that total taxation had also gone up led to the ironical comment from extreme *laissez-faire* ideologues that this was the most 'socialist government since the war'.

It is also true that no serious in-roads were made into the rigid group structure of British society. Conservatives, even of an individualist persuasion, are by no means immune to the promptings of special privilege. Owner-occupiers continue to enjoy tax relief on the interest paid on their mortgages. Despite conclusive evidence that this redistributes income from poor to rich and involves a breach of a classical liberal principle of just taxation, Conservatives continue to be its most enthusiastic supporters. Furthermore, the voucher scheme, which would produce a dramatic increase in people's choice in education, appears to have been shelved.

The new conservatism has clearly not established the 'social market economy' in Britain as its major 'theorists' (especially Sir Keith Joseph) had clearly hoped. Yet it can nevertheless boast some positive achievements. The conquest of inflation is thought to be the most important. This did not look possible until the establishment of the Medium-Term Financial Strategy (MTFS) in 1980. In the first year of office the Thatcher Government in fact turned an existing 8 per cent inflation into one of 20 per cent largely through its inheritance of certain public-sector pay obligations from the previous Labour Government and its early ineptitude in monetary policy. Nevertheless, since then inflation has steadily fallen. The difference between the 'Thatcherite' approach and that of almost all predecessors was admirably summarised by Nigel Lawson in his Mais Lecture (1984): 'it is the conquest of inflation, not the pursuit of growth and employment, which is or should be the objective of macro-economic policy.'[44]

These latter are not the direct responsibility of government but can only come from the market. Nevertheless, government does have a limited responsibility to remove artificial impediments to the smooth operation of the exchange process. Here the accumulated mass of impediments has proved to be a formidable obstacle and the failure of the Conservative Government to do much about it has drawn very heavy criticism from the more rationalistic classical liberals. Nevertheless, legislation to restrict the legal immunities of trade unions has gone some way to put them under the 'rule of law' although the ultimate *laissez-faire* aim of repealing the provisions of the 1906 Trade Disputes Act (which make it impossible to sue a union for damages caused by an industrial dispute) remains no more than a theoretical possibility.

The privatisation of state industries is, of course, a basic element in the liberal's economic creed. The rationale of this is obviously to restore the market's role in the allocation of resources: it has nothing to do with raising money to reduce the budget deficit (since this can only be reduced permanently by cutting public spending). The criticism of the Conservative privatisation programme is that its real purpose is the latter rather than the former — hence the sale of public assets at the luxury end of the market. Furthermore, the plan seems to be to sell off these assets as *monopolies* so as to increase their attraction to private buyers, rather than as competitive units. Again no inroads have been made into the vast network of public corporations set up by the 1945–51 Labour Government.

The disappointment which many individualists have felt at the achievements of the new conservatism has not surprisingly led to some reflection on its *nature*. Certainly in practice, it has a lot more in common with a traditionalist pre-Macmillan Toryism than it has with an idealistic classical liberalism. The primary obligation of the state to maintain a sound currency has been re-established and its withdrawal from other economic roles begun. Most important here is the re-emergence of the authority of the state in the traditional conservative sense. For it is a conventional view that that authority can only be maintained if the state is restricted to those tasks for which it is appropriate. What was so striking about the 'corporatist' period of the 1970s was the decline in the authority of the state despite its growth in size and extent. The involvement of groups in governmental decision-making, often independently of Parliament, led to a certain kind of anarchy in British society. 'Pluralism', to a traditional conservative, meant the handing over of authority to groups (especially trade unions); and since these groups could not control their own members, it happened that there was no authority at all. In the Britain of the 1970s, the state, so far from being all-powerful, became the plaything of insubordinate groups.

To the extent that Mrs Thatcher has decisively rejected corporatism and re-established the rule of law in certain areas, her conservatism parallels some aspects of classical liberalism. However, her failure to tackle effectively the vast elements of statism in education, housing, and welfare has dismayed many of her supporters. The slow action taken here betrays a similar conservative *disposition*. This prescribes a cautionary attitude towards wholesale reform of inherited institutions even when our reason tells us that they are manifestly inefficient. Even in Hayek's philosophy, his thesis about the prevailing fact of human ignorance of the future might well indicate an acceptance of much of the existing institutional order, however inconsistent that may be with an *a priori* and rationalistic classical liberalism.

In this analysis, the 'Thatcher revolution' is hardly a revolution at all but a reversion to a traditional conservation. It could be said that it was the corporatist interventionist conservatives (with their 'managerial' view of the role of government) who had discarded a whole sceptical tradition about the necessary limits of political action. Nevertheless, there are aspects of the Joseph-Thatcher ideology which are redolent of a kind of sturdy individualism and anti-statism which do not at all gell with the *paternalism* associated with traditional conservative dogma. Whether those *laissez-faire* whisperings are merely rhetorical flourishes or portents of a more rigorous pursuit of liberty in all its dimensions is difficult to say.

Notes and References

1. Though there were quite tough legislative measures in the first post-war Labour Government.

2. A book believed to have influenced Churchill's election campaign in 1945.

3. (Macmillan, London; 1968). This second edition was published as *The new ordeal by planning*.

4. *The new ordeal by planning*, p. 182.

5. Ibid., chapter 11.

6. Ibid., pp. 78-9.

7. Ibid., p. 95.

8. Ibid., chapter VIII.

9. In M.Oakeshott, *Rationalism in politics and other essays* (Methuen, London, 1962), pp. 37-58.

10. M.Oakeshott, The political economy of freedom in his *Rationalism in politics*, pp. 39-40.

11. Ibid., p.40.

12. Ibid., p.55.

13. Ibid., pp. 48-50.

14. Steel was later re-nationalised by a Labour government in 1967.

15. Keynes was heavily involved in the Bretton Woods Conference 1943-4.

16. For an argument that there are forces that are likely to make stagnation permanent, see N.P.Barry, 'Is there a road to serfdom?', *Government and opposition*, vol. 19 (1984), pp. 52-67.

17. This was in 1971.

18. For the argument that trade unions are inevitably involved in government policy making, see K. Middlemas, *Politics in industrial society* (Deutsch, London, 1979).

19. Secondary and tertiary trade-union actions, which had nothing to do with an original dispute, were legalised and 'closed shops' were protected by law.

20. In a speech to the Labour Party Conference in September, 1976.

21. Set up in 1957 under the direction of Ralph (now Lord) Harris and Arthur Seldon.

22 In addition to works cited earlier, see Hayek's *New studies in philosophy, politics, economics and the history of ideas* (Routledge and Kegan Paul, London, 1978).

23. This must not be confused with a Benthamite or rationalistic utilitarianism.

24. For the best short description of this, see Hayek 'The results of human action but not of human design' in *New studies in philosophy, politics and economics*, pp. 96-105.

25. F.A.Hayek's *The constitution of liberty* (Routledge and Kegan Paul, London, 1960),

26. See Hayek, 'Rules, perception and intelligibility', in *New studies in philosophy, politics and economics*, p. 47.

27. See Hayek, *The constitution of liberty*, chapter 10.

28. See *The mirage of social justice* (vol. ii of *Law legislation and liberty* (Routledge and Kegan Paul, London 1976).

29. The most sophisticated expression of Brittan's political thought is *The role and limits of government: essays in political economy* (Temple Smith, London 1983)

30. See especially 'Three sources of human values', epilogue to *The political economy of a free people* (vol. iii of *Law, legislation and liberty*), pp. 153-76.

31, Brittan, *The role and limits of government*, p. 68 and pp. 71-4.

32. See J. Kay and M.King, *The British tax system* (Oxford University Press, London 1978), pp. 164-70.

33. See J. Le Grand, *The strategy of equality* (Allen and Unwin, London 1982) especially Part Two.

34. S. Brittan, 'The economic contradictions of democracy', *British Journal of Political Science,* vol. 5 (1975), pp. 125-9.

35. For a discussion of this, see N.P.Barry, 'Ideas versus interests', in N.P.Barry *et al., Hayek's serfdom revisited* (Institute of Economic Affairs, London 1984) pp. 45-64.

36. Though the idea was first suggested by Joseph Schumpeter: see his *Capitalism, socialism and democracy* (Allen and Unwin, London, 1943).

37 Hayek, *Rules and order* (vol. i of *Law, legislation and liberty),* p. 47.

38. See J. Burton, 'The instability of the middle way', in Barry *et al., Hayek's serfdom revisited,* pp. 97-9.

39. See. A Seldon, *The riddle of the voucher* (Institute of Economic Affairs, London, 1986).

40. However, this form of redistribution is not without its individualist critics: see chapter 6.

41. See N.P. Barry, 'The state, pensions and the philosophy of welfare', *Journal of Social Policy,* vol. 14 (1985), pp. 468-90.

42. (Macmillan, London, 1938).

43. See K. Joseph, *Stranded on the middle ground,* (Centre for Policy Studies, London, 1976). Also, K. Joseph and J. Sumption, *Equality* (Murray, London, 1979).

44. (Centre for Policy Studies, London, 1984), p.3.

6

America

I

Many of the anti-consensus arguments adumbrated in previous chapters originated in America. Classical liberal economic theories have always had a more secure hold there than elsewhere in the West. Obviously, the history of that country has had a great deal to do with this. A country founded on the principles of individualism, property rights, free enterprise and limited government was bound to generate a philosophical and economic literature favourable to those values. A country that had no experience of feudalism, where land was originally freely available for occupation, and a large part of whose population consisted of refugees from European tyranny, would be more attracted to individualistic economic values and distrustful of government. It is still largely true that in America conservatism (in a dispositional sense) is individualist, *laissez-faire* and rather un-European precisely because the *tradition* in that country is Lockean and libertarian — a point made with great eloquence by Louis Hartz[1] many years ago.

This has of course, posed a difficulty for American political nomenclature, for in that country, liberalism almost invariably means economic interventionism, egalitarianism (albeit somewhat muted), distrust of 'business' and a strong role for the state (i.e. the federal government) in the promotion of welfare. For this reason, I use the word 'liberal', in this chapter only, in the American not the European sense. American liberalism uneasily comprises a commitment to an expansion of liberty in individual moral conduct, literary expression and so on, and a highly regulatory role for political authorities in economic matters.

One clear example of the difference between American liberals and American conservatives is in their attitudes towards the Supreme Court (and judicial review in general): the liberals prefer an *activist* Court charged with interpreting the Constitution broadly so as to ensure a more positive role for political authorities (especially in the expansion of civil liberties), while conservatives yearn for a Court that resists the trend of legislative and executive action and restores what they think to be the original individualistic eighteenth-century constitution. However, there is a complication here, because the liberals, although they want an active Court with regard to civil liberties, prefer the Court to be supine and inert in the face of central and state governmental *economic regulation,* as indeed it has been since 1937. Unlike in Britain, the judiciary plays a major role in American political thought and the question of constitutionalism will be dealt with in more detail at the end of this chapter.

Despite the long tradition of individualism in American political thought, the free market and limited-government social philosophy has suffered a series of almost fatal setbacks this century. The popular image of America may be one that depicts a capitalist haven, but the ruling consensus in political thought and practice there has until very recently not been different from that in Britain and Western Europe. Again, the reaction to it is not intellectually dissimilar, although the American new Right is more robust (and more specifically tied to the American experience) than its European counterpart. Furthermore, the social-democratic economic consensus never quite swamped the intellectual world as it did in Britain: for example, the Chicago University Economics Department resisted Keynesian macro-economics almost completely and kept up a virulent but highly technical 'monetarist' economics during the heyday of demand management. That same department, under the leadership of Frank Knight, also developed a broad libertarian economic and social philosophy which was given a popular exposition by Milton Friedman. This meant that in economics at least there was a fully developed alternative to the consensus when that began to show serious strains in the late 1970s.

In many ways the American social-democratic influence on government policies preceded that in Europe; for the massive federal interventions that produced the welfare state in the 1960s (President Johnson's 'Great Society') were seen by some to be a natural extension of Roosevelt's New Deal, designed to cope with the economic dislocation caused by the Great Depression of the 1930s. It is difficult to abstract contemporary American political and economic thought from that experience. For American liberals this

showed the failure of a self-regulating economy to realise the country's economic and social potential. It was claimed that the
catastrophic drop in output and employment that occurred after
1931 demonstrated that a private property-based, unregulated
economy produced misery for the masses and vast wealth for a
minority. What stood in the way of decisive political action was the
American Constitution itself, with its separation of powers, limited
government and a judiciary that appeared to protect individual property rights against the public interest.

From 1937 onwards, however, the Supreme Court ceased to be
a serious obstacle to interventionism. Furthermore, the 1960s 'war
on poverty' programme, the high-point of post-war American
liberalism, was subject to very little in the way of judicial review. By
then the American economy had been subject to an unparalleled
degree of economic regulation and anti-trust legislation. In addition,
the Supreme Court, under Chief Justice Warren,[2] had handed down
a number of highly controversial liberal decisions in the areas of race,
personal liberties and the rights of suspects in police investigation.

The *laissez-faire* and conservative strands of American economic
and political thought have been equally influenced by the Great
Depression, for libertarians have always claimed that it was government intervention itself, especially the mismanagement of the
monetary system by the Federal Reserve System (the American
central bank, created in 1913), which disrupted what would otherwise be an automatically equilibrating market system. In fact, libertarians claim that not only were the policies and institutions created
by the New Deal intellectually unsound and in practice ineffective,
but also that they permitted the vast growth in federal power and
spending which has threatened the free order.

Although the intellectual problems raised by government
spending, welfare and social justice are common to British and
American political thought, there are two areas in which the recent
experience of the two countries shows important differences: the
question of trade unionism and the race issue. In America unions
have historically been of less political importance than in Britain.[3]
Membership by the workforce has always been less in America (at
present only about 22 per cent of American workers are unionised
and a disproportionate number of these are government employees)
and the unions are not so closely linked to the Democratic Party
as their British counterparts are to the Labour Party. Consequently
there has been less legislation favourable to trade unions (though
legal immunities do exist). Thus the consensus in America did not

sanction 'corporatism', or deals between government, business and unions, in the way that it did in Britain.

The race issue, while clearly not unimportant in Britain, has not had the same constitutional and political significance that it has in America. If there was one position that American liberals unanimously shared, it was the belief in the necessity of reverse discrimination (or, as it is called, 'affirmative action') to relieve the social and economic problem of blacks, and other minorities. Because America nominally has a constitution which protects individual rights (which might be adversely affected by affirmative action), certain crucially important political, jurisprudential and philosophical questions were raised by the race problem. As we shall see below, the new Right in America has been very much concerned with this.

Opposition to the American liberal consensus was especially muted in the first two decades after the last War. Apart from the economists, who were engaged in the narrow, technical exegesis of monetary theory in a small number of universities, it was largely conservative in a broad social and cultural sense. An important event was the publication in 1953 of Russell Kirk's *The Conservative Mind*,[4] which established a body of conservative 'principles', albeit of a rather un-American kind. The first significant intervention into the political field by a classical liberal economist was Milton Friedman's *Capitalism and Freedom* (1962), although it should be pointed out that Friedman had for many years been working on a vast critique of monetary policy and its effect on the Great Depression. There had been, of course, many less well-known figures[5] since the Depression who had rejected the growing consensus but undoubtedly the experience of the rise of the 'New Left' in the 1960s, with its attack on freedom of speech in the Universities, gave the Right a great fillip. Of great significance in the renaissance of conservative thinking was the fact that the New Left launched its attack on specifically *liberal* institutions and policies. This suggested to many social critics that the massive social reforms and interventionist policies of the 1960s had done much to undermine American social stability and traditional values of freedom and responsibility — although much of this may well have been the (temporary) result of the radicalising effect of the Vietnam War.

What became 'neo-conservatism' can be seen very much as a response to liberal excess. Influential figures in this are Irving Kristol and Daniel Bell (founders of the public-policy journal, *The Public Interest* in 1965), Norman Podhoretz, Robert Nisbet and a host of others anxious to re-examine critically the post-war American experience. Many of these neo-conservatives were ex-liberals, still prepared to defend liberal social 'ends' but desperately unhappy about the means (mainly big government) used to bring them about.

On the other hand, there has also been the emergence of a more populist, certainly less intellectual, conservatism which wants to reverse the permissive social tendencies of recent years; it also makes noises about the undesirability of more familiar targets, such as deficit spending, big government, excessive welfare and so on. This is the 'Moral Majority'[6] movement and other associated religious organisations. However critical they may be about the evils of modern government, they certainly want to use all of the political machinery available — Congress, the Constitution, the Supreme Court, and the state legislatures — for the imposition of their values (e.g. anti-abortion law, censorship of pornography, prayers in schools, some action against homosexuality and so on) on American society. In some ways their claim that all this is legitimate because they represent the true majority is rather un-American, at least in a constitutional sense, since that tradition is anti-majoritarian. The paraphernalia of federalism, the separation of powers and judicial review was an intricate constitutional design to *prevent* the imposition of majoritarianism on a free people. Nevertheless, it cannot be denied that there is some similarity between these movements and the 'populism' that was such an important feature of American politics at the beginning of this century.

However important the Moral Majority may be politically, I shall say very little about it in this chapter. The concern here is with the intellectual features of the political and economic thought of the new Right in America. Although the great conservative coalition that produced Reagan's presidential victories included these somewhat authoritarian elements, what is remarkable about it was that it had the backing of some of the foremost figures in American conservative social thinking, many of whom, especially the *economic* liberals, had social views diametrically opposed to those of the Moral Majority. I shall discuss these in the sections that follow.

II

I mentioned earlier that conservatism in America, in the dispositional sense of the word, is liberal individualist because that is the tradition of that country. The implication of this is that there cannot really be an indigenous American conservatism which does not to a

great extent embrace those very ideas which some European conservatives have found wanting. However, this would not be quite
true of all American conservatives; Hartz's description of the
American political tradition as Lockean is not universally accepted.
It is not, evidently, the view of the country's foremost conservative
thinker, Russell Kirk. Although he has not had a tremendous
influence on the contemporary new Right, his policital thought not
only has intrinsic interest but a brief consideration of it is also helpful
in the exploration of the nature of American anti-consensus thought.

In *The Conservative Mind* Kirk introduced Burke to American
political ideas, as if Burkean thought were a replacement for the
prevailing Lockean, natural rights and 'revolutionary' interpretation
of the past. Of course, there is an immediate ambiguity here since,
as I have indicated earlier (see above, chapter 4), Burke has much
more in common with the free-market tradition within conservatism
than is often supposed; so that to see the American political tradition
in Burkean terms is by no means to reject the case for economic
liberty. In addition of course Kirk does not repudiate economic
liberty. What he does, however, is put economic freedom in the
context of a constitutional order which places more emphasis on
spiritual and cultural values than on money-making. Thus his
thought is hostile to much of industrialism and extreme *laissez-faire*
economics as well as the rise of big, federal government. There is,
therefore, *political* virtue in the American tradition of strictly limited
government, judicial review and rule of law; a virtue that made the
American 'revolution' a conservative event since it established, or
re-established, these phenomena which had been undermined by
British colonialism. If there is a specifically American *motif* in Kirk's
conservatism it is its implicit reverence for the Southern political
order and the constitutional doctrine of states' rights. The South
is the only example of aristocratic politics in American history and
its ordered, basically class society has had a particular appeal to
some American conservatives, especially as the dominance of the
federal government began to undermine the traditional *federalist*
political structure. It is from this position that we must view Kirk's
despair at the 'rootless masses' created by urbanisation and industrialisation and his critique of 'Manchesterian economic theory'.

Though much of what Kirk says is at odds with what is today called
the new Right, especially in economic matters, it is a sophisticated
articulation of one strand of American conservatism. The trouble
is that it is really out of date and in many respects too European to
gell easily with American values. Perhaps Goldwater's presidential

platform in 1964, and certainly the political ideas of Senator Robert Taft,[7] reflected something of this conservatism, but the contemporary intellectual Right is much less inclined to reject industrialism and classical liberal economics and much more keen to construct a conservatism that accommodates what it regards as the genuine American tradition, free enterprise, individual rights and so on, and also even certain inescapable features of the twentieth century, such as welfare.

The neo-conservatives are attempting something like this, although it must be said that they have been more successful in the critique of certain prevailing trends in American society and politics than in constructing a coherent conservative alternative. Many of those writers who are associated with the journal *The Public Interest* are in fact ex-liberals, driven to conservatism by the excess of American liberalism, and most have not actually abandoned the ends of liberalism. In the aphoristic words of Irving Kristol (who is actually an ex-Marxist), a neo-conservative is a liberal mugged by reality.[8] Many of the neo-conservatives are social scientists, such as Edward C. Banfield, James Q. Wilson and Nathan Glazer, who came to reject interventionist American liberalism through more or less empirical investigations of typical Great Society social programmes such as the war on poverty, school busing and other attempts at enforced racial integration, and social security. In these studies the conclusions they reach are little different from those of the classical liberal economists.

Nevertheless, although the neo-conservatives do not have the religious impulse of the Moral Majority nor the ethical commitment of the older conservatives, they must be clearly differentiated from the free-market economists. In the writings of Daniel Bell and Irving Kristol especially, the social deficiencies of *laissez-faire* are eloquently exposed. Important here are Bell's *The Cultural Contradictions of Capitalism*,[9] and Kristol's *Two Cheers for Capitalism*[10] and *Reflections of a Neo-conservative*.[11] In their version of neo-conservatism, we find a doctrine or set of ideas which rejects both extreme economic liberalism and socialism.

The basic argument is that there is a crisis in American values which capitalism cannot solve, despite its undoubted practical successes: a crisis which indeed capitalism has generated because the free society which it has produced is internally self-destructive. At one time the capitalist system was underpinned by the Protestant ethic, or some surrogate for this. Not only did this impose a moral constraint on personal excess (in the original bourgeois value system, the end of all human activity was not consumption), but also within it, reward was correlated with effort; wealth was not arbitrarily distributed but intimately connected to virtue. According to the neo-conservatives, however, the link between modern capitalism and bourgeois ethics has been broken. Advanced industrial societies, especially late twentieth century America, are characterised by modern nihilism: there are no values beyond consumption and, for intellectuals anyway, the freedom of the market has included within it the freedom to destroy the market.

Hence, the production of anti-market literature, films, books and Marxist courses in private universities is, in Kristol's pithy phrase. 'just another business opportunity'. The market offers, in a sense, too much freedom and its failure to generate internal bonds of loyalty portends ill for its survival. Furthermore, that selfishness which powers the exchange system in goods and services is potentially fatal to social values. There is, then, no invisible hand at work to produce equilibrium in the moral world as there is in the economic world.

The real threat to a free society does not come from socialist economics, and Kristol is openly contemptuous of the claims made by collectivists that central planning can improve on capitalism in the production of wanted goods and services. The trouble is that the vacuum left by amoral capitalism has been filled by socialist ethics. Egalitarianism will always be more appealing than that pattern of inequality produced by the market, which has no moral justification at all, and is not even claimed to have by its defenders. Kristol makes this point in a clever essay, 'When Virtue loses all her Loveliness'. Here he claims that the famous Hayekian argument that the distribution of income in a market does not necessarily reflect moral *desert* in any way, but merely the value of labour services as revealed in exchange, has fatal consequences for the ethical viability of capitalism. Kristol claims that men 'cannot accept for long a society in which power, privilege and property are not distributed according to some morally meaningful criteria'.[12] He seems to be saying that however fallacious the arguments for social justice (i.e. that income should reflect some extra-market criteria such as merit or need) are in the light of the logic of neoclassical economics, such a stance has destroyed the acceptability of capitalism, not just for the collectivist intelligentsia, but for the rest of society.

Thus although Kristol would argue that American liberal social policies in the 1960s produced unanticipated disasters, and that the new Left's morality is little short of a return to barbarism, the

philosophy of capitalism (or its lack of a philosophy) is as much to
blame for the moral nihilism of our times. In fact he would claim
that whatever success socialism has had is a function not of its
economics but because it is, in effect, *anti-economics*. It rejects the
notion of man as a maximiser, who realises his true 'self' through
accumulation, and who has no values beyond the cash nexus, just
as some traditionalist conservatives do.

It would be a mistake, though, to assume that Kristol and the
neo-conservatives yearn for a value system that transcends
capitalism, that rejects the market in favour of some gnostic per-
fectionism. Neither is there any sympathy for the intrusion into
private life that is entailed by the policy aims of the Moral Majority.
There is certainly no emphasis on religion in neo-conservative social
thought (despite the fact that America is a highly religious society).
In a sense, morality is instrumental for Kristol and Bell, a necessary
means for the maintenance of a liberal capitalist order — an order,
pace Hayek and Friedman, which is not self-sustaining. Nevertheless,
Kristol has on occasions justified some legislative constraint on
pornography, though it is not clear quite what the intellectual
rationale is for this, apart from that kind of paternalism that seems
to accompany almost any conservative disposition. Of course, if a
thinker does not accept the outcomes of an exchange process (subject
to the rule of law) as being *for that reason* legitimate, then all sorts
of *ad hoc* interventions in the process can be justified.

Nor are the neo-conservatives against welfare provided by the
federal or state governments. The particular problem of welfare will
be treated later in this chapter, but at this point it is worth mentioning the neo-conservative position. As might be expected, there
is no *one* neo-conservative attitude to welfare. As I have suggested
earlier many of their criticisms of welfare programmes centre on
means rather than ends, and on the unfortunate expansion of
political power that inevitably accompanies them. Certainly Kristol
is not opposed to state welfare, though it is by no means clear what
form he believes it should take. There would perhaps be a general
preference for welfare to be a state and local responsibility in its
entirety rather than shared between the federal administration and
the other layers of government in America. Also, neo-conservatives
would demand much stricter conditions for the qualification to
welfare entitlement.

III

Conservatism in America in recent decades has been associated with classical economic liberalism rather than high-flown tradition-alistic metaphysics. This is partly because the classical economists have been attacking interventionist economic policies with an economic philosophy that could be readily identified with the (at least) pre-1930s American tradition, and partly because the most sophisticated critiques of the American post-war consensus were almost exclusively derived from economics. Furthermore, in some contrast to the aforementioned neo-conservatives, these economists were not at all concerned with morality: they denied that American capitalism was in a crisis of values; it was simply being mismanaged. Indeed, the Chicago economists especially (but they were by no means unique, an identical position being held by the Virginia School of public-choice economics) were concerned to argue that debate about values was intellectually inconclusive and in practice potentially destructive. In fact, the familiar claim was that among intellectuals and the public at large, there is much less disagreement about (American) values than is commonly sup-posed. To Kristol's question — What if the free-market society generates an anti-freedom ethic? — I assume that the economist would say that it does not. They would further argue that anti-market philosophy is very largely the property of an intellectual elite (many of whom are, ironically, employed in *private* universities). The real danger to the market order came from entrenched groups in American society which were in receipt of government privileges and exemptions from the rule of law, or were employed by the government itself. The members of such groups did not have un-American ideas; they were merely driven by self-interest — a very American idea.

The most dominant voice of conservative economics has un-doubtedly been that of Milton Friedman: for not only has he made formidable contributions to technical economics (which we are not concerned with here) but has also produced, in a series of books and articles, a political economy of freedom. Some of Friedman's ideas have been considered earlier (see chapter 2) and we shall therefore consider here only those which are primarily relevant to the American experience. Although there is much in Friedman's philosophy that gells easily with the 'old-time religion' of sound money and limited government, it would be quite mistaken to brand it as merely conservative — for he is unquestionably a radical, indeed an economic rationalist, who is prepared to take the idea of freedom, in all its aspects, to where it may lead him. The conventional 'Left-Right' political spectrum is never more inappropriate than when applied to Milton Friedman's economic liberalism.

Milton Friedman's politics are quintessentially utilitarian and structured around his scientific economics. Every policy proposal or institutional reform is carefully analysed in terms of its measurable consequences. Throughout his career it is difficult to discern any real changes of ultimate economic principles but only minor alterations (derived from observation and experience) in the methods by which they might be implemented. Most important here is a detectable movement towards a heavy emphasis on *constitutional* control of politicians in his latest writings.

Running through Friedman's political economy there is a fierce anti-elitism, a Mandevillian faith that public benefit will emerge from private, selfish action and an old-fashioned American scepticism of the claims of politicians. The latter point is at the heart even of his most technical expositions of monetary theory and history, for he has always been an advocate of 'rules' against 'discretion' in the conduct of monetary policy. The authorities should be limited by strict rules and not have the latitude to vary the supply of money in order to bring about some particular policy. Friedman (with Anna Schwarz) attempted to show that it was the inept monetary policy of the Federal Reserve Board (in fact, of course, Friedman argues that the Federal Reserve System should never have been established) that turned a mild recession into the Great Depression of the 1930s. By engineering a massive cut-back in credit, many banks collapsed thus creating a severe deflation. It was the catastrophic drop in purchasing power that brought unemployment up to 25 per cent of the workforce and vast under-employment of the capital stock. Thus the results of this research were not merely that the Keynesians were wrong in thinking that 'money does not matter ' (it clearly did then), but also that centralised and therefore discretionary control of the money stock was unreliable. Thus, all attempts at 'stabilisation' policy should be eschewed: the market itself is stable, and it is the political process itself that is potentially disruptive.

This distrust of central banks continues to the present day. The key point is that although the Federal Reserve Board is nominally independent, its obligation to maintain a stable (and predictable) currency is highly vulnerable to political pressure.[13] Under Reagan, for example, Friedman maintains that although an attack on inflation was obviously desirable, the disinflation proceeded too quickly, producing over ten per cent unemployment by the end of 1982. Other commentators[14] have pointed to the erratic and unpredictable behaviour of the Federal Reserve Board even under a government much more disposed to 'orthodox' monetary policy than any other since the War.

It should be noted here that it is not merely inflation to which Friedman and other 'conservative' economists are opposed; even more serious is *unpredictable* change in the general price-level. From the 'natural rate of unemployment' hypothesis it follows that in the long run, unemployment will be the same whatever the rate of inflation. Since the natural rate is determined by structural features of the economy (see chapters 2 and 5), inflation may only *temporarily* succeed in lowering unemployment: once people correctly anticipate it, it will have no effect. The real harm is caused by erratic monetary policy which makes it difficult to anticipate the future price-level.

Whereas at one time Friedman thought that the central bank could be bound by ordinary rules, he now seems to think that it cannot be — neither does he think that it can be relied upon to operate a Gold Standard effectively. Instead, he now suggests that there should be a *constitutional amendment* to oblige the Federal Reserve 'to increase the quantity of money it issues at a fixed rate year in and year out'.[15] This, he assumes, would be much more effective because it would insulate the central bank from political pressure. Constitutionalism, in the strict sense is, of course, a part of the American political tradition in a way that it is not in Britain.

The distrust of the political process extends to other aspects of economic life — most notably the explanation of the inexorable rise in *federal* government spending as a proportion of GNP in America.[16] He has also linked (somewhat crudely) this rise in government spending with a threat to freedom and democracy — at one time suggesting that few domocracies could survive if public spending exceeded 60 per cent of GNP. Although he has never doubted the good intentions of those in government he detects a kind of reverse Adam Smith effect. In *Free to Choose*, Milton and Rose Friedman suggest that individuals are led, as if by an invisible hand, to produce a complex and costly set of regulations and interventions, the sum of which was not specifically intended by any one of them.[17]

It is argued therefore that the massively expanded social-security system, aid to farmers, federal educational assistance and so on, all sum to a *total* of public spending that is clearly inefficient, yet the recipients of such aid have no incentive to forego their advantages. The benefits of a reduction in public spending are too diffused and thinly spread to motivate individuals to refrain from pursuing their private group-interests. Even when public opinion turns against government spending, as it has done in recent years, it is difficult to translate that into effective policy. This is largely due to what Friedman called the 'iron triangle' — a combination of the direct beneficiaries of government largess, the legislative committees and their staffs that make the laws, and the bureaucracies that administer the laws. All of these exercise 'tyranny' over the anonymous public.

What happens under loose democratic rules is that the demands of groups on government generate vast government deficits. Presumably, if the demands for increased public spending had to be met immediately by increased taxation, this would in a democracy dampen the enthusiasm of the electorate substantially. Therefore, a balanced-budget rule is the key to cutting spending. Once again a proposed constitutional amendment (at present a movement to get one passed is under way) enforcing a rule on the federal government is favoured by Friedman.[18] This would not require the federal government to balance its budget each year but over the course of the trade cycle. Thus the argument here is not against public spending in a democracy *per se*, but only against an existing procedure that distorts the true costs of such spending.

Those who have followed Friedman's policy stances over the years will find an over-all consistency. However, other economists in the past decade have pursued a superficially more radical classical liberal economic doctrine — 'supply side' economics.[19] This is not the place to consider even briefly this much talked-about intellectual trend but some mention must be made of it. The Reagan government included many avowed supply siders and its early policy seemed to be based on the principles they espouse.

In fact, all classical liberal economists are supply siders, where this means only that they reject Keynesian emphasis on *demand* management as the route to prosperity and stress the importance of opening up the market to entrepreneurial opportunity, and of reducing government and taxation. The old classical liberals might well claim that the phrase 'supply side' has been simply hijacked. Where so-called supply siders might be differentiated is their belief that tax cuts are more important than balancing the budget. In fact,in some versions it was claimed that such would be the extra economic activity created by massive tax cuts that the government's income would actually rise: there would then be no need to cut government spending. The more traditional classical liberal economists doubt this; they believe that instant tax cuts would create a massive government deficit which would have to be covered by government borrowing (on the assumption that it is not financed by printing money). The effect of this is to drive up interest rates and hence private investment would be 'crowded out' by heavy public-sector borrowing.[20]

The disputes beteen the various strands of free-market economics may seem scholastic to an outsider. In very broad terms, Friedman is a supply sider. Of course, he wants to cut public spending and tax less; it is just that he now takes a constitutional route in an attempt to determine a procedure that will make high public spending difficult for an indefinite future rather than rely on the good-will of transient politicians. That is why the demand for a balanced budget rule *sounds* conservative.

In the light of the demands of classical free-market economics the experience of the Reagan government since 1980 is ambiguous. In comparison with other Western governments that have followed (broadly) anti-collectivist policies, its success seems remarkable. The economy has grown considerably and by the end of 1985 unemployment was down to seven per cent. Unfortunately, the almost complete failure to cut public spending has resulted in a deficit of, by some estimates, $160 billion. All economists agree that this bodes ill for the future: not only that but it has enabled Keynesians to claim that it validates the consensus orthodoxy, since growth and reduced unemployment have coincided with typical fiscal laxity (i.e. the budget deficit). However, what has not occurred is the predicted Keynesian inflation.

The free-market liberals would claim that basic micro-economic factors explain America's recent success. It is still a relatively open economy in which entrepreneurial flair is rewarded. There has also been some important deregulation which has provoked competition and price-cutting, the most spectacular example being the airlines. Perhaps the least discussed fact is the fall in the real wage in America, the classic free-market remedy for reducing unemployment. In all this the relative unimportance of trade unions, at least in comparison with other Western democracies, must not be under-estimated.

Nevertheless, the key problem located by Friedman as the major cause of the breakdown of free economies, the omnipresence of 'politics' and pressure-group activity in economic life, remains virtually undiminished. It was the presence of powerful groups, especially in welfare, education and defence, that prevented those cuts in public spending on which a proper supply-side economics depended. In Congress, almost all Democrats represent groups; very few can genuinely claim to represent the public interest. Friedman is probably more far-sighted than most in his claim that group privileges must be attacked *all together* (in a rather un-political manner) and that constitutional protection is required to prevent further political encroachment on individual choice in the market.[21]

It is this emphasis on individual choice that differentiates Friedman from genuine political conservatives. The contrast with neo-conservatives like Kristol is instructive, and with 'European-ised' conservatives such as Russell Kirk, it is spectacular: for markets, although they require a framework of rules and procedures to be effective, do not require some special kind of morality to sustain them; free exchange systems generate an appropriate personal ethic. Thus Friedman is by no means indifferent to personal responsibility; on the contrary, he believes that only the removal of government from vast areas of life, especially welfare and education, will bring forth that responsibility. Unlike many apocalyptic conservatives who repeatedly express despair at modernity, at rootless and amoral 'mass man' and at industrial society, Friedman has almost unbounded faith in the ordinary man, if only he is left free to choose and has to pay for his choices.

It is, however, a faith tempered by empiricism, for it is as much the demonstrable folly of government that drives him to apparently extreme positions. To take one topical example, the consumption of addictive drugs. Even though Friedman concedes that there might be a *moral* case for government intervention here, the consequences of such intervention are, he claims, so counter-productive that they negate the moral argument. Thus, with simple economic reasoning, it can be shown that by banning drugs a black market is immediately created which raises their price above what the free-market price would be, hence encouraging an increase in crime, especially street crime, from which we all suffer. I cannot envisage many conservatives endorsing Friedman's conclusion that the drug laws should therefore be repealed.

IV

The question of welfare, and more especially government's role in its delivery, has greatly excited new-Right anti-consensus intellectual thinking in America. Dissatisfaction with the 1960s 'War on Poverty' (which it is estimated cost more than the Vietnam War) has in many important ways united both traditional conservatives and the more radical *laissez-faire* economists. It is not just a cost-benefit question which is at issue: as we shall see, there is a general agreement that the anti-poverty programmes of the 1960s have been largely ineffective, but also involved is the moral problem of welfare itself. To what extent do generous welfare provisions undermine personal responsibility and the role of the family? Is redistribution morally justifiable (even if it were efficient)? Does the desire for equality adversely affect liberty? These and similar questions are as much part of moral and political thought as they are social accounting. In addition, in America the very fact that historically blacks have been disproportionately poor in comparison with whites has inevitably and inextricably tied the race question to the general welfare problem.

There was, in fact, a welfare consensus (which to some extent still exists) that embraced almost everybody in America, including conservatives and, ironically, *laissez-faire* economists, such as Milton Friedman. Although there is a strong belief in the importance of eleemosynary activity in the solution of the problem of poverty, nevertheless, practically all conservatives believed that there should be an additional role for the state. The favourite response is a more simplified cash-transfer system to the poor (popularly known as the negative income tax, or NIT) to replace the complex web of entitlements, many in-kind, that welfare states normally develop. However, as we shall see, even this, when tried, has produced spectacularly disappointing results. The backlash against welfare has therefore been against a much wider consensus than is commonly thought.

There have been two important books that have influenced contemporary anti-consensus thinking on welfare: George Gilder's wide-ranging and somewhat polemical *Wealth and Poverty*[22] and Charles Murray's sober, scholarly but ultimately devastating critique of President Johnson's Great Society anti-poverty programme, *Losing Ground: American Social Policy 1950-1980*[23]. While these studies mainly concentrate on the counter-productive nature of government's attempts to alleviate the genuine indigent, there is another strand of critical welfare thinking: this is about the unintended redistributive effect of the whole range of welfare policies — there is an observed transfer of resources from poor to better off and young to old brought about mainly by the Social Security Act (1935).

The aim of the War on Poverty was not just to help the needy (in 1950 it was reckoned that one-third of Americans were below the poverty line) but ultimately to reduce the numbers of those who depended on government (either federal or state) for an acceptable standard of living. Of course, it has been a feature of *laissez-faire* social thought that as prosperity increased, the 'welfare state' would gently wither away. The 'left wing' welfare programmes were (perhaps unwittingly) an endorsement of this philosophy; they were indeed targeted at those who for social reasons had been unable to realise the American dream of individual independence and economic self-sufficiency, especially blacks who had suffered systematic discrimination. According to the critics, what happened was the reverse; social dependency *increased* and the original philosophy of individual responsibility gave way almost completely to the idea that 'society' was somehow to blame for all the ills and misfortunes individuals might suffer in contemporary America.

Throughout the 1970s the 44 major welfare programmes (paid by the federal government and administered by a variety of local bodies) grew two-and-a-half times faster than the growth in GNP and (excluding the social-security benefits nominally paid for by past payments) paid out $200 billion in grants and services to about 50 million people a year. The major programmes are AFDC (Aid for Families with Dependent Children, Medicaid and food stamps).[24] For many families the gap between what they could receive in welfare payments and the average American wage was remarkably small. There were also many agencies involved in job creation, employment training and establishing economic opportunities, much of whose work was aimed at equalising opportunities for minorities.

There is growing evidence that despite this vast expenditure, the problems of poverty are in fact getting worse. Murray reports the changes in the percentages of 'latent' poverty i.e. those who could be in poverty but for the existence of government assistance. This is an important concept because it measures how successful welfare policies have been in enabling people to gain individual independence. Latent poverty fell from about one-third of the population in 1950 to 21 per cent by 1965 and to about 18 per cent by 1968. However, as the programmes began to take effect the figures began to rise: latent poverty rose to 19 per cent in 1972, 21 per cent in 1976 and had reached 22 per cent by 1980.[25] Despite massive government intervention, job opportunities for (especially young) blacks actually declined. Between 1965 and 1980 4.9 million new low-skilled jobs were taken up by whites but blacks suffered a net loss of 117,000 jobs. Also, there seemed to be a growing correlation between welfarist policies and the break-up of the traditional family structure. Again the black community shows the most striking figures. In 1950 20 per cent of all live births to black mothers were illegitimate; today the figure is very nearly 50 per cent.[26]

These figures seem to confirm a belief long-held by critics of state welfare in classical liberal tradition — that is, they generate the phenomenon of 'moral hazard'. This is the idea that the existence of a policy designed to help a group simply encourages the size of that group to grow. It occurs in private insurance markets where protection offered against a hazard attracts people most likely to experience that hazard. Classical liberals identified a problem endemic to all state welfare: there is no set of extra-market anti-poverty measures which will not have the effect of encouraging more people to become poor. Milton Friedman and others, who have pioneered the idea of a negative income tax, were well aware of this; they merely argued that a cash transfer to the indigent would be more efficient, less demanding and more consonant with freedom and choice, than the prevailing complex of in-kind payments.[27] They also thought that private charity ought to be encouraged because, although it does not eliminate moral hazard, it is likely to have stricter eligibility rules than state welfare. It is also to be noted that *laissez-faire* theorists do not attach any moral opprobrium to claimants of state welfare; they are behaving quite rationally in response to a signal. It is doubtful that the more moralistic conservatives are so tolerant of such action.

In effect, Murray argues that the experience of the War on Poverty proved the existence of moral hazard on a massive scale. To the chagrin of liberal (in the American sense) social scientists much of the popular prejudice about welfare was born out by the evidence. The popular prejudice can be formalised into three respectable propositions:

(1) people respond to incentives and disincentives;
(2) people are not naturally industrious or moral; and
(3) if society is to function people must be held responsible for their actions.[28]

The American welfare system has failed, he claims, because these propositions, which are common to conservative and classical liberal thought, have been ignored. Predictions that ignored them, especially those related to the economic conditions of blacks, turned out to be almost completely false. A particularly damning statistic was the rise in black unemployment among 20 to 24 year olds, which had reached 40 per cent by 1980. The inescapable conclusion for Murray is that the benefits accruing to unemployment were just too attractive. The breakdown of the family was encouraged by the economic advantage of being an unmarried mother through the AFDC scheme. Many commentators have noticed the plight of the unemployed black youth, who turned out to be the major victim of well-intentioned but unsuccessful welfare policies.

The only positive achievements of the War on Poverty are the markedly improved employment and career prospects of (surprisingly) blacks in the older age-cohort (45-54 years old) and the noticeable increase of blacks in middle class occupations.[29] It seems to be the case that an attitude favourable to independence and individual responsibility persisted in the older age-groups while those in the younger groups had no opportunity to acquire such a morality because of the welfare programmes: these produced a kind of welfare culture rather than a work culture.

It should be stressed that Murray's case does not rest solely on the monetary value of the various welfare benefits (in fact the *real* value of AFDC and food stamps declined between 1970 and 1980) but on the whole complex of political and court rulings that eased the eligibility requirements. Important here are two Supreme Court decisions — one that struck down state residency requirements for welfare and one which allowed payments to be made to unmarried mothers when there is 'a man in the house'. In normative terms, the critics claimed that the whole system abolished the distinction between the deserving and the undeserving poor. Gilder proposed a blunt and decidedly unfashionable solution: 'The crucial goal should be to restrict the system as much as possible, by making it unattractive and even a bit demeaning.'[30]

To add to the despair of American social-welfare theorists came the disappointing results of some NIT experiments conducted by the OEO (Office of Economic Opportunity) in the late 1960s and early 1970s. Although this has always been the favoured anti-poverty policy of *laissez-faire* conservatives, it is obviously in breach of Murray's three fundamental axioms. It is, indeed, a spectacular example of 'throwing money at a problem' — a charge economic liberals repeatedly make against interventionists. There had always been a fear that in principle its cost would be horrendous. In fact, one of its supposed virtues has turned out to be a vice: the complete absence of *stigma* in the scheme (it is paid automatically through the tax system whenever income falls below a specified level). Furthermore, take-up is obviously 100 per cent.

The results from Seattle and Denver (1971-78)[31] showed the same results as other welfare schemes. NIT reduced incentive to work by 9 per cent for husbands and 20 per cent for wives. For young males, who were not heads of households, hours worked per week were down 43 per cent. The effects on the family were equally disastrous: dissolution of marriage was 36 per cent higher for whites who received the NIT compared with those who did not; and for blacks the figure was 42 per cent.

After results like this the conservatives had really no way to go except back to recommending a much harsher system of social welfare — indeed, one more consonant with certain pessimistic principles of human nature, principles which moralistic conservatives and classical economic liberals had always believed to be true anyway. Of course, proponents of the NIT could always claim its disincentive effects will fall, the lower the amount that is paid, but how low would it be allowed to fall? More traditional conservatives now claim that schemes like the NIT miss the whole point. The problem of welfare is ultimately a moral one, that the prevailing system inculcates a 'welfarist' mentality quite unconducive to individual responsibility. They would claim that a distinction must be made between the undeserving and the deserving poor, that welfare must be difficult to obtain, and some element of stigma has to be attached to those in receipt of it. On these criteria, the NIT fails more than any other existing welfare scheme.

The prevailing mood of conservative welfare thinking can only be described as one of profound pessimism. There is a movement now towards designing institutions and policies that cultivate in some way a work ethic and make the notion of individual responsibility respectable again. Economic liberals undoubtedly believe in these virtues but their own proposals do little to encourage them. There is, nevertheless, a burgeoning idea, common to conservatives and *laissez-faire* liberals, that responsibility for welfare should be shifted away from the federal government to the localities and, most importantly, to voluntary bodies. This has not yet been fully worked out, but when it is articulated it will have as profound an effect on the American consensus as did the revolution in monetary theory.

It is not only the attempts to solve the poverty problem that have disturbed conservative critics of the American welfare system. There are many other aspects of it which dispel the illusion that it might some day 'wither away'. It is a consistent theme that much of government expenditure consists of paying back to the same individuals money collected from them in taxes — 'churning', as it is called by public-choice theorists.[32] This is simply inefficient. There is, however, a more serious problem to do with social security: this is the existence of 'unfunded' obligations to pay social security to future generations. This has implications for both efficiency and equity and indeed the long-run stability of American democracy.[33]

The most important feature of the American social-security system is the obligation to pay index-linked pensions, financed not out of funds invested in the stock market, but from the current yield of the (federal) pay-roll tax. The ability of the government to pay them depends entirely upon speculative assumptions about the economic growth rate and future demographic changes, and these are not encouraging. At present, the unfunded liability is reckoned to be eight trillion dollars and if the commitment is to be honoured, massive pay-roll taxes will be required by the middle of the next century. There is nothing egalitarian about this arrangement since higher pensions are paid to higher earners — people who can be assumed to be well able to take care of their own retirement arrangements. It also involves a massive transfer of resources from the young to the old, a system which each generation has every incentive to keep going.

To almost all conservatives the system illustrates too well the inadequacies of ill-thought-out welfare arrangements. Most importantly, it indicates the failure of liberal legislators to anticipate the remote consequences of their actions, and more particularly the inability of American political institutions in the twentieth century to protect individuals against central government — the very purpose for which checks and balances, the separation of powers and judicial review, were designed. As many classical liberals have argued, a major difficulty with extensive government involvement in welfare (and indeed the economy in general) is that it makes reform very difficult because any change is bound to hurt some people who have 'invested' heavily in the system: often, as in the case of social security, through no fault of their own.

V

I have suggested above that the consensus about welfare in American society inextricably involved policies to improve the well-being of racial minorities, especially blacks. It is appropriate at this point to review the general conservative reaction to the massive changes in law and policy with regard to minorities which have occurred in the last thirty years. It is difficult in American intellectual society to discuss the question of race dispassionately. All too often, critical attention is directed towards the *motives* behind the support or rejection of particular policies rather than towards an objective analysis of their consequences. It is almost always the case that biased or racist motives are attributed to any conservative or classical liberal who might question the wisdom of some of the legislative and political efforts made to improve the conditions of blacks in America.

This is not to deny that there has been some overt or covert racism in American conservative thought. However, the rational criticism of the consensus on the minorities question has tended to come from that individualist tradition in social and economic thought which would obviously eschew any relevance to policy questions of classifications based on race. Indeed, one of the most stringent criticisms of discriminatory policies in favour of, say, blacks as *a whole* is that they involve, inevitably, injustice to particular individuals in a way quite alien to the American legal and moral tradition. Furthermore, no conservative or classical liberal would deny that grave injustices have been inflicted on blacks and other minorities in America's past. Nor would they object to all of the judicial and legislative measures of the past thirty or so years that benefited minorities: the Supreme Court decision in *Brown v. Board of Education* (1954) which ended state enforced segregation in the public schools, and the 1964 Civil Rights Act which forbade discrimination in public employment and the public 'accommodations', were generally acceptable. However, cogent anti-consensus arguments have been raised against *enforced* integration and against what may be called a political and administrative attitude of mind which constantly seeks alleged examples of discrimination appropriate for correction by government action. Now that women and Hispanics have become the objects of anti-discriminatory action, it has been sardonically remarked that over two-thirds of the American population consists of exploited minorities! What is particularly objected to by economic liberals is the claim that *all* cases of inter-racial inequality are a product of genuine discrimination and that this can be solved by government action. As has frequently been observed, the most spectacular examples of racial discrimination, from South Africa to the southern states of America, emanate from political institutions of one kind or another.

The particular economic liberal argument about race and discrimination derives from the general theory of markets. Thus, although individualists stress the importance of equal rights and just and impartial laws, the bulk of their case against positive government intervention here rests upon a theoretical and empirical demonstration of its counter-productive effects. Furthermore, a cold and dispassionate analysis of discrimination, it is claimed, reveals some misleading impressions about its extent. A good example here is the explanation of the persistent lower wage-rates of blacks in comparison with whites: it is argued that the real correlation here is between *age* and lower pay, and since black workers and other minority races tend to fall disproportionately in younger age groups than whites, it is not surprising that they earn less.[34] Again, those who claim that there is widespread discrimination in the market ignore differentials that have a geographical explanation. The national average income for blacks is low, but outside the South (where more than half still live) it is higher than for some white groups, e.g. Mexican Americans and Puerto Ricans. What these data strongly suggest is that it is a methodological mistake to treat blacks holistically, as one whole group exhibiting common characteristics — but this is what many anti-discrimination laws and affirmative action policies typically do.

The anti-consensus argument about race rests on the proposition that the market is the least discriminatory of social and economic institutions. If men are driven by the desire for profit, then it will not pay them to discriminate on grounds of colour, or any other characteristic irrelevant to securing the most efficient use of resources. The more competitive an industry is, then the less discrimination there is likely to be. Activities not subject to price, such as non-profit organisations, can therefore discriminate at zero cost. Thus it is that from the (alleged) baser motive, the desire for profit, a benign outcome, a colour-blind economy, is likely to emerge. In governmental activities, because there is no price constraint, the absence of racial discrimination depends entirely on political goodwill. Throughout American history, government policy on minorities has lurched backwards and forwards in a more or less unpredictable manner.

The man who has made these and other related points with unparalleled sophistication and painstaking documentation is the brilliant black economist, Thomas Sowell. It would be a gross error to represent Sowell simply as a black economist since he has established his reputation as an orthodox neo-classical economist in the broad Chicago tradition.[35] His work on the economics of race is not self-contained but is logically derived from his *magnum opus* in social science and political economy, *Knowledge and Decisions*.[36] This is a theoretical and empirical demonstration of the virtues of the market as an information co-ordinating and signalling mechanism. The market represents an ongoing process of *incremental* change which allows mistakes to be corrected, whereas government is an organisation based on power which, because it makes *categorical* and final decisions, prevents that co-ordination process from taking place.

Sowell claims that minorities will always do better under the market than by depending upon the caprice of politics. He once said: 'I don't have faith in the market, I have the evidence of the market'. The role of government is to provide strict rules to make life predictable for economic transactors; if it goes beyond this to impose 'end-states' or particular results, it coagulates the incremental processes of the market. Federal minimum-wage laws, for example, had a disastrous effect on the employment prospects of young blacks (a point virtually ignored by Murray). By fixing the minimum wage above the market wage, this rendered many young blacks unemployable because for historical and social reasons their skills were not equal to the minimum wage. Interventions such as this reduce the costs of discrimination. In all societies, governments have the power to implement decisions but they do not have the local knowledge to make the correct ones.

Sowell does not oppose all of the legislative and judicial reforms of the 1960s aimed at eliminating discrimination. The 1964 Civil Rights Act was consistent with the legitimate role of government as the maker of general rules but 'affirmative action' programmes and 'job quota' schemes are not. These place an obligation on employers to provide appropriate representation for ethnic groups (and women) in the workforces, irrespective of the state of the labour market: demographic and age factors mean that some groups are bound to be 'under-represented' in certain occupations. Perhaps equally important is that such changes came about through administrative pressure from government agencies and not through a clear political decision. Furthermore, Sowell argues that affirmative action is implicitly in breach of the 1964 Civil Rights Act since the establishment of quotas must involve classification by race. Unfortunately, in key cases involving just this, the Supreme Court has been ambiguous.[37] Sowell insists that there is no evidence to show that affirmative action programmes have improved the economic well-being of blacks.

Like all neo-conservatives and economic liberals, Sowell makes a crucial distinction between the ending of politically imposed segregation (in schools, employment and so on) and the enforcement of integration, a process which imposes public choices on private actions. The latter reflects that localised knowledge on which effective decision-making depends. Thus he was not opposed to the Brown decision (although he has denied that segregated schooling is the cause of the lower IQ measures of blacks), but he is openly hostile to the later Supreme Court decisions, especially *Green v. County School Board* (1967), which led to 'busing' to guarantee an appropriate racial mix in public schools. This involved an intolerable degree of judicial intervention in the running of schools in an attempt to generate particular outcomes, whether they are desired or not by individuals.

In general, Sowell's conclusion is that blacks and other minorities in America have historically done better in the market than in government; even the ethically desirable goal of integration, he claims, was being gradually achieved by spontaneous processes in the late nineteenth century.[38] Far too many enthusiasts of the consensus, he argues, were eager to attribute the bad economic conditions of certain identifiable groups to malign forces at work in society rather than to economic necessity; he maintains that: 'Inherent constraints are not as exciting as sin but they are more central to economics.'[39]

Sowell provides a sophisticated expression of many of the vague doubts and badly articulated misgivings that conservatives have repeatedly held about the race question in American society. Hitherto, conservative opposition to special measures to help minorities came from either outright racists or Southern 'states righters' who used a constitutional argument against the federal government in order to perpetuate unjust practices against blacks. More important intellectually is the effect Sowell's analysis has had on 'optimistic' consensus social science. It is claimed that the interventionist measures of the 1960s were justified in terms of contemporary social science: indeed, many studies were produced showing evidence of poverty and discrimination which, it was assumed, government could correct. However, Sowell produced causal explanations, derived from more or less orthodox economic theory, as to why such phenomena exist and drew startlingly different conclusions and policy recommendations. He turned an emotionally charged argument about race into a sober analysis in social and economic science.

Political thought in America usually begins and ends with the Constitution, and particularly the role of the Supreme Court and judicial review. We have noted on several earlier occasions that classical liberalism and conservatism share a preference for law over politics, for strict rules over the discretion of authorities (elected or otherwise) and a distrust of majoritarianism. Freedom is inextricably bound up with law and procedures. Individualists' dissatisfaction with the British political system stems largely from the fact of the permissive nature of its 'constitution', which grants a *de jure* legislative authority to Parliament. However, they can take little comfort from the experience of America, for despite an apparently 'rigid' Constitution, the typical consensus policies have been pursued there with little formal restraint. That they have not proceeded as far as in Britain is as much a tribute to the temper of the American people, which is still broadly sympathetic to the free market, rather than to the presence of a significant institutional constraint. Nevertheless, as we have seen in the political economy of Friedman, American classical liberals still seek procedural and constitutional solutions to social and economic problems. The 'constitutional attitude' may have wilted over past decades but it is by no means moribund.

American economic liberals and conservatives maintain that their tradition is individualistic. The Founding Fathers designed the Constitution to limit government, to disperse power and to protect individuals from majorities. Their faith in the people was not so unbounded that they thought that government could be eliminated altogether but political leaders and centralised authority had, nevertheless, to be narrowly confined. Madison's classic observation on the delicate balance between anarchy and autocracy is still relevant to American individualism today. In *Federalist* No. 51, he wrote: 'But what is government itself but the greatest of all reflections on human nature? If men were angels, no government would be necessary. If angels were to govern men, neither external nor internal controls on government would be necessary.' Clearly, the present power of the federal government and its intrusion into private affairs have extended way beyond the intentions of the framers of the Constitution. It is true that the federal structure does permit a variety of different institutions, laws and tax policies among the component states, and this allows individuals and organisations (as Olson has shown — see chapter 3) to flee to areas more favourable to enterprise, but the hand of the federal government is present in areas undreamt of 50 years ago.

James Buchanan, the public-choice economist, argues that America is fast approaching a state of constitutional anarchy. In perhaps one of the finest statements of constitutional liberalism (of the eighteenth-century classical variety), *The Limits of Liberty*,[40] he maintains that the 'blocking mechanisms' of the American political system (and other Western liberal democracies) have broken down. In his view a stable constitutional order requires a body of 'higher law', represented in what he calls the 'Protective State', which is a product of virtually unanimous agreement. This states standards of just conduct, rules of contract, and entitlements to property. While not immutable, such a body of law should only be changed by general agreement. The actions of government, what he calls the 'Productive State', should be limited to the production of public goods and services in accordance with procedures laid down by agreed upon rules. The role of a judicial body, as part of the Protective State, is to enforce impartially the basic rules, of contract, for example. It should not endeavour to make law or to respond to the particular and momentary desires of the citizenry.

Buchanan's abstract contractarian political philosophy can be translated into terms which enable us to understand the present 'crisis' in American constitutionalism. The Productive State (Congress, if you like) has gone beyond the delivery of essential public services and taken over large parts of the private economy. It has taxed not merely in order to finance its essential operations, but to redistribute income; and not only that, but the very structure of Congress produces majority votes on the basis of coalitions of interest groups rather than on the representation of a genuine majority will. Equally important is the fact that the Supreme Court, instead of enforcing neutrally and impartially the fundamental rules of the Protective State, has actively engaged in law-making itself.

This latter point is most noticeable in the Warren Court which in a number of decisions concerning civil liberties, the rights of suspects in criminal cases, electoral reapportionment, 'busing' to enforce integrated schools and affirmative action, has usurped the functions of legislatures. Perhaps more important is the fact that since 1937, the Court has exercised amazing judicial *restraint* in the face of legislative encroachment on the rights of private property and on freedom of contract. The general conservative and economic liberal point here would be that the switches in opinion that the Supreme Court has made on various issues has meant that it is no longer a neutral enforcer of agreed upon law but the mouthpiece of the prevailing intellectual fashion. That element of predictability which a genuine liberal-individualist order requires has been badly compromised.

Anti-consensus political thought on the Constitution in America has centred on the role of the Supreme Court (in fact, there has been one attempt to clip its powers). One tradition holds that the judicial body should uphold neutral principles, i.e. interpret the Constitution in such a way that it favours no political ideology. The difficulty here is that it is impossible to specify uncontroversially what such neutral principles might be. The general orthodoxy in American political science suggests that in some way or another the decisions of the Court will reflect changing opinion in society. It should also be noted that such a position of neutrality is not necessarily conservative, for it might well imply that the Court should refrain from too great an interference with the legislative branch.[41]

Both Right and Left in the American political spectrum have reason to be highly critical of the Court. Conservatives maintain that after 1937, when it abandoned substantive economic due process, rights of contract and property were continually violated as the New Deal progressed. However, American liberals have always claimed that the Supreme Court was not interpreting the Constitution neutrally but imposing its *laissez-faire* economics and untrammelled freedom of contract on the American people. Furthermore, they claim that the Court was resisting the will of the American people, which had given President Roosevelt and the Congress a mandate for substantial economic reform. Arthur Selwyn Miller argues that the period between the Civil War and 1937 represents 'the most blatant attempt at judicial economic Government ever attempted in this country'.[42] Now, of course, the Left in American politics admires the Court precisely because it has retained substantive due process for non-economic matters and has clearly resisted the majority will in a number of civil-liberty cases. The Warren Court ruled that evidence extracted from a suspect who had not been informed of his rights was inadmissible, extended school desegregation, struck down state-sponsored school prayers and created a fundamental 'right of privacy' amongst other exercises in judicial law-making.[43] Much of this continued under the Burger Court[44] in which for some years the conservatives were still in a minority; especially important was *Roe v. Wade* (1973) which prevented the states legislating on abortion.

The conventional position now seems to be that personal rights and civil liberties have a higher priority than economic liberties. Substantive due process applies here, i.e. the Court will look very closily at the content of a state of federal statute to see whether it conflicts with the constitution, but not in economic matters (normally those involving property and contract) where legislatures have virtually been given a free hand.

In political thought a standard conservative and economic liberal argument is that the presumption in favour of personal liberties has no constitutional foundation but is a typical piece of judicial activism. However, the argument goes further than this. At the theoretical level it is maintained that liberty is indivisible, that no categorical distinction can be drawn between economic liberties and other liberties. As Friedman has often maintained,[45] the mere declaration that there is a civil right to free expression would be vacuous unless there were also economic rights to property and private income. A collectivist society, through economic compulsion, could significantly restrict a free press while formally acknowledging it. Although this *general* argument has little applicability to contemporary America, economic liberals nevertheless claim that the abandonment of economic due process has left both the protection of private property and freedom to contract to 'unreliable' legislatures.

This is not to say that all conservatives necessarily oppose the widening of civil liberties under the Warren Court and its successor. It is certainly true that the religious new Right has been infuriated by, for example, the school-prayers decision and the judgements concerning abortion and contraception, but my main concern is with the political thought of economic liberals (of libertarians) and the more theoretical conservatives. Here, the argument is the Court should be more neutral in its judgements and less supine towards the legislature's persistent whittling away of property rights. What they would like to see would be the Supreme Court merely *vetoing* suspect legislative and executive action on the basis of more or less unchanging principles of constitutional law. What is particularly objectionable to conservatives is the fact that judicial activism has involved the Court in administration. This is especially apparent in its desegregation decisions which have involved Court officials in the indirect management of school boards.

Conservative and economic-liberal legal theorists want the Supreme Court to reassert this veto power to restrain economic legislation by Congress or the states. This is as much a political theory as it is a legal theory since it incorporates the notion of judicial review into a general philosophy of limited government. It presupposes that the job of the Court is to declare the 'higher law' of the Constitution against the 'positive' law of legislatures. Its intellectual rationale depends upon a sophisticated critique of the economic doctrine that the Supreme Court has drawn upon in its validation of economic legislation and on a scepticism concerning the claim of legislatures to represent a genuine popular will. Both these problems, as well as an economic liberal theory of law, are explored in Bernard Siegan's path-breaking study, *Economic Liberties and the Constitution.*[46]

The period when the Supreme Court recognised substantive economic due process operated from the adoption of the Fourteenth Amendment in 1868 until 1937, when the High Bench 'switched' in the face of Roosevelt's threat to 'pack' it (although the turn around was presaged by an important decision in 1934). During this era the Court used the prohibition against the taking of property without compensation contained in the Fifth Amendment and the clause in the Fourteenth Amendment, which prohibits depriving 'any person of life, liberty or property, without the due process of law', to strike down legislation from the states which was designed to regulate the economic affairs of individuals. This legislation regulated working hours, factory conditions, pay and prices and granted trade-union recognition.[47] The Supreme Court did not deny that legislatures could regulate health and safety under the 'police power', but such purported legislation was subject to stringent tests: there was, indeed, a presumption in favour of individual economic freedom, especially liberty of contract.

The most notorious case was *Lochner v. New York* (1905) in which a statute limiting the hours that could be worked in bakeries was struck down. The individual's right to contract was, in this case, sacrosanct. In *Lochner*, the dissenting Justice Oliver Wendell Holmes made his famous observation that the American Constitution did not implement Herbert Spencer's *Social Statics*. In defence of the period up to 1937, Siegan argues that the regulations and controls that were struck down were largely made at the behest of big business anxious to eliminate competition.[48] Also, the proposed limitations on workers' freedoms would have hit the poorest in the community and caused unnecessary unemployment. According to Siegan, what is conventionally assumed to be a black period of American history was in fact an era of unprecedented prosperity and freedom (at least up until the Great Depression).

The end of substantive economic due process was signalled by

Nebbia v. New York (1934), a case in which price regulation of milk was upheld. Substantive economic due process did survive briefly but the end of the (alleged) *laissez-faire* court can be traced to the 1937 case of *West Coast Hotel v Parrish,* in which a Washington State statute establishing minimum wages for women and minors was upheld. This was followed by the acceptance by the Court of major items of Roosevelt's New Deal programme, the Railway Labour Act, National Labour Relations Act and the Social Security legislation. From this date onwards the Court upheld all economic regulation of private industry and the view became accepted that judicial review should not be used against the legislature on economic matters, apparently because the remedy, if required, was to be found in the political process itself. However, it was argued at the time that substantive due process should be relevant to issues affecting minorities who, it was assumed, had limited access to the political system.[49] This was the beginning of that distinction between personal freedom and minority rights on the one hand, and economic liberties on the other, which conservatives and libertarians find so objectionable.

It is perhaps a forlorn hope that the Supreme Court will reassert its power to review economic legislation, but there are conservatives who think that it should do so. It is argued that, for example, the minimum-wage laws could be challenged as breaches of the contracts clause in the Constitution, and that the prohibition on the taking of private property for public use without just compensation be used more aggressively. However, the political infeasibility of an activist Supreme Court in the economic sphere has presumably caused economists, such as Milton Friedman, to favour constitutional amendment as an alternative.

The case for a more adventurous conservative judiciary is largely based on criticism of the economic thought alluded to by the Supreme Court. The acquiescence in the fact of economic legislation seems to be derived from the belief that the market is not self-regulating and the idea that a *laissez-faire* economy would lead to undesirable business concentration. Yet conservatives maintain that regulation tends to favour established businesses, which 'capture' the regulatory agencies and, in fact, restricts competition.[50] Furthermore, the reliance on the political process is, it is claimed, misplaced because modern political economy has shown that simple majority-rule procedures do not reflect the common good (if there is such a thing) but only coalitions of interests. In a comparison between the likelihood of judicial error and legislative error on economic matters, it cannot be assumed that the legislature is necessarily right.

The conservative who demands the restoration of substantive economic due process, or at least some kind of control over the economic activities of legislatures, might appear to be vulnerable to the charge that he is sanctioning the very kind of judicial activism he finds so objectionable in the Supreme Court of recent times. However, it could be argued that this would not be judicial activism; it would simply be the enforcement of the rights that already exist in the Constitution. Thus, so far from the period from 1868 to 1937 being one in which the Supreme Court imposed its conception of economics on the legislatures and the American people, it was merely *declaring* what the Constitution said. It is, of course, claimed that this was not so, that such excessive judicial control of legislative action is not sanctioned by the Constitution, and that indeed, the wide liberty of contract which the Justices invoked is not expressly granted by the document. It is of course true that much of Siegan's argument could be seen as an exercise in political theory — a reconstruction of the American 'higher law' as a body of indivi-dualistic rules and procedures. His argument is that the constitu-tional tradition (and the intentions of the Founding Fathers) is one that emphasises economic liberty, private property and freedom of contract even if the document does not explicitly state this.

Notes and References

1. See L. Hartz, *The liberal tradition in America* (Harcourt and Brace, New York, 1962).
2. Some recent decisions of the Burger Court have, however, been more conservative.
3. See J. Burton, *The political future of American trade unions* (Heritage Foundation, Washington D.C., 1982).
4. (Faber London,).
5. Notably the journalist H.L. Mencken.
6. For an account, see G. Peele, *Revival and reaction* (Oxford University Press, London, 1984), chapter III.
7. The Republican Senator who lost the presidential nomination to General Eisenhower in 1952.
8. Quoted in R. Nisbet, 'The conservative renaissance in perspective', *The Public Interest*, no. 81 (1985), p. 135.
9. (Basic Books, New York, 1976).
10. (Basic Books, New York, 1978).
11. (Basic Books, New York, 1983).

12. I. Kristol, 'When virtue loses all her loveliness' in D. Bell and I. Kristol (eds), *Capitalism today* (Basic Books, New York, 1971), p. 8.

13. M. and R. Friedman, *The tyranny of the status quo* (Penguin, Harmondsworth, 1985), pp. 93–9.

14. See D. Fand, 'Paul Volcker's political legacy', *Policy Review* Fall, 1985, *34* pp. 58–63.

15. Friedman, *The tyranny of the status quo*, p. 99.

16. In 1930 *federal* spending was less than 4 per cent of US national income; it is now 30 per cent. For details see the Friedmans, *The tyranny of the status quo*, pp. 25–32.

17. M. & R. Friedman, *Free to choose* (Penguin, Harmondsworth, 1979), pp. 5–6.

18. The Friedmans, *The tyranny of the status quo*, p. 58. Most state constitutions already contain 'balanced-budget' rules. It should be noted that the Friedmans also favour a presidential 'item veto' on the budget.

19. See P. Craig Roberts, *The supply-side revolution: an insider's account of policymaking in Washington* (Harvard University Press, Cambridge, 1984).

20. David Stockman, originally a supply sider and Reagan's budget director, resigned in 1985 because he could not get increased taxes to reduce the deficit: see his *The triumph of politics* (The Bodley Head, London, 1986). This was regarded as an act of betrayal by the purist supply siders.

21. Friedman, *The tyranny of the status quo*, pp. 157–9.

22. (Basic Books, New York, 1981). This is actually a book on supply-side economics.

23. (Basic Books, New York, 1984).

24. Murray, *Losing ground*, p. 67.

25. Ibid., pp. 64–6.

26. Ibid., p. 140.

27. The Friedmans, *Free to choose*, pp. 119–24.

28. Murray, *Losing ground*, p. 146.

29. Ibid., p. 142.

30. Gilder, *Wealth and poverty*, p. 143.

31. Murray, *Losing ground*, chapter 11.

32. See Tullock, *The economics of wealth and poverty* (Wheatsheaf, Brighton, 1986), chapter 3.

33. See P.J. Ferrara, *Social security: averting the crisis* (Cato Institute, San Francisco, 1982).

34. See T. Sowell, *Markets and minorities* (Basic Books, New York, 1981), pp. 10–11.

35. Sowell is also a fine historian of economic thought, specialising in classical economics.

36. (Basic Books, New York, 1980).

37. In *Bakke v. Regents of University of California* (1978), a white student who argued that he had been discriminated against by an affirmative action programme was admitted to the University, but such programmes were not struck down.

38. See Sowell, *Markets and minorities*, p. 116.

39. Ibid., p. 81.

40. J. Buchanan, *The limits of liberty* (University of Chicago Press, Chicago, 1975); see especially chapter 4.

41. The leading exponent of constitutional neutrality was H. Wechsler: see his 'Toward neutral principles of constitutional law', *Harvard Law Review*, vol. 73 (1959), pp. 26–35.

42. Miller, *The Supreme Court and American capitalism* (Free Press, New York, 1968), p. 54.

43. Perhaps the most controversial decision was *Miranda v. Arizona* (1966), involving a suspect's constitutional rights.

44. See T. Eastland, 'Are we all judicial activists now?', *Policy Review*, no. 28 (1984), pp. 14–19.

45. M. Friedman, *Capitalism and freedom* (University of Chicago Press, Chicago, 1962), pp. 16–20.

46. (University of Chicago Press, Chicago, 1980).

47. See ibid., chapter 6.

48. Ibid., pp. 136–8.

49. This was the opinion of Justice Stone. For a critical discussion, see ibid., pp. 185–8.

50. For a critique of regulation, see G. Stigler, *The citizen and the state* (University of Chicago Press, Chicago, 1975).

7

West Germany

I

Throughout this study I have been talking about the reaction of conservatives and economic liberals to a semi-collectivist consensus, yet an analysis of the economic and political thought of postwar West Germany reveals almost the reverse process at work. Thus, throughout the 1950s and much of the 1960s, the Federal Republic of West Germany pursued a social and economic policy known as the *Soziale Marktwirtschaft* (or Social Market Economy) which embodies many of the principles described in the preceding chapters. There was at the time, and to some extent still is, a genuine consensus about its main features — they were enacted by the Christian Democrats (West Germany's conservatives) and the Social Democrats whenever they were in power. Two significant events illustrate the hold which this consensus had on the political establishment: firstly, the formal abandonment of Marxist socialism and the acceptance of the basic private-enterprise market economy by the Social Democrats at Bad Godesberg in 1959 (although only after much initial opposition); and secondly, the formation in 1966 (albeit temporarily) of a 'grand coalition' between the Christian Democrats and the Social Democrats, in which the latter seemed to be the more enthusiastic supporters of the market. Although in recent years the Social Democrats have reverted to a more orthodox socialist policy, their period of determined co-operation with the forces of capitalism was truly remarkable.

Yet just as in the early 1970s, political thinkers in Britain and America were first beginning to experience a reaction against Keynesian ideas and 'economic management' in general, and to doubt the efficacy of pressure-group involvement in policy-making, these same doctrines began to make headway in West German politics. From 1967, quasi-Keynesian demand management policies began to be adopted and a partial retreat from the Social Market Economy began in the early 1970s. A prominent market economist, Hans Lenel, wrote an important article in 1971 entitled, 'Do We Still Have a Social Market Economy?',[1] and Karl Schiller, the Social Democrats' Minister of Economics, resigned in 1972 because of the statist trend in government policy (although he had been instrumental in advocating Keynesian fiscal policies). In the past decade, West Germany has begun to exhibit many features of the British disease, especially in relation to welfare spending; but nevertheless, the economic system there still retains those basic elements of freedom and constitutionalism which are deemed to be worthy of imitation. The major works of the theorists[2] of the Social Market Economy are now being translated and exported to Britain and America; indeed it is somewhat ironic that they are today being received with greater acclaim than they ever were in the heyday of the system.

Before examining in detail the economic and political thought of the Social Market Economy, it might be helpful to look briefly at the circumstances in which it arose. From 1936–48, during both the Hitler and the Allied Occupation periods, the German economy was subject to rigid controls. Price fixing, rationing and a hopelessly inefficient monetary system had produced ruinous economic results: output plummetted, the black market flourished and barter had replaced normal monetary exchange. The Allied Occupation powers, engaged in the process of denazification, were determined that West Germany should not have a liberal market-economy. In fact, the economic advisers at the time were Keynesian and broadly sympathetic to economic planning. However, it was realised that currency reform was essential and Ludwig Erhard (chief official of the Administration for Economic Affairs for the British and American Occupation Zones), the architect of the German 'economic miracle' and later West Germany's Chancellor, used the occasion of the establishment of the new Deutschmark to secure (by the use of not a little chicanery) the immediate lifting of a whole range of price and other controls.

This was greeted with scepticism by the Allied economists. None other than John Kenneth Galbraith was economic adviser to the American Military Government and he made the following comment on the liberalisation programme: 'There has never been the slightest possibility of getting German recovery by this wholesale repeal, and it is quite possible that its reiteration has delayed German recovery. The question is not whether there must be planning . . . but whether that planning has been forthright and effective.'[3] Yet the subsequent events showed Galbraith, and almost all conventional economic observers at the time, to be spectacularly wrong.

As the liberalisation of the hitherto controlled economy proceeded throughout the 1950s, West Germany quickly recovered.[4] From 1953 to 1963, GNP grew at an annual average rate of 6.7 per cent, compared with 4.7 per cent in France and 2.7 per cent in Britain. Alongside that of Britain, West Germany's performance in industrial output and exports was phenomenal, and by the 1960s the country was on top of the European economic league. Although other factors than the Social Market Economy were important, such as a vast surplus of labour from Eastern Europe which reduced pressure on wages and ensured (relative) trade-union docility, the application of that particular economic philosophy was instrumental in securing this remarkable transformation. There was no German economic 'miracle' but merely the result of the pursuit of well-tried economic orthodoxies (although by then they had become almost radical). Some credit must also be given to Erhard, as senior Economics Minister in the Adenauer government, for sticking to free-market principles against many pressures, not least from interest groups which, if they had been as successful as they were in Britain, would have disrupted the process of economic recovery. Nevertheless, there was no 'pure' market economy in post-war West Germany. There were many state interventions of which perhaps the most significant was the deliberate use of fiscal policy to encourage personal savings.

It is a significant fact that the Social Market Economy was imposed on the German people almost as if it were a 'rational plan'. Most commentators doubt that it had much support from the major political groups, and but for the ruinous situation at the time it might never have been given a hearing. It is also pertinent to note that Germany's defeat had effectively destroyed all those special interest groups that have succeeded in undermining the market system in Britain and America. However, once the success of the Social Market Economy became manifest, the doctrine came to be embraced by all the political parties.

What is also surprising is that the doctrine should take root in a country whose intellectual traditions in economics, philosophy and politics were collectivist. Nineteenth-century German economists were 'historicist': they resisted the claims of abstract theorists, who derived complex doctrines from fairly simple and purportedly universal propositions about human behaviour, in favour of an economics which stressed the uniqueness of particular epochs. One epoch of which they were critical was the contemporary capitalist era. The rapid industrialisation of the nineteenth century was blamed for the misery and poverty of urban life which they observed. There is a long practical and intellectual tradition in Germany which favours positive state action to produce that 'welfare society' which it is felt that an untrammelled market cannot generate: it is a tradition that lingers on even in the theories of the Social Market Economy.

That small group of liberal thinkers that worked either outside or inside Germany during the Hitler period was therefore something of an aberration in German intellectual history. Yet a coherent strategy for a post-war market society was worked out and its theoretical foundations laid down in the years immediately following the ending of hostilities. The thinkers in this movement are often called German neo-liberals, but a more appropriate collective title might be the 'Ordo Group', named after their annual publication, *Ordo: Jarbuch für die Ordnung von Wirtschaft und Gesellschaft.*[5]

II

Many economists and social thinkers were, and still are, involved in Ordo.[6] Although there is a theme common to them all, they may be conveniently divided into two strands: the Freiburg Group, a faction concerned mainly with economics, in which the outstanding names were Walter Eucken, Franz Böhm and F. Meyer, and a more socially and politically oriented movement, whose major figures were Alfred Müller-Armack, who originally coined the phrase, Social Market Economy, William Röpke, and Alexander Rüstow. Röpke is particularly important because his social thought is suffused with a deep, pessimistic conservatism which threatened to suffocate his undoubtedly liberal economics. Also, Müller-Armack should be singled out because his almost obsessive concern with the 'social' features of the Social Market Economy gave an intellectual licence to the straying from rectitude, especially in relation to welfare, that occurred in the 1960s and 1970s.

The first characteristic to notice about the philosophy of the Ordo Group is that its members dismissed both central planning and *laissez-faire*. The rejection of collectivism is easy to explain on grounds of both experience and theory. Central planning in Germany had been a disaster which they had personally witnessed: it had produced shortages and a gross misallocation of resources; it had achieved full employment but, as Eucken shrewdly observed, this was only secured by virtually conscripting workers into producing goods that nobody wanted. The absence of the price mechanism produced industrial chaos, but the cost of this was more than economic: the destruction of personal responsibility for action that collectivism entailed also generated a certain kind of moral deformity.

The scepticism about *laissez-faire* is perhaps surprising but it is expressed with varying intensity by all the writers in the Ordo Group. Rüstow claimed that it was neither 'worthy of preservation nor capable of preservation'. Röpke claimed that 'like pure democracy, undiluted capitalism is intolerable'. In Erhard's published writings there are disparaging comments on 'Manchesterism' and repeated declarations that he was 'unwilling to accept without reservation and in every phase of development the orthodox rules of a market economy according to which only demand and supply determine price'.[7] Thus, despite a clear recognition of the virtues of free exchange, the prevailing theme of the Ordo writers was that the market was not autonomous and self-sufficient, in sociological, economic or ethical terms. It had to be constantly shaped and moulded so as to bring about some kind of harmony, or social optimum, that transcended merely economic considerations, and which could not be generated spontaneously.

The rejection of unalloyed *laissez-faire*, however, should not be interpreted as a commitment to the 'middle way' or the 'mixed economy', even though Röpke occasionally referred to the Social Market Economy as the 'Third Way' (as being distinct from both capitalism and socialism). Its theorists did not simply borrow bits and pieces of *laissez-faire* and planning on pragmatic grounds but articulated a fully autonomous social philosophy in which the market played a predominant but not exclusive role. This was, of course, why the Austrian *laissez-faire* theorist, Ludwig von Mises, rejected it and why Hayek had some doubts about it.

The objections to an uncorrected market were both technical and moral. The technical objections were based on the argument that the market showed a tendency to self-destruction, i.e. that unlimited free exchange would produce monopolies, cartels and a level of industrial concentration that would destroy economic freedom. In addition, though I think that this was less significant for the theorists of the Social Market Economy, an uncorrected free-exchange system produced economic cycles which may require some overall direction (though not of a Keynesian kind). The moral deficiency of the market lay in the fact that as an institution, it was ethically neutral, no more than an instrument which was required as a preliminary for individuals in their pursuit of higher, more 'spiritual' ends. As Müller-Armack put it: 'No economic order is of itself ethical . . . We merely believe that the market economy places fewer obstacles in the path of applying ethical principles to economic life.'[8] Encompassed within this ethical dimension is the view that income distribution may have to be altered by extra-market criteria on the grounds that a free exchange does not necessarily provide a level of welfare for everyone which a humane political economy requires. It is worth looking at these three objections in more detail.

Undoubtedly, the historical record of the German economy inclined the Ordo writers to the view that a free market would spontaneously generate ultimately fatal (to both efficiency and freedom) imperfections. German industry had showed a tendency to concentration, a process which was said to be hastened by a decision of the Supreme Court in 1897 which legalised cartel arrangements. Before the last War, the German iron and steel, coal and chemical industries were dominated by nine cartels, and banking by three large banks. Just how effective cartelisation was in the reduction of competition is disputed but, nevertheless, Eucken and other Ordo economists were convinced that an economy subject to no guiding hand from the state and law showed a chronic tendency to the 'closure' of the market.

Thus, although Eucken, for example, maintained that the state undeniably closed the market more effectively than any other social institution, there were still serious problems that were *endogenous* to the free-exchange system. These would come to the fore through unlimited freedom of contract. The state should therefore constrain those freely-negotiated contracts that had a tendency to bring about the destruction of freedom itself. In a perfectly competitive economy there can be no such thing as 'market power', since no one agent can influence price, but this is highly unlikely to be realised in the real world, and therefore the state had a duty to maintain competition should spontaneity fail. The Allied Occupation administration managed to break up the major cartels but the problem continued to bother the German Federal Republic until anti-cartel legislation was passed in 1958.[9]

Whether a *laissez-faire* economy produced a tendency to chronic unemployment was disputed by the theorists of the Social Market Economy. They were by inclination micro-economists who saw unemployment as emanating from defects in the competitive system. At the macro-level, then, their main concern was that government should provide a stable currency. Macro-policy should be limited to monetary policy — with the object of preventing both inflation and deflation. Although they speculated on the possibility of contra-cyclical policy, they feared that whatever success it might have in the short run, it would have long-term deleterious effects on the competitive conditions obtaining in a market economy. Certainly Eucken eschewed the deliberate pursuit of a 'full employment' policy by Keynesian methods; indeed, he stressed the inevitability of frictional unemployment if an economy was to adapt to changing circumstances.

The alleged ethical neutrality and mere instrumentality of the market led to the inclusion of the adjective 'social' in the Social Market Economy, but it is perhaps the most difficult element in the doctrine to describe. All that seems to be clear is that the market should serve a particular form of desirable society: a form of social freedom that transcended the freedom to exchange. This would entail some considerable welfare and, in the doctrine of Müller-Armack at least, a state-directed form of income distribution which altered the familiar determination of wages by marginal productivity. Nevertheless, all the Social Market Economy writers expressed a hostility to conventional 'welfarism' which, through undiscriminating payments, destroyed that sense of personal responsibility on which a free society depends.

III

From this critique of pure *laissez-faire*, it is apparent that the notion of a Social Market Economy represents an understanding of society in more than economic terms: it is an order of inter-related parts. The German word used to describe this is *Wirtschaftsordnungspolitik*. This means that an economy is not just a system of exchange but a 'constitution', a set of rules and practices, within which economic transactions themselves form only a part. An economy may be self-correcting in terms of formal quantity and price, but it is not the autonomous creator of those rules in the absence of which transaction is impossible. Eucken talks of an *Ordnungspolitik* consisting of *constitutive* and *regulative* principles.[10] The constitutive principles include the rules for the ownership and use of private property, a stable currency, (qualified) freedom of contract and personal responsibility for action. The regulative principles include control over monopolies and other general rules to preserve the functioning of a competitive order. A system of rules would provide that control which a market economy needs, but would exclude the necessity of a personalised and centralised system of authority.

Müller-Armack was more ambitious and metaphysical in his explanation of the Social Market Economy. In his view it was a balanced or 'irenical'[11] order which recognised the plural and competitive nature of men's goals. A purely competitive system was mechanical and therefore indifferent to men's goals. In his somewhat arcane language, a society is a 'magic triangle whose corners are marked by the goals of economic freedom, economic and social security and growth'.[12] Only a corrected market, guided and modified by irenical principles could harmonise the conflicting goals which had led to destruction in the past.

The principles that govern state intervention flow naturally from these observations. There should be intervention to preserve the rules and procedures of the competitive system itself, not to interfere with the workings of that system. Government control should not be used to steer the economy in any particular direction, except to prevent spontaneous development from proceeding in a way which would be destructive of the price mechanism. In Böhm's illuminating image, the role of the state should be like that of a gardener 'tending his plants'. The favourite word used to describe and evaluate proposed interventions was *Marktkonform*. Did a particular intervention conform to the needs of a competitive order or did it impede it? Thus, in housing policy, accommodation assistance to the poor conforms to the market, rent control does not; cash payments to the poor aids the market, a minimum-wage law does not; the breaking-up of monopolies is permissible, nationalisation of industry is not; tariffs can never conform to the market. Müller-Armack was prepared to go beyond this. So concerned was he to maintain balance and harmony in society that he was prepared to tolerate subsidies to declining industries, payments to those adversely affected by changes brought about by the natural processes of the market, and even aid to agriculture.[13] Though he did say that such interventions should not impede the market, in practice, however, they always do.

More than any other liberal thinkers of their time, the Ordo writers were aware of the corrosive influence organised groups could have on the functioning of the competitive system. Their writings in the 1950s showed just that kind of disdain for 'group politics' that was to become standard in individualist writings in Britain and America in the 1970s. However, whereas in these two countries the influence of pressure groups, trade unions, business groups, farmers and so on, was attributed to an all-powerful state, Rüstow, perhaps more correctly, saw this as a sign of the state's 'lamentable weakness'.[14] It was unable to resist the pressure from organised interests to secure a price-control measure, an exemption from the rule of law, a subsidy or the grant of a monopoly privilege. No doubt, Rüstow and others were influenced here by their experience of the Weimar Republic, under which the state institutions were too weak to detach themselves from social conflict to lay down and enforce impartial rules.

Eucken was particularly perceptive in noticing the 'public-good' features of the Social Market Economy. It is a system of interrelated parts of great complexity, and neither its technical efficiency nor its virtues are likely to be comprehended by individuals. People may be quite competent in their own fields but incapable of understanding the economic and social order in its entirety.[15] More to the point, even if people were aware of the virtues of the market order they have no incentive to act in its interests as long as they cannot be sure that others will be so enlightened. This argument was insufficiently stressed by the theorists of the Social Market Economy. They tended to criticise 'rent-seeking' by interest groups in terms of moral failing rather than seeing it as an inevitable consequence of group action in the face of uncertainty. Therefore, their discussion of the *Ordnungspolitik* contained inadequate consideration of those *institutional* devices which are required to prevent the Social Market Economy from collapsing into a collection of warring groups.

The ideal form of political rule for the Ordo writers was a version of the *Rechtsstaat*, a body of impartial law administered without regard to personal or group interest. It depended ultimately on a kind of Hegelian conception of the state, an abstract institution above the competitive struggle of social life. It was only after the rise of public-choice theory in America that it began to be perceived that such a conception was headily unrealistic. It turned out to be the case that the Constitution of the Federal German Republic, although it contained many admirable features, was inadequate to constrain that pressure-group activity which is such a prominent feature of contemporary democratic politics.

I have shown that the Ordo theorists rejected 'economism', the idea that a free society can be conceived of entirely in mechanical terms. A Social Market Economy, according to Müller-Armack, is ultimately a moral order.[16] Their notion is vague, imprecise and capable of either a liberal or a conservative interpretation. It was given a more conservative meaning in the social philosophy of Röpke, much of whose work evinces that pessimism, if not outright despair, which has come to be so symptomatic of conservatism in the English-speaking world. Though he was a prominent figure in the Social Market Economy movement and made significant contributions to its pure economic doctrine, his later more speculative works exhibit a generalised critique of 'modernity' which is not always harmonious with liberal political economy. One study, *A Humane Economy*,[17] has had some considerable influence on new-Right thinking outside Germany, although this is one of a trilogy[18] concerned with the ills and deformities of modern civilisation.

Röpke's qualifications on the market reflect the conventional views of the Ordo Group. The 'catastrophic' error of classical liberalism was to assume that the free-exchange system was morally autonomous: according to Röpke a true philosophy of liberty has to go 'beyond supply and demand'.[19] The dogmatic believer in *laissez-faire* is simply yet another exponent of that crass rationalism which has dogged European history and civilisation since the French Revolution. In Röpke's view, we have to delve more deeply into history and culture if we are to discover those principles of human conduct that are essential for a humane social and economic order. Hence his reverence for peasant communities; they have communal values and social bonds that transcend the pure individualistic cash nexus. The specific errors of modernity identified by Röpke are positivism, 'proletarianisation', consumerism, urbanisation and uniformity (*Vermassung*).[20] If the liberal order is to survive it must cope with the problems posed by these phenomena. Like many conservative thinkers, Röpke felt that the threat to Western civilisation came not from communism, the economic failures of which were manifest, but from that spiritual vacuum that rationalism had bequeathed.

Positivism, the philosophical argument that there are no transcendental moral values, that ethics is a matter of subjective choice, had done much to create that spiritual vacuum. It is noticeable that positivism is a feature of much classical liberal thinking. Some liberals claim that moral rules are at most artifices and contrivances which transactors need in order to bring about an essential predictability to human action. However, Röpke claimed that if it is denied that there are values that are to some extent 'natural' and universally shared,[21] then even a market economy can have no permanence and stability.

'Proletarianisation' is not a feature of modern society that describes only workers in large-scale industries: it is a characteristic of the form of employment which the modern economy has spontaneously generated — it is, in effect, the tying of the worker, whether he is in a factory, an office or a university, to a form of organisation. He becomes *dependent* and easily manipulated. This explains Röpke's somewhat romantic attachment to the independent peasant proprietor, a fast disappearing species that he was prepared to support by some form of state aid.[22] The decay of the rural economy has therefore produced a chaotic urbanisation. People have lost their identities in large centres of population and have become atomised 'abstract individuals who are solitary and isolated as human beings, but packed tightly like termites in their role of social functionaries'.[23] It is a mistake, claims Röpke, to suppose that an unending supply of consumer goods can be sufficient to create independent individuals, morally self-sufficient and therefore able to resist modern mass ideologies.

I have picked out these somewhat gloomy features of Röpke's thought (in fact, much of it does consist of sober economic analysis of a kind favourable to the market) to pin-point that strain in the thought of the Social Market Economy which is critical of *laissez-faire* for its moral inadequacies. It is noticeable that many of the features of modernity that Röpke regards as undesirable have emerged spontaneously. In fact, most classical liberals would not regard them as undesirable at all, especially consumerism. Röpke was by no means alone in his worries about ethics. Müller-Armack constantly talked of a 'Second Stage of the Social Market Economy';[24] a stage which would build on the economic success of liberalism to produce both a virtuous and prosperous order. It would be quite wrong to dismiss those thoughts as romantic speculations that have no relevance to liberal political economy, for it is the case at the height of its success, the Social Market Economy failed to excite the affection of large parts of the German population, especially its youth and intelligentsia. In the late 1960s, the advances of the German economy were openly condemned and Marxism, despite its proven economic failure and the close proximity of communist regimes to West Germany, began to flourish. Whether this was because the Social Market Economy had failed to generate an appropriate moral order, or that Marxism became just a fashion, it is difficult to say. However, Röpke had accurately diagnosed a problem in liberal political economy: material success is not enough and, paradoxically, too much prosperity may be harmful to its long-term prospects.

V

Hard-headed observers of the Social Market Economy would argue that these questions about morality and mass society are peripheral to more pressing problems that began to beset the West German system in the 1960s. The more cynical among them might also argue that a 'Second Stage' of the Social Market Economy has indeed occurred — a degeneration from its true form brought about by the importation of alien ideas.

It is certainly true that certain key departures from the original principles of Ordo-liberalism took place from the early 1960s. Whether these were in response to economic difficulties, or actually precipitated them (as the purists maintain), is not really at issue here. What is important to note is that from about 1963 the Social Market Economy was gradually eroded:[25] by the subtle intrusion of Keynesian methods of economic management, by a rise in welfare spending, and by the open involvement of organised groups in the decision-making process. An important political event was the electoral defeat of Erhard in 1966; he had in fact been a more successful Economics Minister than Chancellor, but already, in 1964 a Council of Economic Experts had been appointed — an ominous sign, even though it had no formal power.

What happened throughout the 1960s was a gradual movement towards contra-cyclical macro-economic policy. The gathering of data, the setting of targets and concentration on 'aggregates' became the prevailing themes of government economic policy. The process was made more formal by the passing of the Law for Promoting Stability and Growth in 1967. This law proclaimed four overall targets of government policy: stable prices, high employment, balance of payments equilibrium and continued economic growth.[26] Of course, these goals were supposed to be reached *spontaneously* in the pure theory of the Social Market Economy. Perhaps the most objectionable feature of all this, from an Ordo point of view, was the development, under the Law, of a 'programme for concerted action'. This involved the representatives of business, trade unions and government officials in the process of achieving the four goals of economic policy. All this looks suspiciously like the 'corporatism' which was so conspicuous a feature of the Heath-Wilson-Callaghan years in Britain.

Although no coercive machinery was involved in the new German macro-economic policy, it marked a definite change in style from the 1950s and early 1960s. Throughout the 1970s targets were set, financial plans drawn up and moral persuasion used to bring decentralised transactors into line with national policy. A move towards Keynesian fiscal policy was made with the federal government running deficits, even though there is a constitutional provision that decrees balanced budgets. Again, the same sort of government by exhortation that characterised Britain's consensus years also occurred in West Germany, especially in relation to incomes policy. The new approach to economics even acquired an ideological slogan: the Social Market Economy now became the 'Enlightened Market Economy'. Schiller, who had been instrumental in introducing the new macro-economic ideas, eventually found the departures from orthodoxy too great and resigned from the Social Democratic Government in 1972. The Ordo purists now argue, not surprisingly, that the recent poorer performance of the West German economy dates precisely from the introduction of the new macro-economics.

From the 1960s there was also an increasing emphasis on state welfare policy in the Federal Republic, largely in the form familiar to observers in America and Britain. There has been a long process of decreasing reliance on private insurance for such things as sickness and old age; and the typical signs of a 'welfare culture' are beginning to appear.[27] The Constitution of the Federal Republic has proved powerless to prevent the vote-maximising process from inexorably pushing up the cost of state welfare. Just as in America and Britain, expenditure on welfare has exceeded the growth of GNP. The politicisation of welfare services has created a complex range of entitlements which have to be honoured irrespective of the state of the economy. The cost of these only becomes visible when the rate of economic growth slows up, as it has done in the past decade in West Germany.

Those who still hold to the basic tenets of the Social Market Economy argue that unrestrained electoral competition shortens the time-horizons of politicians. The short-run desire to be re-elected leads politicians to promise electors policy packages which are paid for in the future. The most spectacular example of this is the promise of earnings-related pension provisions financed on a 'pay as you go' basis. In West Germany the problem may be even worse than in America, for retirees are guaranteed a pension of 95 per cent of their working wage. Given that the West German workforce is ageing more rapidly than in any other comparable Western democracy, young workers there are going to be landed with truly massive taxes to honour this commitment before the end of this century.

Given that there was a strong welfare commitment in the original philosophy of the Social Market Economy, especially in the ideas of Müller-Armack, it might be thought that this process is unexceptionable. Indeed, the original plan was first to bring about German economic recovery by free-market methods and then to concentrate efforts on establishing a more humane and socially conscious order. However, there is little similarity between the present West German welfare system and the social thought of the Ordo Group. Böhm, Eucken, Erhard, Röpke, and even Müller-Armack to some extent, rejected the conventional form of the welfare state. Irrespective of its effects on efficiency, they argued that the level of *dependency* entailed by blanket state-provision of welfare services eliminated personal autonomy and individual responsibility for action. They would have recommended a much wider spread of private insurance against the vicissitudes of life and that state aid should be confined and limited by considerations of morality and economics. They were aware of the fact that welfare provisions have a tendency to increase the numbers dependent on welfare (see chapter 6) but were naïve in not anticipating the extent to which this would operate in a democracy. Nevertheless, they would not have approved of minimum-wage laws and the whole range of welfare provisions that now operate in West Germany to discourage workers from seeking employment and employers from hiring them.

Thus, despite their emphasis on *Ordnungspolitik*, or an economic constitution, they failed to devise adequate institutional arrangements which would prevent the decline of the Social Market Economy. Sometimes the impression is given, especially in the work of Müller-Armack, that the new economic order would produce an autonomous 'man', morally equipped to resist the economic seductions of the welfare state. From this perspective, the old *laissez-faire* school had a more realistic view of human nature: man is a maximiser who responds to signals, whether they are of a kind favourable to the market or conducive to its ultimate destruction.

Notes

1. '*Ordo: Jarbuch für die Ordnung con Wirtschaft und Gesellschaft*', vol. 24 (1971).
2. See *Standard texts on the social market economy* (Ludwig Erhard Institute, New York, 1982). For accounts of the intellectual foundations of the German Social Market Economy, see H. Oliver, 'German neo-liberalism', *Quarterly Journal of Economics*, vol. LXXIV (1960), pp. 117–49; and K. Zweig, *The origins of the Social Market Economy in Germany* (Adam Smith Institute, London, 1980).
3. Quoted in H. Willgerodt, 'Planning in West Germany' in A. Lawrence Chickering (ed.), *The politics of planning* (Institute for Contemporary Studies, San Francisco, 1976), p. 64.
4. For an account of West Germany's post-war economic history, see A. Gruchy, *Comparative economic systems* (Houghton Mifflin, Boston, 1977), chapter 5.
5. First published in 1948.
6. Major contemporary Ordo writers are Hans Willgerodt, Hans Lenel and Christian Watrin.
7. L. Erhard, *Prosperity through competition* (Thames and Hudson, London, 1955), p. 120.
8. A. Müller-Armack, 'Economic systems from a social point of view' in J. Thesing (ed.), *Economy and development* (Konrad-Adenaur-Stiftung, Mainz, 1979), p. 115.
9. Though some observers thought that this was unsatisfactory since exemptions are possible.
10. See W. Eucken, *The foundations of economics* (Hodge, London, 1950).
11. A. Müller-Armack, 'The principles of the Social Market Economy', *German Economic Review*, vol. 3 (1965), p. 94.
12. A. Müller-Armack, 'The socio-political model of the Social Market Economy', in *Economy and development*, p. 130.
13. Ibid., p. 135.
14. For an account of Rüstow's political thought, see C.J. Friedrich, 'The political thought of neo-liberalism', *American Political Science Review*, vol. XLIX (1955), pp. 509–25.
15. See Eucken, *The foundations of economics*, p. 29.
16. 'Economic systems from a social point of view' in Thesing (ed.), *Economy and development*, pp. 95–122.
17. (Wolf, London, 1960).
18. The two other titles are *Civitas humana* (Hodge, London, 1948); and *The social crisis of our time* (Hodge, London, 1950).
19. See Röpke, *A humane economy*, chapter III for a detailed discussion of the limits of the market.
20. Ibid., p. 36.
21. For Röpke's belief in objective moral standards, see his *The social crisis of our time*, p. 4.
22. Ibid., pp. 201–6.
23. Ibid., p. 10.
24. A. Müller-Armack, 'Thirty years of Social Market Economy' in Thesing (ed.), *Economy and development*, pp. 156–62.

25. For an account, see Gruchy, *Comparative economic systems*, pp. 152–60.
26. See ibid., pp. 153–4.
27. See W. Hamm, 'The welfare state at its limit', *Ordo*, vol. 34 (1982).

8
Conclusion

I

It should be apparent from the preceding chapters that despite serious differences between individual thinkers, and between the political traditions of the three countries studied, there is a common theme of 'new-Right' or anti-consensus political thought. The common theme is not merely anti-socialism (there have been anti-socialists ever since the genesis of socialism) but a more complex set of political attitudes, philosophical presuppositions about man and society, theories of market economics and doctrines of individualism, which sum to a general *movement* of ideas: a movement associated perhaps more with the critique of a prevailing intellectual fashion than with theoretical innovation — though, here it should be mentioned that individualist social philosophy has been innovative at the level of pure theory.

In this concluding chapter, I shall endeavour to draw together the various strands of this movement by focusing upon a number of general themes — namely, the nature of 'society', the value of politics, the theory of constitutionalism and democracy. In this brief overview I hope to suggest (yet again) certain differences between the liberalism and conservative variants of the anti-consensus movement of ideas, and indicate the kind of problems with which they are typically concerned.

II

The word 'society' has had peculiar significance in twentieth-century political thought. Of course, all political theorising is about society

190

in a trivial sense, but what is significant about interventionist or consensus thought is that society is treated as if it were an object or entity that has little or no self-sustaining and self-correcting mechanisms. In practical terms, this means that every problem is a 'social problem', requiring immediate attention through central action, rather than an individual problem that can be settled by following decentralised rules. To take the example of crime: the prevailing attitude has been that this is a social problem in the sense that delinquent behaviour is *caused* by malignant conditions that are somehow correctable. In a not (logically) dissimilar explanation, crime is a *disease* which requires treatment for the offender rather than punishment.

To an individualist, crime is not a social problem in this sense at all, it is the case of a person (or persons) breaking rules: actions for which he is responsible — for 'society' is not a person but a convenient label to describe the interactions of individuals under rules. It is of course true that we are born into a society whose structure and rules are not of our individual choice (a point stressed by conservatives against extreme individualists), but this does not diminish the crucial element of personal responsibility for action. Hence the conservative would make retribution the basis of punishment and reject the notion of 'treatment' entirely. Liberals (somewhat crudely) tend to treat crime as individual rational maximising action and therefore subject to cost-benefit analysis: it is reduced simply by raising its costs, e.g. stiffer sentences.[1] It is sometimes said, ironically, that if 'society' is to blame for crime, then everybody should be in the dock except the criminal!

This simple example exhibits a logic that could be extended across the whole of public policy: the social-science consensus always proposed a 'solution' to a problem rather than enquired into the reasons for its occurrence. The liberal view is that in many cases, once the explanation of an event has been discovered the 'social problem' simply disappears. A spectacular example is the phenomenon of homelessness in Britain. As the number of homeless people rises, the standard political response is to build more houses. Yet in this country we are witnessing the paradox of rising homelessness alongside increases in the number of housing units (and a more or less stagnant population). The liberal social scientist explains this by showing how rent controls and aids to home-ownership (through tax relief on mortgage-interest payments) distort the housing market. Rent controls dry up the supply of rented accommodation and the stimulus to owner-occupation drives up the price of housing beyond the reach of significant numbers of people. The liberal argument is that if the market were left alone, it would allocate the stock of housing more efficiently than the government. What this example shows is that a 'social problem' is quite often created by short-sighted government action. Left to itself 'society' generates few problems which individuals cannot solve themselves.

It is, of course true that conservatives are less rigorous in the elimination of the 'social'. The housing case itself exemplifies the desire of conservatives to qualify the logic of the market by social considerations: no political grouping has been more assiduous in the protection of homeowners from the vicissitudes of economic life than the Conservative Party in Britain. Nevertheless, conservative thinkers do show a general scepticism about the claims of 'society' and about the possibility of solving social problems. This scepticism, however, stems perhaps more from a belief that *other* problems will arise from attempts at social engineering than from a doctrinaire belief in the self-correcting processes of market society. Conservative despair at the possibility of social amelioration often goes hand-in-hand with liberalism's rational demonstration of the efficacy of the price system.

This latter point is nicely illustrated by the reaction against social reform, as evidenced by Murray's book on the anti-poverty programme in the US, *Losing Ground* (see chapter 6). Here fairly orthodox assumptions about human nature proved to be extraordinarily reliable predictors of the effects of ameliorative social policy. The fact is that individuals respond to 'signals', and if welfare is made easily available, as it has been in Britain and West Germany as well as the US, more people are attracted to it. The anti-consensus view is that certain social problems become intractable because political solutions to them often run counter to well-established propositions about human nature. It is the recognition that society is not a 'thing' that can be easily manipulated, but an ordered collection of acting and choosing individuals who, if they are allowed some freedom, will 'trade away' from the social state desired by reformers, which constitutes the basis of anti-consensus thought.

It is this last point that underlies the famous 'road to serfdom'[2] theme that is such a feature of liberal (and to some extent, conservative) thought. This is the idea that social reforms that go against the facts of human nature will fail and produce undesirable consequences; further interventions will then be required to correct these, producing more unwelcome effects so that eventually, the whole of society has to be controlled in a totalitarian manner. In other words, the danger is that a society is subverted by stealth rather than revolution. This grim prognosis, when first formulated by Hayek, was probably unduly pessimistic. As we have seen, stagnation and not totalitarianism has been the fate of those Western democracies that have been governed by the social principles of the consensus. Nevertheless, this stagnation has been sufficiently intense to provoke a revival of individualistic doctrines.

III

The most significant feature of the consensus has been the dominance of 'politics'. This requires some explication. To anti-consensus thinkers, a world without politics is inconceivable: after all, they are engaged in a political exercise themselves and peaceful reforms are expected to come about through the political method. Furthermore, even *laissez-faire* economists have to accept in some sense the 'primacy of the political', i.e. the theory that the survival of an exchange process depends on a set of rules and political arrangements which are not derived from exchange itself. However, the necessity for such political arrangements does not entail that politics as a *decision-making method* should predominate over all other possible decision-making methods, such as market mechanisms, and voluntary actions outside the realm of price. Both conservatives and liberals, then, have protested strongly against the 'politicisation' of modern society.

What is going on in anti-consensus thought is a 'demystification'[3] of politics — an unravelling of its essential features, and an attempt to show that behind its benign façade lie malign forces. Politics, when this means bargaining between groups and the competitive electoral process, seems superficially to be a healthy process, a way of generating a modest conception of the public interest in necessarily diverse and pluralist societies. It seems to be ethically superior to both coercion and the cold efficiency of the market. Yet the dominance of politics has produced nothing like the public interest, but only the elevation of sectional interests, especially trade unions, farmers and employers' associations, which are eager to seek exemptions from the rule of law and the rewards of economically inefficient subsidies. As we have seen, this process has been most apparent in Britain. Indeed, inflation can be given a sociological as well as a monetary explanation, for in order to secure electoral victory, political parties have been driven to offer bribes to *politically* significant groups which are paid for by devaluing the currency. In a society dominated by group interests, no one has any incentive to protect the public interest. Hence, the pressure of politics during the consensus gradually eroded the rule of law; and the febrile activity of legislators in passing statutes to satisfy the demands of their client groups undermined those elements of certainty and predictability in legal processes that a free society requires.

Curiously enough, the anti-consensus intellectual movement could legitimately complain that despite its over-arching power over the economy and society, the typical social-democratic state was weak. This was so precisely because it could not resist the incessant demands of pressure groups. To the conservative, it was not so much that the state itself was predatory: the fact was that it was unable to resist the demands of predatory groups. The weakness of the state was often stressed by German neo-liberals. Thus it is the case that conservatives now demand both a strong and a limited state. They have an Hegelian vision of a powerful sovereign state that stands above the conflict within egoistic market society and impartially delivers law and order. What many conservatives have not enquired into is the question of how this strong state can be so limited. They seem to neglect the lessons of public-choice theory: it tells us that since the state is manned by ordinary flesh-and-blood individuals, no less immune to the promptings of self-interest than ordinary market transactors, its expansion is inexorable under modern democratic conditions. This is why, on the whole, liberals have been much more interested in constitutional reform than have conservatives.

The scepticism about the claims of politics leads naturally to an emphasis on law and constitutionalism in the explanation of a more desirable social order. The doubt that political discretion can be relied upon to generate the public interest meant that liberals (and to some extent, conservatives) have sought stability through the following of more or less fixed rules rather than political action. However, for most of this century 'constitutionalism' has been an unfashionable doctrine: almost all the ameliorative social programmes of the consensus involved a repudiation of the notion that political action should be subject to constraint. This is, of course, not to say that they were 'illegal', but to suggest that the constitutional arrangements of most Western democracies were too flimsy to resist the imposition of many schemes which had a dubious support from public opinion.

This is most obviously the case in Britain where parliamentary sovereignty and the absence of a written constitution place individuals not actually at the mercy of majorities but vulnerable to a House of Commons majority which invariably represents a minority of the electorate. One of the achievements of anti-consensus thought has been the destruction of that complacency that once ruled all constitutional debate in Britain. The very fact that individuals have taken grievances to the European Court of Human Rights (whose decisions Parliament and government are only morally obliged to accept, given the prevailing doctrine of sovereignty) is indicative of the current dissatisfaction.[4] Furthermore, the fact that governments normally 'lose' the cases suggests strongly that internal constitutional protections in that country are inadequate. Although some liberal constitutionalists regard such European, extra-parliamentary, institutions as desirable, there is by no means a unanimous acceptance of them by anti-consensus thinkers. Almost all conservatives resent this 'foreign' intrusion into Britain's domestic affairs and are wedded to the traditional idea of sovereignty and the rule of law (despite the obvious tension between those two concepts). Many liberals argue that although the European Court of Human Rights has been effective in upholding *civil* liberties, and in enforcing non-discrimination, it has been largely ineffective in the area of *economic* liberty (indeed, the Protocols of the European Convention on Human Rights give governments wide discretion in matters of taxation and general economic policy).

The example of the American Constitution is not particularly encouraging, for although the federal system permits a great variety of tax systems, laws and institutions (indeed, the flight of business from the highly taxed and regulated East Coast to the 'sun-belt' states of the West is a remarkable feature of recent American economic history), it has not prevented a massive growth in central-government power and spending. The constitutional document, so far from being a stable body of permanent and more or less inflexible rules, has been regularly interpreted and modified in accordance with the prevailing intellectual and political fashions. As we have seen, although the American Constitution is often interpreted as a liberal document, certain aspects of its individualistic features, especially freedom of contract and the right to property, have been systematically eroded since the New Deal. Since so much of American constitutional practice depends upon the *personnel* of the Supreme Court, the ideal of a fixed body of general rules has become somewhat remote. On the desirability of this latter ideal at least, American conservatives and *classical* liberals are at one. The

American Constitution does of course allow amendment and it is towards this process that conservatives and classical liberals in the US have increasingly gravitated as a way of avoiding a 'politicised' Supreme Court.

In general, conservatives are less favourable to constitutional reform in existing, stable democracies. They would argue that the upholding of traditional modes of political conduct (styles of behaviour which are not expressible in formal rules) is a better guarantor of order than constructing elaborate constitutional rules. Indeed, the record of constitutional reform is not particularly favourable. However, in Britain at least, there is a growing recognition that internalised, or tacit rules of political conduct, have simply failed to constrain government. A conservative constitutional writer, Nevil Johnson, conceded this in his influential *In Search of the Constitution* and even suggested a 'convention' to re-write the rules of the political game in Britain.[5]

Constitutionalism presents something of a special problem for the more sophisticated liberal, for to be fully consistent, the liberal cannot impose his conception of an individualist constitution on a possibly unwilling people.[6] As far as possible the constitution should be 'neutral' between differing political values. However, the argument is that under the prevailing institutional arrangements of most liberal democracies, policies can be implemented which have little in the way of public support. At the very minimum, the liberal constitutionalist demands that governments of *all* political persuasions should have to appeal to a much wider section of the community than is required at present. Some liberals (especially American public-choice theorists) are prepared to admit that the introduction of stiffer constitutional rules would mean that many features of the semi-collectivist consensus would have to remain until a wide body of opinion emerged to secure their removal.

One of the innovations that liberal constitutionalists have introduced into the debate is the desirability of the revival of the idea of a 'monetary constitution'. One of the main political legacies of the Keynesian revolution in macro-economics has been the ending of all restraint on governments' and the central banks' power of money creation. As we have seen in earlier chapters, the attempt was made to stimulate employment by raising demand. This was inevitably accompanied by more or less permanent government deficits, financed largely by inflation since raising taxes for this is politically unpopular. The collapse of the Gold Standard in the twentieth century and the falling into desuetude of the convention that governments ought to balance their budgets (at least through the course of the trade cycle) gave governments great economic discretion. West Germany has a constitutional rule prescribing balanced budgets but in crises, this proved to be surmountable. America is in a much better position to restore the 'monetary constitution' than Britain since constitutional amendments could be passed (and made effective), limiting the federal government's power of money creation and enforcing a balanced budget. Under Britain's present constitutional arrangements, all this depends upon the vagaries of the electoral system with no possibility of a permanent rule binding all governments.

The constitutional debate is closely connected to the question of democracy. Almost all anti-consensus thinkers are critical of simple majority-rule democracy. Instead of constitutions imposing constraints, they have been seen, via the democratic procedure, as mechanisms for transmitting the 'people's will': it is tacitly assumed that this 'will' requires no constraint. However, as we have shown in earlier chapters, the conventional majority procedure is a very inadequate mechanism for this, even if it were desirable for the majority will to be implemented — a proposition seriously questioned by all classical liberals and conservatives. The inefficiency of majority procedures has meant that much of the policy-making of the consensus was dictated by elites and politically influential pressure groups, rather than a product of a wide public opinion.

Conservative theorists are rather more critical of democracy in principle than are liberals. The (theoretical) egalitarian impulse in democracy runs counter to the conservative idea of an hierarchically ordered society. The participatory element which is common to much contemporary democratic ideology is specifically frowned upon because it is disruptive of the idea that 'governing' is a specialised activity which should be informed by experience than driven by popular enthusiasm.

The liberal critique is rather different from this. The individualist makes a distinction between the *range* of government and the question of *who* does the governing: it is more important that government be limited than democratically elected. The affection liberals feel for democracy stems from the historical evidence that democratic procedures tend to be more consistent with freedom and the open society than do the varieties of authoritarianism. There is certainly no *logical* connection between democracy and freedom. It is, indeed, the declining empirical connection between liberty and democracy that has provoked the liberal critique of majority-rule procedures.

Nevertheless, liberals maintain that in a free society, government should be a product of subjective choice rather than the activity of a wise and gifted elite. It is the public-choice perspective on the self-interested actions of politicians that engenders the liberal's healthy disrespect for *all* government. The upshot of this is that liberals want to mitigate the potentially anti-individualistic tendencies of democracy rather than eliminate it altogether. The more radical liberal suggestions for the reform of democratic government include the replacement of simple majority rule with weighted majorities and the taking out of politics altogether certain areas to do with fundamental individual rights (including economic ones). Of course, in Britain, one simple reform, the introduction of proportional representation, would end the distortion of the people's will produced by the prevailing electoral system. Although this is only a small item on the philosophical liberal's political agenda, it does have one positive (and deliciously ironical) advantage from an individualist's point of view: it produces weak governments that are forced to form coalitions and seek broader support in order to get anything done.

The liberal is as sceptical as the conservative of the contemporary demands for 'popular' participation in politics. This, unless it is accompanied by a genuine reduction in the range of government activity, is likely to lead to an over-investment in politics and the domination of public life by groups and individuals who are prepared to allocate much of their time to politics. Most people display a healthy apathy towards politics, an indifference which is only harmful if society is heavily 'politicised'. For all liberals the best form of participation is in economics and voluntary action, and the purest form of 'democracy' is individual choice in the market.

IV

It is undoubtedly the case that classical liberalism rather than conservatism has made most of the intellectual running in the revival of anti-collectivist social philosophy. This is for three reasons. Firstly, in a world increasingly dominated by economics, classical liberals have a clear and (they would say) well-tried set of economic doctrines which can be used to understand the contemporary economic malaise: indeed, they had worked with considerable success in West Germany throughout the period of the consensus. Secondly, conservatives traditionally distrust any kind of doctrinaire reasoning in politics: although the traditionalist's scepticism about abstract reform proposals might almost accidentally coincide with a *laissez-faire* economic philosophy, the fact that this was never articulated into a 'dogma' meant that conservatism was peculiarly vulnerable in contemporary ideological warfare. Thirdly, and perhaps most importantly, conservatism itself had been badly compromised by the consensus. Furthermore, there is a long tradition of conservative thought and practice that is favourable to a more active state than that espoused by a more rationalistic individualism. At the philosophical level, Roger Scruton's claim that social and political relationships cannot be reduced to choice is especially significant.

Nevertheless, it is conservative political parties that have accepted the implications of the new revitalised liberalism. With the exception of the Social Democrats for a short period in West Germany, socialist parties remain hostile to the market. The fact that in Britain now the business interests ally themselves to the Conservatives (when in the nineteenth century that party was predominantly linked to the landed interest) gives the mistaken impression that classical liberalism is the party of capital: as a social and economic doctrine its major claim is that it advances the interests of anonymous members of society. Yet undoubtedly its current association with conservatism does much to undermine this claim.

A further difficulty in classical liberalism's connection with conservatism is that the latter's concern with the realities of power is greater than its commitment to abstract principles. This means that conservatives are inevitably much more political animals than they are theorists and are more likely to respond to the prompting of an election than the lure of an idea. Indeed, the current attraction that practising conservatives have for free-market ideas may be (somewhat cynically) described as another piece of political opportunism. This is probably unfair to many genuine conservatives, but it certainly points up the clear anti-political stance of many philosophical liberals.

The remarkable feature of a genuine liberal society is that almost all of its benefits are long-term; and they accrue not to members of identifiable groups but to anonymous members of the community. In other words, the liberal political philosophy, despite its alleged connection with 'capital', has no natural *political* constituency. In a world accustomed to expect immediate benefit from political action, the message of liberalism is all too-often a depressing one. Conservative politicians normally do not have the patience to wait for its long-term advantageous effects. Most liberals in Britain expected the tightening of monetary policy that the Conservative Government engineered after 1979 to be accompanied by a sharp increase in unemployment. Their *micro-economic* diagnosis of the country's ills indicated that many enterprises were only kept in business because of inflation and that they would have to be liquidated if long-term economic stability was to be guaranteed. Britain probably had (has?) more rigidities in her economy than any other comparable Western democracy and recovery was therefore bound to be slower. This clearly is not politically 'sellable' to many conservatives.

Nevertheless, one should not over-emphasise the differences between theoretical conservatism and liberalism. An older tradition (common to both Britain and the US) put 'sound' money, the rule of law and the public interest over sectional interest. Although expressed more prosaically than classical liberalism this doctrine encompassed much of what is valuable in the individualist's political creed. The anti-consensus intellectual movement involves, then, not just a revival of old liberal ideas but also a clearer and sharper articulation of traditional conservative doctrine.

Notes

1. For an extremely sophisticated example of the liberal 'economic' approach to crime, see G. Becker, *The economic approach to human behavior* (University of Chicago Press, Chicago, 1976), Chapter 4.

2. See F.A. Hayek, *The Road to Serfdom* (Routledge & Kegan Paul, London, 1944).

3. I am indebted to John Gray for this observation and for his comments on my unpublished lecture 'End states, processes and politics' (University of Buckingham, 1985), in which this theme is explored in more detail.

4. For a discussion, see M. Zander, 'The United Kingdom and the Bill of Rights', *Catalyst*, vol. i (1985), pp. 13–22.

5. N. Johnson, *In search of the constitution* (Pergamon Press, Oxford, 1977), pp. 224–5.

6. Some classical liberals stress that we have to start from the *status quo*; if this happens to be a semi-collectivist welfare state then it would be illegitimate to impose a *laissez-faire* order on its inhabitants without their consent. The major exponent of this view is the public-choice economist, James Buchanan.

Index

adversary politics 125
agriculture 99, 101, 118-19
Alchian, A. 22, 37-8, 54
Allen, W.R. 22
analytical philosophy 5
anarcho-capitalism 64
Austrian school of economics 26

Bakke v. Regents of University of California (1978) 172
balanced-budget rule 20, 24, 72, 130, 153
Banfield, E. 146
Barry, B. 84
Barry, N.P. 21, 22, 52, 53, 83, 139, 200
Bastiat, F. 65
Becker, G. 26, 55, 200
Bell, D. 143, 146
Bentham, J. 50, 65
Block, W. 83
Böhm, F. 177, 181, 187
Bretton Woods 112, 114
'British disease' 123, 125
Brittan, S. 55, 83, 116, 121-5, 126, 128, 138, 139
on democracy 122-5, 134
Brown v. Board of Education (1954) 161
Buchanan, J. 27, 53, 65, 72-3, 83, 85, 124, 172, 200
on constitutionalism 166-7
Burke, E. 89, 93-5, 99, 101
Burton, J. 53, 54, 83, 139
Butler, R.A. 111

Callaghan, J. 115
capitalism 14-15, 16, 31-3, 57, 64, 106, 177, 178, 199
cartelisation 179
Chicago school of economics 26
Chickering, L. 188
Churchill, W.S. 137
classical liberalism 14, 15, 19, 20, chapters 2 & 3 *passim*,
115, 127, 198-200
and law 62-3, 86-7, 128, 134
and the state 58-60, 64-8
closed shop 41
Coase, R.H. 84
competition *see* market
consensus chapter 1 *passim*, 39-40, 52, 94, 113-14, 116, 127, 141, 161, 164, 190
conservatism 7, 19, 20, chapter 4 *passim*, 115, 130-1, 196, 198
neo-conservatism 143, 144, 145-6, 146-8, 160
constitutionalism 8, 9, 27, 61, 98, 126, 129, 194-5, 196-7
Britain 9-10, 104, 115, 124, 129-30, 165
U.S. 143, 144, 165-71, 195, 196
corporatism 113, 132, 136, 143
Craig Roberts, Paul 172
Cranston, M. 85
Crick, B. 74, 75, 84
crime 191

Dahl 74-5, 85
democracy 1, 7, 10, 15-16, 18, 59, 70-2, 75, 125, 126, 197-8

Eastland, T. 173
economic rent 3, 77
economism 25-6, 183
education 15, 67, 79, 80-1, 126-7, 135, 163-4
Eisenhower, D. 171
empiricism 5-6, 29
Enlightened Market Economy 186
entrepreneurship 36-7, 107, 153
equality 2, 7, 17-18, 52, 56-7, 82, 122-3, 128, 147
equilibrium 4, 35-6
Erhard, Ludwig 175, 176, 178, 185, 187, 188

Eucken, W. 177, 178, 180, 182, 187, 188
European Court of Human Rights 195
evolution 30, 38, 65, 90, 122
externalities 15, 18, 34, 66-7

Federal Reserve Board 40, 142, 150-1
federalism 97, 146, 165-6
Ferrara, P. 172
freedom 28, 31, 39, 50-1, 64, 99, 134, 199
free-rider problem 75
Friedman, D. 83
Friedman, M. 26, 40, 41, 49, 53, 54, 65, 67, 141, 143, 148, 149-54, 155, 157, 165, 168, 170, 172, 173
  iron triangle 152
  monetary rules 47, 79, 85, 151
  on constitutional amendment 150, 151, 152
Friedman, R. 26, 53, 151, 172
Friedrich, C.J. 188

Gaitskell, H. 111
Galbraith, J.K. 14-15, 16, 22, 54, 175-6
Gilder, G. 155, 158, 172
Glazer, N. 146
Gold Standard 9, 13, 46-7, 73, 93, 151, 196
Goldwater B. 145
Gough, I. 21
Gray, J. 52, 53, 83, 200
Great Depression 1, 44, 131, 143, 150, 169
Great Society 155-6
Greenleaf, W.H. 101
Gruchy, A. 188

Hahn, F. 54
Hailsham, Lord 88, 101
Hamm, W. 189
Hamowy, R. 83
Harris, Lord 139
Hartz, L. 140, 145, 171
Hayek, F.A. von 27, 29, 30,

44, 45, 53, 65, 85, 94, 99, 101, 103, 105, 107, 113, 116, 117-22, 124, 126, 137, 138, 147, 148, 178, 200
  conservatism 86-7, 88
  consumerism 51
  evolution 118
  money 47
  reason 117-18
  rule of law 120-1
  serfdom 77
  social justice 121
Heath, E. 114, 133
Hegel, G.W.F. 182
historicism 176-7
Hobbesianism 59, 97, 126
housing 6, 41, 79, 123, 134, 191
Hume, D. 5, 27, 29, 53, 68, 88
Hutchison, T.W. 22

Industrial Relations Act (1971) 14
inflation 13, 20, 42, 45, 49, 72
Institute of Economic Affairs 116, 126
International Monetary Fund 115

Jenkins, R. 21
Jewkes, J. 106-8, 111, 113, 124
Johnson, L.B. 144, 155
Johnson, N. 22, 83, 196, 200
Joseph, Sir K. 134, 135, 139
justice 2, 63, 81
  social justice 2, 17, 34, 52, 81-3, 96, 98, 147

Kay, J. 138
Keynes, J.M. 8, 9, 11-12, 13-14, 20, 43, 49, 73, 104, 117, 124
Keynesianism 4, 11, 13, 23, 42, 43, 44, 49, 51, 72-3, 99, 103, 111, 112, 114, 115, 117, 152, 174, 180, 185-6
King, M. 138
Kirk, R. 143, 145, 154
Kirzner, I. 36, 54
Knight, F.H. 35, 141

Kristol, I. 143, 147-8, 149, 171
Kuhn, R. 21

Laffer, A. 54
laissez-faire 31, 78, 83, 88, 92,
    111, 123, 131, 133, 135,
    137, 140, 145, 155, 170,
    177-80, 190
Lange, O. 53, 54
Laslett, P. 22
Lavoie, D. 53
law, 7, 9, 25, 31-2, 39, 59, 64,
    71, 82, 91-2, 194
  and state 58-9, 91-2
  common law 31-2, 59-60,
    61, 68, 83, 91
  rule of law 28, 58, 62-3,
    100, 110, 149, 193
  statute 31-2, 113
Law for Promoting Stability
    and Growth 185-6
Lawson, N. 136
Le Grand J. 85, 138
Lenel, H. 175
Letwin, S. 83
liberalism (American) 24, 140-1
libertarianism 23, 117
Littlechild, S.C. 54
Lochner v. New York (1905) 169
Locke, J. 129, 140, 145

Macmillan, H. 100, 131-2, 133,
    136
macro-economics *see*
  Keynesianism
Madison, J. 165
Mandeville, B. 57
Marcuse, H. 15, 22
market 14, 15-16, 16-17, 23,
    31, 32-8, 46, 50, 136
  and conservatism 89
  and race 162-4
  and regulation 170-1
  process 35-7
  socialism 51
Marktkonform 181
Marxism 1, 7, 11, 16, 51, 60,
    70, 95, 184
Medium Term Financial
    Strategy 135

Mencken, H.L. 171
Menger, C. 26
Meyer, F. 177
micro-economics 11, 25, 26, 40
Middlemas, K. 138
Mill, J.S. 37, 53, 54, 56, 62,
    65
Miller, A. 167, 173
minimum wage laws 163
Miranda v. Arizona (1966) 173
Mises, L. von 27, 37, 53, 54,
    56, 65, 178
Moggridge, D. 22
monetarism 42-4, 45, 46, 47-8,
    72, 130, 135, 141, 143, 180
  quantity theory of money 42
money illusion 11, 20, 43
monopoly 35, 36, 39, 106, 107,
    136, 181
moral hazard 18, 157
Moral Majority 144, 148
Müller-Armack, F. 177, 179,
    180, 181, 183, 184, 187, 188
Mundell, C. 54
Murray, C. 155, 156-9, 163,
    171, 192

National Economic Develop-
    ment Council 132
Nebbia v. New York (1934), 170
negative income tax (NIT)
    79-80, 155, 158-9
New Deal 141, 195
Nisbet, R. 101, 171
Nozick, R. 22, 28, 53, 101

Oakeshott, M. 88-9, 94-7, 99,
    109-11, 130, 132, 138
O'Connor, J. 21
Olson, M. 27-8, 53, 75-7, 85
Ordo Group 176-80, 183, 186

paradigm 3-4, 19
Pareto principle 66, 81
parliamentary government 9,
    10, 39, 60, 62, 121, 130,
    165, 194-5
paternalism 80, 99, 137
Peacock, A.T. 22, 84
pensions 18, 72, 78, 80, 128,

160, 186-7
Phillips curve 43, 54
Pigou, A.C. 67
Podhoretz, N. 143
Polanyi, M. 30, 53, 107
politics 6, 8, 25, 38, 46, chapter 3 *passim*, 153-4, 193-4
Popper, Sir K. 21
positivism 5-6, 26, 183-4
poverty trap 79
pressure groups 38-40, 60, 68-9, 73, 74-7, 113, 121, 136-7, 181-2, 194
presumptivist argument 18, 22, 82
prices and incomes policies 13, 29, 31, 49-50, 133
prisoners' dilemma 119
privatisation 136
property 17, 25, 33, 36, 37, 60, 64, 67-8, 91, 110, 122-3, 129
public choice 27, 65, 124, 194, 196
public goods 15, 65-8, 69
public interest 28, 38, 70-2
public spending 20, 111, 115

Quinton, Lord A. 101

race 142, 143, 161-4
Rawls, J. 17, 22
Reagan, R. 144, 152
reason 29-31, 52, 183
Rees-Mogg, Sir W. 22
Rechtsstaat 182
rent control 31, 129, 191
rent-seeking 77, 126, 182
rights 5, 9, 10, 28, 60, 61, 87, 95, 97, 128-9, 162, 167-8
Robbins, Lord L.C. 8, 22, 103
Roe v. Wade (1973) 167
Roosevelt, F.D. 141, 169
Röpke, W. 177, 178, 183-4, 185, 187, 188
Rothbard, M. 53, 83, 84, 85, 101
Rowley, C. 84
rule of law *see* law
Runciman W.G. 22

Rustow, W. 177, 178, 182, 188

Schiller, K. 175, 186
Schumpeter, J.S. 139
Schwartz, A. 54, 150
Scottish Enlightenment 27, 29
Scruton, R. 97-9, 133, 199, 200
self-interest 29, 56-8, 71, 149
Siegan, B. 169-70, 171
Smith, A. 7, 27, 29, 35, 53, 57, 65, 94
social democracy 1, 7, 10, 15-16, 18
Social Market Economy 76, 135, 174, 175, 176, 177, 182, 185
society 156, 190-3
Sowell, T. 162-4, 172
Spencer, H. 62, 169
state 2, 6, 7, 8, 16, 18, 31, 35, 65, 70, 89, 91, 94, 98-9, 137, 194
steel nationalisation 138
Stewart, M. 54
Stigler, G. 26, 173
Stockman, D. 172
Stone, H. 173
substantive due process 167, 169
Sugden, R. 84
Sumption, J. 139
supply side economics 152-3
Supreme Court (U.S.) 10, 140-1, 158, 163-71
syndicalism 126-7

tacit knowledge 13, 30-1, 107
Taft, R. 146
Tawney, R. 6, 17, 21, 22
Thatcher, M. 115, 133
The Public Interest 143, 146
time preference 18-19
Titmuss, R. 17, 18
Tollison, R. 85
Trade Disputes Act (1906) 2
trade unions 2-3, 13, 16, 20, 39, 41, 49, 76, 119-20, 136, 138, 143
tripartism 39, 114
Tullock, G. 27, 53, 65, 124

unemployment 2, 8, 12, 13-14,
40, 134, 150, 151
natural rate 20, 42, 43, 134,
151
Urmson, J. 21
utilitarianism 13, 15, 28, 29,
30, 36, 63, 87, 95, 117, 122,
127, 134

Vietnam War 143
Virginia school *see* public choice

Wagner, R. 72-3
Warren Court 141, 166, 167,
168
Watrin, C. 188

Weimar Republic 182
welfare 17, 18, 20, 21, 52,
60-1, 77-8, 79, 92, 148,
186-7
American 155-60
West Coast Hotel v. Parrish (1937)
170
Willgerodt, H. 188
Williams, B. 22
Wilson, Q. 146
Wirtschaftsordnungspolitik 180-1,
182
Wiseman, J. 22

Zander, M. 200
Zweig, F. 188